STUDIES IN PHILOSOPHY AND HEALTH POLICY

The Misfortunes of Others

STUDIES IN PHILOSOPHY AND HEALTH POLICY

Edited by
DANIEL I. WIKLER
Program in Medical Ethics, University of Wisconsin Medical School

Advisory editors
RUDOLPH KLEIN, MARY WARNOCK,
DAVID P. WILLIS, UWE REINHARDT

The books in this series will address the conceptual issues and moral problems arising from health policy and the practice of medicine. Issues of a social and political nature facing policy-makers and administrations, as well as issues primarily affecting individuals in medical relationships, will be discussed. The series will include works by philosophers and by philosophically inclined writers from other disciplines whose distinctive methods can be brought to bear on the questions. Only in this way will a proper understanding of the problems be achieved, as a basis for sound policies and decisions.

THE MISFORTUNES OF OTHERS

End-Stage Renal Disease in the United Kingdom

Thomas Halper
Baruch College and the Graduate School
of the City University of New York

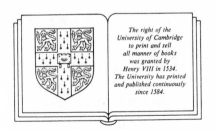

The right of the
University of Cambridge
to print and sell
all manner of books
was granted by
Henry VIII in 1534.
The University has printed
and published continuously
since 1584.

Cambridge University Press

CAMBRIDGE

NEW YORK   NEW ROCHELLE   MELBOURNE   SYDNEY

Published by the Press Syndicate of the University of Cambridge
The Pitt Building, Trumpington Street, Cambridge CB2 1RP
32 East 57th Street, New York, NY 10022, USA
10 Stamford Road, Oakleigh, Melbourne 3166, Australia

First published 1989

Printed in Canada

Library of Congress Cataloging-in-Publication Data
Halper, Thomas.
The misfortunes of others: end-stage renal disease in the United
Kingdom/by Thomas Halper.

p. cm. – (Studies in philosophy and health policy)

Bibliography: p.

Includes index.

ISBN 0-521-35047-6

1. Chronic renal failure – Great Britain.   2. Medical policy – Great
Britain.   I. Title.   II. Series.
[DNLM: 1. Health Policy – Great Britain.   2. Kidney Failure,
Chronic – occurrence – Great Britain.   WJ 342 H195m]
RA645.K5H33   1989
362.1′96614′0094 – dc19
DNLM/DLC
for Library of Congress   88-22857
CIP

British Library Cataloguing in Publication Data
Halper, Thomas
The misfortunes of others : end-stage
renal disease in the United Kingdom. –
(Studies in philosophy and health policy).

1. Great Britain, Medical services for
renal failure patients
I. Title   II. Series
362.1′96614′00941

ISBN 0-521-35047-6

For Pauline –
a misfortune to none, a joy to all

We all have strength enough to endure the misfortunes of others.

(La Rochefoucauld, *Maxims*)

Contents

Tables

Acknowledgments

The data on which this study is based were gathered from dozens of interviews conducted in 1983–5, as well as from the pertinent published literature. Specifically, the following people graciously consented to be interviewed either in person or by telephone: Sir Douglas Black, M.D., former president, Royal College of Physicians; J. Stewart Cameron, M.D., Guy's Hospital, London; Sabri N. Challah, M.B., European Dialysis and Transplant Association; Hugh de Wardener, M.D., Charing Cross Hospital, London; Rodney Deitch, the *Healthcare Parliamentary Monitor*; John Fanshawe, Yorkshire Television; Sir George Godber, M.D., former chief medical officer, Ministry of Health; D. Kassop, M.D., North West Thames Regional Health Authority; Harry Keen, M.D., Guy's Hospital, London; the late Ruth Lupton, honorary secretary, National Federation of Kidney Patients Associations; Ian B. Monroe, M.B., editor, the *Lancet*; Guido Pincherele, M.D., senior medical advisor, Department of Health and Social Security; Anthony Smith, M.D., British Medical Association; Paul Walker, M.D., North East Thames Regional Health Authority; Mrs. Elizabeth Ward, president, British Kidney Patients Association; and Anthony J. Wing, D.M., St. Thomas' Hospital, London. Several other persons, who requested that their names be withheld, must be thanked anonymously.

I am grateful to Daniel I. Wikler of the University of Wisconsin Medical School and three anonymous readers, who read the entire manuscript and offered invaluable suggestions and words of encouragement. For shepherding the manuscript from submission to production, an enterprise that consumed well over three years, Professor Wikler deserves much more than these few words can suggest.

Portions of the manuscript were also read by Norman Daniels, Tufts University; H. Tristram Engelhardt, Jr., M.D., Ph.D., Baylor College of Medicine; Rudolf Klein, University of Bath; Stanley J. Reiser, M.D., University of Texas Health Science Center at Houston; Richard A. Rettig, Illinois Institute of Technology; David Rosner, Baruch College of the City University of New York; Frederick T. Sherman, M.D., Huntington (N.Y.) Hospital; Barbara Stocking, director, King's Fund Centre of Health Services Development, London; David P. Willis, the *Milbank Quarterly;* and, again, Anthony J. Wing, D.M. Their criticism, advice, and support were of great value.

Special thanks are also due Shiela R. Dykes, administrator of the European Dialysis and Transplant Association, for innumerable kindnesses and Maria C. Dueno and Joan Flatley of the Department of Political Science, Donna M. Lambert and Eva M. Mattina of the Center for the Study of Business and Government, and Antoinette Georgiades, Moyee Huei-Lambert, and Ann Marie Sheehan of the Word Processing Service, all of Baruch College of the City University of New York, for the preparation of this manuscript.

A generous Professional Staff Congress/City University of New York award helped make this book possible.

Marilyn and Pauline have earned a groveling apology for activities forgone as a consequence of this project.

The mere enumeration of all these names only hints at the extent of my gratitude and indebtedness.

Portions of this book appeared as articles in the *International Journal of Technology Assessment in Health Care* (Cambridge University Press) and the *Milbank Memorial Fund Quarterly* (since retitled *Milbank Quarterly*). They are reproduced here by kind permission. Many of the data on which my analysis rests were graciously made available by the European Dialysis and Transplant Association.

1. End-stage renal disease in the United Kingdom

This is a case study of how a national health system in an advanced Western democracy confronts an affliction posing a life-or-death issue for thousands of its citizens every year. The health system is the National Health Service, the democracy is the United Kingdom, and the affliction is end-stage renal disease (ESRD).

This case is not unique; if it were, it could hardly serve as an illustration. Nor is it without the ambiguities that real life attaches to phenomena, like bits of fried fish sticking to a pan. But what makes the case intrinsically compelling and heuristically useful is that it embodies three factors of unusual contemporary importance. First, ESRD therapies are rather new and technologically advanced. Their introduction and dissemination had few precedents on which to build; from the beginning, though, these therapies have attracted the attention of some of the brightest and most aggressive elements in the nation's medical community. Second, ESRD therapies reliably extend life. That they extend life gives them a drama, a mystique, a public visibility, a role in the main medical mission; and that they do so reliably means that they cannot be ignored or dismissed. Third, ESRD therapies are expensive. This requires all parties concerned to confront the unforgiving issue of scarcity in all its guises – ethical, economic, and political. Thus, one finds at the center of the factual situation in the United Kingdom an extraordinary and unrelenting starkness, for the life-or-death question is less often whether the medically indicated therapies will succeed than whether they will even be tried.

It is not, therefore, that ESRD policy can be taken as a paradigm of resource allocation or patient selection. Indeed, an observer would be hard put to discover – or even to construct – a typical policy. Rather, what makes ESRD policy worth investigating is not what it typifies, but what it exemplifies (cf. Schwartz and Aaron, 1984).

END-STAGE RENAL DISEASE

The two kidneys are the body's main organs of excretion. About four inches long and two and a half inches wide, each kidney contains millions of filtering tubes (nephrons) with tiny cups (glomeruli) that surround clusters of very small blood vessels (capillaries). Blood carrying wastes – urea, toxins, mineral salts, and so forth – enters the cups, flows through the tubes, and leaves through the vessels. In the process, the wastes together with excess fluids are removed and sent onto the bladder, while the now purified blood resumes its circulation.[1]

The kidneys are remarkably durable organs, and if only one is functioning – and that at less than a normal rate – an individual may experience no obvious symptoms. At the same time, however, kidneys are subject to serious, progressive, and irreversible deterioration, usually as a result of glomerulonephritis, or Bright's disease (an inflammation of the glomeruli), pyelonephritis (due to scarring from reflux – the return of urine from the bladder to the kidneys – or infections), diabetes mellitus, polycystic kidney disease, or vascular disease (chiefly, hypertension). This condition is called chronic renal failure – in contrast to temporary, reversible acute renal failure – and is marked by, among other things, a decline in the capacity of the kidneys to extract excess fluids and poisonous wastes from the blood. Anemia, edema, and infection frequently accompany the condition, and the functioning of the brain, intestine, heart, skin, and other organs is impaired. In almost all cases, chronic renal failure eventually reaches the point where it is termed end-stage renal disease, which, as the name suggests, is fatal.[2]

[1] The kidneys also help to control the electrolyte balance of positive and negative electrically charged atoms (or ions) in the blood.

[2] In a small number of patients with chronic renal failure, residual functioning may remain stable, even over a period of years (Nahas and Coles, 1986).

DIALYSIS

Viewed from the plane of technology, the history of renal medicine over the past four and a half decades seems a stunning confirmation of the possibility of progress.

In 1943 a saintly Dutch physician, Willem Kolff, designed a machine for treating renal failure. Based on the principle of dialysis, the procedure involved diverting a continuous flow of the patient's blood to a semipermeable membrane (initially, cellophane tubing designed for sausage casings), which permitted excess fluids and wastes to pass through its tiny holes like water through a sieve. The blood, now with only a tolerable level of fluids and wastes remaining, was then returned to the patient (Kolff, 1965, 1986). Kolff treated his first patient in 1943 (Kolff et al., 1944), and two years later dialysis saved its first life (Kolff, 1947).

Each dialysis session with Kolff's machine, however, required surgery that destroyed sections of blood vessels. Therefore, the procedure was feasible for only short periods in cases of temporary acute renal failure[3] and was of no use to patients suffering from ESRD.

In 1960 the blood vessel problem was solved by a device invented by Scribner and his colleagues in Seattle (Quinton et al., 1960). They devised a shunt made of Teflon and siliconized rubber, which could be surgically implanted into a superficial artery and adjacent vein in an arm or leg. During dialysis, the shunt was disconnected, so that the blood was sent through the machine; after dialysis, the shunt was simply reconnected. Though there were some problems of clotting, infection, and discomfort, this shunt represented a breakthrough that made dialysis an acceptable treatment for ESRD.

Subsequent researchers have added a number of refinements and improvements,[4] and from the beginning, machine dialysis has

---

[3] Acute renal failure, which arises from poisoning, surgical shock, or battlefield trauma but not from a degenerative kidney disease, requires only short-term dialysis to sustain life until spontaneous recovery ensues.

[4] E.g., the forearm fistula. In place of a shunt, a large vessel is produced by the surgical connection of an adjacent superficial artery and vein. The large vessel is then punctured with large-bore needles, through which the patient's blood flows to and from the dialysis machine. The danger of clotting is markedly reduced, and the problem of a patient's running out of access blood vessels is eliminated. See Brescia et al. (1966) and Khalid et al. (1986).

remained by a large margin the most widely used therapy for ESRD in the world.

Even at the purely mechanical level, the dialysis machine was a marvel. For most of human history, tools have simply been extensions of the individual, enhancing capacities he already possessed. A stethoscope, for example, enables the physician's ear to detect internal bodily sounds that, unaided, it might fail to discern. And even as the stethoscope improved the physician's ability to hear, it reminded him that, on his own, his powers were quite modest.

The dialysis machine, however, is one of a growing class of devices that differs from this traditional, simple model. It does not enhance ordinary human powers, but rather, by literally altering the volume and composition of bodily fluids, asserts extraordinary powers of its own. Thus, far from humbling man by emphasizing his physical limitations, it emboldens him by suggesting an intellectual potential that can hardly be imagined (see Mumford, 1934, p. 321).

At first, dialysis was believed to be so complicated and dangerous that it required a hospital setting (de Wardener, 1966, pp. 115–17), but after the feasibility of performing dialysis at home was demonstrated (Merrill et al., 1964; Baillod et al., 1965), many physicians and patients began to conclude that, when appropriate, home dialysis was preferable to hospital-based therapy. Although preparation, operation, and cleanup are time-consuming and sometimes stressful, the risk of infection is lower, and the patient's convenience, comfort, and sense of control over his own life are greater. Home-dialysis patients tend to have superior survival and rehabilitation rates; and the hazard rate for home patients is particularly low during the crucial first eighteen months of treatment (Capelli et al., 1985).

For patients using the kidney machine, dialysis is typically necessary three times per week for approximately three to six hours each session. Preparation and cleanup take at least another two hours, and dietary restrictions and fluid intake must be carefully followed. Enervating side effects, in addition to depression (Gentry and Davis, 1972; Loury, 1979; Livesley, 1982), excessive emotional dependency (Kaplan De-Nour and Czaczkes, 1968; Reichsman and

Levy, 1972), sexual dysfunction (Milne et al., 1978; Levy, 1983), and profound emotional and interpersonal strain (Czaczkes and Kaplan De-Nour, 1978, chs. 5 and 6), are common, as are debilitating psychological disorders. Indeed, even stabilized dialysis patients average one symptom (hypotension, hypertension, nausea, vomiting, muscle cramps, or headache) per session (Rosa et al., 1980). Thus, dialysis can be said to have transformed ESRD from a terminal to an interminable illness (cf. Register, 1987).

All of these factors – the life-threatening character of ESRD, the nature of the dialysis regimen, the impaired bodily functions associated with ESRD and dialysis, and such secondary consequences of the condition as marital difficulties, financial problems, and unemployment – may combine to produce stress that "can be too great a burden on the patient's psychological resources" (Maher et al., 1983, p. S-50). Indeed, so stressful is dialysis that some patients choose to terminate it, despite the certain knowledge that this means death (Farmer et al., 1979; Levy, 1979; Neu and Kjellstrand, 1986). As an American nephrologist put it, "There are patients who just curl up and die far sooner than necesary" (Freeman, in Malcolm, 1986a).

None of this has changed significantly for many years, for the improvements in machines, disposables, and techniques have been fairly minor and have not basically altered the patient's experience. Discomfort, dependence, tedium, and often worse remain the price that many dialysis patients pay for survival.

In the late 1970s following the development of a safe, permanent peritoneal access device (Tenckhoff and Schecter, 1968; Striker and Tenckhoff, 1971), continuous ambulatory peritoneal dialysis (CAPD) began to appear as an alternative treatment in certain cases, chiefly for patients who were old, diabetic, or frail.[5] Here, a catheter

[5] Another technique is hemofiltration, which duplicates the filtration process of the normal kidney by sending solutes through a semipermeable membrane in much the same way that they are transported through the glomerular membrane (Quellhorst et al., 1980). The process was developed in 1967 (Henderson et al., 1970), and by 1980 was receiving scattered use in Western Europe (Jacobs et al., 1981; Quellhorst, 1983). There is evidence that hemofiltration patients require significantly less hospitalization than dialysis patients (Quellhorst et al., 1983),

is inserted into the patient's abdominal cavity, and wastes and excess fluid pass through the cavity's natural lining, the peritoneum, into a bag, which, when full, is simply discarded and replaced. This procedure is repeated four times per day and, in all, consumes about two and a half hours.[6]

CAPD is much less grueling than conventional dialysis, permits a normal diet, and ordinarily eliminates the need for transfusions due to blood loss; it also has a survival rate comparable to that of hospital/center dialysis (Capelli et al., 1985, p. 48). Still, it is not without its own major problems: It is not suitable for all patients, CAPD patients average more days in hospital than do regular dialysis patients (principally, because of peritonitis), and fears have been expressed that the high CAPD dropout rate may force so many patients onto hospital dialysis (typically, they are considered unsuitable for home dialysis) that the system may become severely overextended. "The success of CAPD," as one scientist bitingly expressed it, "is a strong indictment of conventional hemodialysis and the antipathy that patients feel for it" (Lysaght, 1985, p. 277).[7]

that they suffer less from hypotension, muscle cramps (Baldamus, 1983; Haas et al., 1985), and hypertension (Martin-Malo, 1984), and that patients over the age of sixty or with cardiovascular diseases or diabetic nephropathy have improved survival rates when treated with hemofiltration (Schaefer et al., 1984); in addition, treatment time may be cut in half (Fischbach et al., 1984). Despite promising technical developments, however, hemofiltration remains more costly than dialysis and, therefore, has not come into widespread use as a treatment for ESRD; also, knowledge of the long-term consequences of hemofiltration is still scanty.

[6] This was a result of improved catheter technology (Tenckhoff and Schecter, 1968), before which each dialysis required a new assault on the peritoneal cavity in order to gain access. CAPD superseded the preexisting intermittent peritoneal dialysis (IPD), which had undergone a comparable improvement about a decade earlier (Maxwell et al., 1959). IPD remains the dominant method used with peritoneal dialysis machines. However, it is so time-consuming – requiring three 9-hour sessions per week or even more – that it has never seemed very practical for hospital use, though it has sometimes been effective with certain kinds of high-risk patients (Schmidt and Blumenkrantz, 1981); its survival rate is also poorer than that of other therapies (Capelli et al., 1985, p. 50).

[7] In a renewal of interest in dietary therapy, some clinicians now believe that, under certain circumstances, even severe chronic renal failure can be stabilized by a

Conventional and peritoneal dialysis, however, are alike in this: Where traditionally the governing cliché dichotomizes medicine into caring and curing, these two therapies plainly are neither. Instead, like much open heart surgery, for example, dialysis postpones death and belongs in a third category, which a distinguished neurosurgeon has labeled "rescue" (Jennett, 1984).

TRANSPLANTATION

"Seldom in the history of medicine," a pair of leading clinicians observed, "have two different life-saving treatments for the same previously fatal disease appeared almost simultaneously" (Blagg and Scribner, 1976, p. 1721). Yet at the same time dialysis was emerging, kidney transplantation also was developing as a complementary therapy, promising satisfactory performance not only of the excretory function but of the secondary metabolic and endocrine functions as well.

From the outset, a principal problem in transplantation was rejection, the immune system's efforts to destroy foreign cells (Carpenter and Strom, 1982). When certain cells in the immune system detect foreign cells, antibodies and other substances are mobilized to attack the invaders. Normally, of course, the process is of great survival value in beating off disease. But a transplanted kidney that provoked such a response could, through a terrible biochemical irony, lead the body to kill the sole agent of its potential salvation.

In 1954 Merrill and his colleagues in Boston bypassed the rejection problem by transplanting a kidney with an identical-twin donor and recipient (Merrill et al., 1956).[8] This was the first successful

dietary treatment featuring very little protein and phosphorus plus calcium supplements (Giordano, 1982; Bennett et al., 1983; Acchiardo et al., 1986; Giovannetti, 1986; Rosman et al., 1986).

[8] Actually, in 1947 Hufnagel, Landsteiner, and Hume, three young surgeons at Peter Brent Brigham Hospital in Boston, had attempted the first successful kidney transplant, but as the patient suffered only temporary acute renal failure, the graft functioned for only two days (Moore, 1972, pp. 39–42). A steady stream of experimentation connected the 1947 operation with the first identical-twin transplant seven years later.

transplantation for ESRD patients, and generated considerable attention worldwide. If kidney transplantation were to come into common use, however, it was clear that the rejection problem would have to be confronted. It was particularly significant, therefore, that four years later, transplants from genetically different donors became feasible with the development of drugs that suppressed the rejection of the new kidneys. At first, UK nephrologists were skeptical (e.g., *Lancet,* 1961), but before long a vigorous program had been established at Edinburgh (Woodruff and Robson, 1962).

Over the past quarter century, innumerable improvements have been made in transplantation. Among them have been advances in tissue typing, the isolation of antibodies that attack the immune system cells causing rejection, and the use of pretransplantation blood transfusions that generate a tolerance for certain substances that trigger rejection and thus ease the acceptance of the transplanted kidney.

The most widely discussed change, however, has been the introduction of the immunosuppressive drug cyclosporine. This drug, derived from a soil fungus, was initially intended for use against infection. It failed in that, but was then found to possess extraordinary utility as an immunosuppressive, for instead of indiscriminately reducing the immune system's defenses, it reduces its defenses only against foreign tissue (see Shevach, 1985). Accepting a transplant thus need not entail weakening the body's defenses against infection.

Cyclosporine's properties were first described by Borel and his associates in the late 1970s (Borel, 1976; Borel et al., 1976, 1977), and shortly thereafter encouraging reports on its use in cadaveric kidney transplantation began to appear (Calne et al., 1978, 1979, 1981; Starzl et al., 1980, 1981). A randomized trial in Canada (Canadian Multicentre Transplant Study Group, 1983, 1986) and a five-year retrospective analysis in England (Merion et al., 1984) reinforced this cautious optimism, though the long-term consequences of taking the drug remain unknown.

In 1987 another immunosuppressant, OKT3, attracted considerable attention. Developed by Schroeder and his associates at the University of Cincinnati Medical Center, the drug is a specially prepared antibody that attacks the patient's lymphocytes (or white blood cells), thus preventing them from inducing rejection. Early reports were very encouraging, though fears of higher infection rates were expressed.

Transplant survival rates are rather variable. In Europe, about two-thirds of the cadaver transplants made in 1980 survived a year, about 60 percent two years, about 53 percent three years, and about 50 percent four years.[9] Live donor transplants, which are only about an eighth as common, have a 15 to 20 percent higher success rate.

But although failure is hardly unknown, the potential quality of life benefits – far greater physical and mental vigor, as well as freedom from the oppressive dialysis routine – have always seemed so impressive that since the earliest days patient demand for transplantation has far exceeded the supply of available kidneys. For some patients, in fact, transplantation appears to provoke fantasies of a return to complete health, if not of a figurative rebirth (Abram, 1972).[10] Thus, although the number of transplants in the United Kingdom increased by 77 percent from 1979 to 1986, the waiting list for transplants zoomed by 122 percent. By 1986, the number of patients awaiting transplants exceeded the number receiving them by a margin of well over 2 to 1.

INCIDENCE OF ESRD

Rising living standards and improved public health practices, one nephrologist observed, have vastly reduced the incidence of ESRD since early Victorian times. Today, however, effective preventive measures are difficult to identify. Hypertension regimens may help,

---

[9] In many cases, the cadaver transplants come from donors who died as a result of traumatic head injuries or cerebrovascular accidents. An acceptable donor must have no history of renal disease or abnormalities and must also be free of infection and malignancy at the time of death.

[10] Data presentations typically exaggerate the survival rate advantages of transplantation over dialysis by treating transplantation and dialysis groups as two distinct populations; in fact, the transplant group is essentially a subset of the dialysis population – and a subset notable for its relative health and youth (Garcia-Garcia et al., 1985, p. 17).

for if left unchecked, hypertension can significantly add to the process of renal deterioration; urinary tract obstructions should be treated early in order to avoid infection that can imperceptibly but irreversibly destroy the kidney; and a combination of aspirin and dipyridamole may slow the development of ESRD in certain cases (Donadio et al., 1984). But the kidney's remarkable adaptability to adversity is often the source of its own undoing, for the patient may not notice any difficulties until long after the period of early detection has passed. For some conditions, moreover, there is no treatment other than dialysis or transplantation anyway, so early detection is quite pointless.

There is some dispute about the incidence of treatable ESRD. When dialysis and transplantation were still quite new, it was estimated that about thirty new patients per million total population (PMP) could benefit from treatment in the United Kingdom (de Wardener, 1966, p. 104). In the early 1970s, studies of England (Branch et al., 1971), Scotland (Pendreigh et al., 1972), and Northern Ireland (McGeown, 1972) suggested that the intake rate should be about forty PMP, a rate until recently often regarded as a "reasonable" benchmark (Joint Renal Services, 1982, p. 45; Kennedy, 1983, p. 120).

Others contend that in excluding those under the age of five, over the age of sixty, or with complicating diseases (like diabetes), these estimates are much too low. American nephrologists, for example, estimate the acceptance rate in their country at 100 PMP (Selected Profiles of Medicare Certified Suppliers, 1981; Luke, 1983, p. 1593; Sugimoto and Rosansky, 1984),[11] and if age and the presence of complicating diseases were ignored completely, the number might soar to 150 (Laing, 1978, p. 18; Berlyne, 1982, p. 189).

The UK Office of Population Censuses and Surveys reports that well over three thousand persons die from renal failure in England and Wales each year (Office of Population Censuses and Surveys,

---

[11] The incidence of ESRD in the United States appears to be somewhat greater than that in the United Kingdom, partially because blacks are especially susceptible to the condition and there is a much higher proportion of blacks in the United States (Prottas et al., 1983).

1984, table 2).[12] It is generally conceded, however, that death from ESRD is frequently – perhaps usually – ascribed to a more proximate cause, like ischemic heart disease, cerebral hemorrhage, or pulmonary infection. Furthermore, at least in the United States, the deaths of dialysis patients are ordinarily attributed to cardiac causes if the true reasons are thought to reflect badly on the dialysis team (Plough and Salem, 1982). "Death certification," according to one London nephrologist, "is notoriously unreliable as a source of . . . data." True ESRD mortality, then, is unknown, though it clearly far exceeds official figures.

UK TREATMENT PATTERNS

As Table 1 indicates, the mix of therapies prevailing in the United Kingdom has changed fairly gradually over the years. From 1971 to 1978 the incidence of transplantation increased steadily, surpassing, after 1977, all other means of therapy by a steadily widening margin. Hospital/center hemodialysis, meanwhile, declined slowly, from involving nearly a third of the patients to less than a sixth. Home hemodialysis, after remaining fairly constant from 1971 through 1978, has fallen off markedly since that time, as CAPD has gained favor. Since 1979, the two methods have served about 35 percent of the United Kingdom's ESRD patients, though in a steadily shifting mix. By 1986, the lead that home dialysis enjoyed over hospital/center dialysis since 1969 had evaporated. Intermittent peritoneal dialysis (IPD) barely retains its peripheral role.

More generally, as Table 2 shows, the United Kingdom has always strongly preferred non-hospital-based therapies to hospital-based ones. Indeed, the ratio of non-hospital- to hospital-treated patients increased from just over 2.1:1 in 1971 to 5.4:1 in 1986.

Compared with other large Western European nations, the Federal Republic of Germany (FRG), France, Italy, and Spain, the United Kingdom is unique in stressing transplantation, CAPD, and

---

[12] To be precise, 3,064 died from clearly designated ESRD and 3,056 from various kinds of renal failure that were not specified as to acute or chronic but that were almost certainly very largely chronic.

Table 1. *Percentage of UK ESRD patients receiving different methods of treatment, 1971–86*

Method of treatment	1971	1972	1973	1974	1975	1976	1977	1978	1979	1980	1981	1982	1983	1984	1985	1986
Transplantation	27.0	27.7	33.3	33.9	36.0	37.7	40.2	44.0	43.4	44.0	41.7	44.7	45.2	48.3	47.5	49.2
Hospital/center hemodialysis	31.3	27.5	25.2	22.8	21.4	20.4	19.5	18.6	18.4	17.8	15.8	16.7	16.9	15.9	15.8	15.6
Home hemodialysis	39.8	39.3	40.4	42.0	36.0	40.4	38.5	38.7	32.9	28.9	25.1	24.8	21.9	18.3	16.7	14.1
IPD	0.1	0.1	1.0	1.2	1.4	1.3	0.9	1.0	1.0	2.0	1.0	1.0	0.7	0.1	0.1	0.1
CAPD	—	—	—	—	—	—	0.6	0.7	2.1	5.5	9.2	12.7	15.3	16.9	19.5	21.0
Treatment uncertain	1.9	5.5	0.1	0.1	5.2	0.2	0.3	—	2.2	1.8	7.2	—	—	—	0.4	—
Total	100	100	100	100	100	100	100	100	100	100	100	100	100	100	100	100

Source: European Dialysis and Transplant Association.

Table 2. *Percentage of UK ESRD patients receiving hospital- and non-hospital-based therapies, 1971–86*

Therapy base	1971	1972	1973	1974	1975	1976	1977	1978	1979	1980	1981	1982	1983	1984	1985	1986
Nonhospital	66.8	67.0	73.7	75.9	72.0	78.1	79.3	80.4	78.4	78.4	76.0	82.2	82.4	84.0	83.7	84.4
Hospital	31.3	27.5	26.2	24.0	22.0	21.7	20.4	19.6	19.4	19.8	16.8	17.7	17.6	16.0	15.9	15.6
Treatment uncertain	1.9	5.5	0.1	0.1	5.2	0.2	0.3	—	2.2	1.8	7.2	—	—	—	0.4	—
Total	100	100	100	100	100	100	100	100	100	100	100	100	100	100	100	100

Source: European Dialysis and Transplant Association.

home dialysis (Table 3). Where in the United Kingdom almost half
the patients were treated by transplantation, in the other large Western European nations the percentages ranged from 12.2 to 24.0;
where in the United Kingdom nearly a seventh were treated by
home dialysis, in the other nations the percentages were from 2.0 to
11.8. In contrast the United Kingdom treated 15.6 percent of its
patients by hospital/center dialysis, while the other nations treated
between 58.1 and 77.0 percent of their patients by this method. In
1985, the United States dialyzed about 81.9 percent of its patients,
19.6 percent at home and 80.4 percent in hospitals/centers (General
Accounting Office, 1986, p. 9).

More broadly, where the United Kingdom relies on non-
hospital-based therapies, the other nations rely on hospital-based
ones (Table 4). Thus, the United Kingdom has many more functioning transplant, home-dialysis, and CAPD patients PMP than the
other large Western European nations (Table 5).[13] Indeed, the United Kingdom treats nearly three times as many patients PMP on
home-based therapies as do Italy and the FRG, and nearly twice as
many as its closest competitors, France and Spain.

On the other hand, the United Kingdom has fewer hospital/
center dialysis patients PMP than the other large Western European
nations (Table 6). In fact, in 1986, UK hospital/center dialysis rates
trailed by large margins those of a number of much poorer countries, including Bulgaria, Cyprus, Czechoslovakia, Greece, Ireland,
Portugal, Tunisia, and Yugoslavia. The United Kingdom's high
transplantation and low hospital/center dialysis rates do not coexist
by coincidence, for as one Glasgow clinician observed, "A major
stimulant to the development of [transplantation] has been the con-

---

[13] By 1985, the United Kingdom's intake rate of 27.5 transplants PMP had almost
been overtaken by Spain (24.8), and France (21.0) and the FRG (20.8) were not
far behind. Italy was a distant last, with 6.6 transplants PMP. That Spain may
soon surpass the United Kingdom is suggested by the fact that 43.9% of its
patients on dialysis were on waiting lists for cadaver transplants, whereas in the
United kingdom the percentage was 41.5; France (15.4), the FRG (20.3), and
Italy (17.7) trailed. In 1985 in the United Kingdom, 102 PMP had received a
transplant, a rate exceeded by only one other large nation, the United States,
with 108.

Table 3. *Percentage of German, French, Italian, and Spanish ESRD patients receiving different methods of treatment, 1986*

Method of treatment	FRG	France	Italy	Spain
Transplantation	14.9	24.0	12.2	23.4
Hospital/center hemodialysis	77.0	58.1	75.2	68.4
Home hemodialysis	5.3	11.8	4.3	2.0
IPD	0.1	0.1	0.1	0.1
CAPD	2.1	5.2	7.7	5.6
Total	100	100	100	100

Source: European Dialysis and Transplant Association.

Table 4. *Percentage of German, French, Italian, and Spanish ESRD patients receiving hospital- and non-hospital-based therapies, 1986*

Therapy base	FRG	France	Italy	Spain
Hospital	77.0	58.1	75.2	68.4
Nonhospital	23.0	41.9	24.8	31.6
Total	100	100	100	100

Source: European Dialysis and Transplant Association.

Table 5. *UK, German, French, Italian, and Spanish ESRD patients with functioning transplant, home dialysis, or CAPD, 1986 (PMP)*

Method of therapy	UK	FRG	France	Italy	Spain
Transplantation	117.6	49.6	72.2	37.2	78.9
Home dialysis	33.7	17.6	35.8	13.1	9.4
CAPD	50.2	7.0	15.8	23.5	18.9
Total	201.5	74.2	123.8	73.8	107.2

Source: European Dialysis and Transplant Association.

Table 6. UK, German, French, Italian, and Spanish ESRD patients
receiving hospital/center hemodialysis, 1986 (PMP)

Method of therapy	UK	FRG	France	Italy	Spain
Hospital/center hemodialysis	37.3	256.4	176.0	279.4	230.5

Source: European Dialysis and Transplant Association.

tinuing under provision of dialysis resources" (Macpherson, 1986, p. 505).

The relatively low rate of hospital/center dialysis in the United Kingdom is reflected in the relatively low number of dialysis centers (Table 7). While the number of centers PMP in the four other nations since 1971 has increased from 208 percent (France) to 960 percent (Spain), the number in the United Kingdom has grown only 50 percent. Not only does the United Kingdom have only a small fraction of the centers PMP of the other large Western European nations. In addition, its rate is exceeded by those of Bulgaria, Cyprus, Czechoslovakia, Greece, Ireland, Lebanon, Poland, Portugal, Tunisia, and Yugoslavia; England has fewer centers than Sicily.

This is not to say that the United Kingdom would be well advised, say, to quadruple its numbers of centers. The staffing problems would be insuperable, and as a small, densely populated country, it simply may not need as many centers as some others. Moreover, it is possible to have too many centers (as in Italy), so that a number of them may not attract sufficient patients to maintain a high level of staff competence. Finally, as a UK Department of Health and Social Services official pointed out, "Given the present level of center dialysis, we don't really need more centers."[14]

How, then, does the United Kingdom compare in its treatment by all therapies of persons suffering from ESRD? Table 8 discloses the answer. The United Kingdom's treatment rates range from 78.8 percent of those treated in France down to 70.9 percent of those

---

[14] Yet it is the present treatment rate of hospital/center dialysis that is precisely in question.

Table 7. UK, German, French, Italian, and Spanish dialysis centers, 1971–86 (PMP)

	1971	1972	1973	1974	1975	1976	1977	1978	1979	1980	1981	1982	1983	1984	1985	1986
UK	0.8	0.8	0.9	0.9	0.9	1.0	1.0	1.0	1.0	1.0	1.1	1.1	1.1	1.2	1.2	1.2
FRG	1.3	2.0	2.5	2.8	3.2	3.6	3.8	3.8	4.1	4.3	4.4	4.1	4.9	5.3	5.4	5.7
France	1.3	1.7	2.0	2.4	2.5	2.8	3.1	3.3	3.4	3.5	3.7	3.5	3.9	4.0	3.9	4.0
Italy	1.0	1.3	2.1	2.7	3.1	4.0	4.3	4.3	5.0	5.1	5.9	4.6	6.4	6.8	6.9	7.0
Spain	0.5	0.5	0.9	1.2	1.3	2.1	2.2	2.7	3.6	3.8	4.3	4.2	5.0	5.3	5.2	5.3

Source: European Dialysis and Transplant Association.

Table 8. *UK, German, French, Italian, and Spanish ESRD patients treated by all therapies, 1986*

	UK	FRG	France	Italy	Spain
Patients treated (PMP)	239	333	303	305	337

Source: European Dialysis and Transplant Association.

treated in Spain. (In 1985, the United Kingdom's treatment rate was 45.4 percent of the U.S. rate.) The United Kingdom's reluctance to support hospital-/center-based therapies has been so marked that even its leadership in transplantation, home dialysis, and CAPD has been unable to compensate.

Nor is this only a recent development. The United Kingdom has lagged behind the other four large Western European nations since 1978, and behind the FRG, France, and Italy since 1973. It is hardly surprising that the United Kingdom trails the FRG and France, where per capita health expenditures are substantially higher; in 1985 the United Kingdom spent only 64 percent of what the FRG spent per capita on health and only 58 percent of what France spent. Italy and especially Spain, however, are poorer countries, and though Italy spent slightly more per capita on health than the United Kingdom, Spain spent only about 73 percent of what the United Kingdom spent (Schieber and Poullier, 1987, p. 107). The comparatively high Italian and Spanish treatment rates, therefore, would seem to reflect different allocation decisions, rather than a higher level of resources supplied across the board.

REHABILITATION

On the question of patient rehabilitation, the United Kingdom's record is about average compared with that of the twenty other nations registered with the European Dialysis and Transplant Association, at least according to the latest available complete data, which were gathered in 1979. In general, the United Kingdom trails slightly in the rehabilitation of hospital hemodialysis patients and leads slightly in the rehabilitation of transplant patients. When com-

Table 9. *Percentage of UK, German, French, Italian, and Spanish*
ESRD patients in rehabilitation categories, 1979

	1	2	3	4	5	6
UK						
Hospital/center hemodialysis	33.2	16.3	19.1	14.1	14.9	2.5
Cadaver transplant	81.0	3.1	6.5	4.8	4.4	0.3
FRG						
Hospital/center hemodialysis	27.7	18.7	15.7	13.6	20.7	3.6
Cadaver transplant	63.0	11.5	10.7	9.2	5.3	0.4
France						
Hospital/center hemodialysis	38.6	22.4	12.4	14.1	10.7	1.8
Cadaver transplant	68.3	12.2	8.3	6.7	4.4	0.2
Italy						
Hospital/center hemodialysis	62.9	17.5	7.1	6.7	5.1	0.6
Cadaver transplant	85.0	9.5	3.0	1.5	.5	0.5
Spain						
Hospital/center hemodialysis	40.7	25.4	12.4	10.6	9.9	1.0
Cadaver transplant	79.6	4.1	10.2	4.1	2.0	0.0

Rehabilitation categories: 1, able to work and working full time (including house-work); 2, able to work and working part time (including housework); 3, able to work but not working (no work available); 4, able to work but not working (earning capacity less than social security benefits); 5, unable to work (living at home, able to care for most personal needs); 6, unable to care for self (requires hospital care or the equivalent at home).
Source: European Dialysis and Transplant Association.

pared with the four other large European democracies, the United Kingdom leads only the FRG in the rehabilitation of hospital hemodialysis patients, but trails only Italy in the rehabilitation of transplant patients (Table 9).

These data, however, may understate the United Kingdom's rehabilitation achievements by substantial margins. First, the relatively poor performance among hospital hemodialysis patients is partially offset by the relatively small number of patients in that category. Second, the relatively strong performance among transplant patients is enhanced by the relatively large number of patients in that category. Third, the 1979 survey omitted home-hemodialysis patients, whose rehabilitation rates according to a 1976 analysis were nearly as good as those of transplant patients.

What sets the United Kingdom apart from the other nations, the data suggest, is not superior rehabilitation rates for each kind of therapy. Instead, the United Kingdom differs in its much heavier utilization of high-rehabilitative therapies – home dialysis and transplantation – and its much lighter utilization of the low-rehabilitative therapy – hospital/center hemodialysis. If each nation's ESRD patient population is judged as a whole, therefore, the United Kingdom ranks first in the proportion of patients in the high-rehabilitative categories.[15]

THE UNITED KINGDOM'S NEEDS

How well does the United Kingdom meet its needs? Table 10 indicates the rates at which new ESRD patients were admitted to treatment in the years 1973–86. For many years, the "often quoted" (Laing, 1978, p. 16) rule of thumb was that forty new persons PMP per year were suitable for treatment (Branch et al., 1971; Pendreigh et al., 1972; McGeown 1972), though even a chief medical officer for the Department of Health and Social Security conceded that the old figure was "now regarded as an underestimate" (Yellowlees, 1982, p. 116). Finally, in 1986 the United Kingdom reached and surpassed that goal.

Until the United Kingdom's remarkable increase in 1986, all the other large Western European democracies far outstripped its long-term rate of gain (Table 11). Even after its 1986 leap of 24.1 percent, the United Kingdom's rate of gain was still surpassed by those of the FRG and Spain.[16]

---

[15] Rehabilitation rates, however, are a function not only of the health care system and the patient's fitness, but also of the nation's employment patterns and sickness payments, which influence whether appropriate jobs are available and whether the patient has financial incentives to seek them.

[16] The United Kingdom's intake rate surpassed forty in 1986, exceeding that of France whose rate has sometimes dropped in recent years.

Table 10. *New UK ESRD patients admitted to treatment, 1973–86*

	1973	1974	1975	1976	1977	1978	1979	1980	1981	1982	1983	1984	1985	1986
New patients (PMP)	13.4	15.3	16.3	16.4	17.4	21.1	21.6	24.6	26.7	29.5	33.4	33.9	37.7	46.8
Increase over previous year (%)	14.8	14.2	6.5	.6	6.1	21.3	2.4	14.8	7.7	10.7	13.2	1.5	11.2	24.1

Source: European Dialysis and Transplant Association.

Table 11. *New UK, German, French, Italian, and Spanish ESRD patients admitted to treatment, 1972–86 (PMP)*

Year	UK	FRG	France	Italy	Spain
1972	12.8	17.1	17.6	14.8	3.9
1975	16.3	31.6	30.6	20.9	10.3
1978	21.1	37.3	29.1	38.1	26.7
1981	26.7	49.7	42.3	43.1	36.7
1982	29.5	47.3	37.9	39.8	36.4
1983	33.4	55.8	44.3	45.5	61.3
1984	33.9	67.1	49.2	42.5	58.7
1985	37.7	59.4	42.9	46.8	45.0
1986	46.8	66.2	44.2	49.4	50.6

Source: European Dialysis and Transplant Association.

BIASES IN UK TREATMENT PATTERNS

Though the United Kingdom's health system may well be "the most egalitarian in any industrialized country" (Hollingsworth, 1981, p. 198), its pattern of ESRD treatment is not constant throughout the population, but instead is skewed by other factors. The most important of these is age (Table 12). According to the latest age-specific acceptance rates – those of 1984 – the United Kingdom treats persons under the age of thirty-five at about the same rate as the FRG and Italy; France's levels are slightly higher and Spain's are by far the highest. Even for the group from age thirty-five through sixty-four, the United Kingdom maintained its respectability, trailing France and Italy by about only 20 percent; the FRG and Spain led by great margins. But the gap that grew wider for the middle group grew still more in the oldest, as the four other nations outpaced the United Kingdom in the over-sixty-four category by ratios of from 2.3:1 to 3.2:1. In the over-seventy-four category, finally, physicians agreed that the United Kingdom treats almost no one at all.[17]

[17] By contrast, in 1985 in the United States 35.5% of those treated were aged sixty-five or over (11.9% were aged seventy-five or over); the proportion of elderly Americans under treatment, 169 PMP, approached that of all UK patients under treatment, 216 PMP.

Table 12. *Age-specific acceptance rates, 1984 (PMP)*

	Male				Female			
	0–14	15–34	35–64	>64	0–14	15–34	35–64	>64
FRG	4.0	28.3	132.3	155.7	4.4	22.5	88.5	92.7
France	7.5	30.0	89.9	121.8	8.0	17.3	59.3	62.5
Italy	4.0	27.3	93.9	133.1	4.1	14.9	62.4	77.7
Spain	7.2	49.8	129.8	120.2	6.7	27.9	88.2	54.5
UK	6.7	30.1	73.7	51.8	4.0	12.4	51.3	21.7

The differential age rates reflect prior decisions on which therapies are to be stressed. The United Kingdom's traditional emphasis on transplantation and home dialysis, that is, naturally led it to treat a smaller percentage of older patients, who are ordinarily considered less suitable for these therapies, though the more recent growth of CAPD has significantly counterbalanced this tendency. In the other three nations, where hospital/center dialysis is dominant, advancing age has less often been a disqualifying factor.

There is also a bias against treating patients who are afflicted with other serious disorders. Probably the most important group in this category is composed of diabetics, for whom ESRD is a common complication. Given that diabetics are far more costly to treat than other ESRD patients (Shyh et al., 1983), that half who are treated die within three years (Cameron and Challah, 1986, p. 966), and that such severe problems as arthritis, retinopathy, or even cardiac death frequently cannot be avoided, this is hardly surprising. Still, the United Kingdom has moved from treating almost no diabetics to treating a sizable number; in 1975, 1.4 percent of the 16.3 PMP admitted to treatment were diabetic, and by 1985 the figure had risen to 11.4 percent of the 37.7 PMP – more than an 1,800 percent increase. At 4.3 diabetic patients treated PMP, however, the United Kingdom lags far behind the leader, Finland, and leaves approximately two-thirds of its new diabetic ESRD patients untreated.

A third bias factor is gender. For all except the tiny category of patients under the age of fifteen, males are somewhat more likely to receive treatment than females. The differentials are, in fact, consistent and marked, especially in the largest group, the elderly. This pattern holds in each of the four nations. The higher treatment rates, however, may simply reflect higher incidence; in the United States, male ESRD incidence is substantially higher than female (Mausner et al., 1978; Hiatt and Frieman, 1982; Rostand et al., 1982; Eggers et al., 1984, p. 73).

In addition, though no data on the subject are available, the general impression seems to be that the UK therapy pattern is biased against the lower classes. Specifically, the stress laid on home dialysis is said to put a premium on certain middle-class attributes, like education and self-discipline, to the relative disadvantage of the working class (Fox 1975, p. 710; Simmons, 1979, p. 202; Bryan, 1981, p. 412). Non-English-speaking resident aliens – who are believed to be difficult to train for home dialysis – and nonwhites generally are also thought by some observers to have special difficulties in getting admitted to treatment.[18] Underlying this is the NHS's generalized orientation toward the better-off classes (Titmuss, 1968, p. 196; Stacey, 1977, p. 898; Le Grande, 1978, pp. 125–42).[19] Since the creation of the NHS, the health of members of the skilled, unskilled, and partly skilled classes, while improving in absolute terms, has declined in comparison with the health of members of the professional and managerial classes.

More marked are the differences among the United Kingdom's various health regions. As Table 13 makes plain, very sizable differences in the rates at which new patients are admitted to treatment are not at all uncommon. The intake rate of the North East Thames region is nearly three times that of Wessex. And regions that in

---

[18] But cf. Challenger-Gumbs (1985), in which a nurse in the Leicester General Hospital renal unit argues that despite a host of complicating cultural problems, immigrants (chiefly, Asians) were accepted for dialysis treatment at approximately the same rate as native-born Britons.

[19] Also, middle-class patients are more likely to have general practitioners who have hospital appointments, received their education at British medical schools, have further professional qualifications, and have less that 3,000 patients, though working-class patients "have a somewhat closer relationship with the general practitioners" (Cartwright and Anderson, 1981, p. 177).

Table 13. *UK patients receiving treatment by region, 1985 (PMP)*

Region	New patients	Total patients
Northern	45.2	257.4
Yorkshire	37.2	107.2
Trent	45.7	232.4
East Anglia	52.6	285.8
NW Thames	40.0	211.7
NE Thames	66.0	305.9
SE Thames } SW Thames }	41.4	257.8
Wessex	24.6	149.6
Oxford	43.8	241.3
South Western	42.6	215.2
West Midlands	37.3	104.4
Mersey	34.2	260.8
North Western	42.5	211.5
Scotland	44.1	232.4
Wales	56.1	196.4
Northern Ireland	25.0	189.4
Isle of Man	50.0	100.0

general are underfunded, like Trent, East Anglia, and Oxford, sometimes exceed the national intake average, whereas regions that are overfunded, like Mersey and Northern Ireland, sometimes do not.

Treatment patterns also vary widely. A 1984 survey disclosed, for instance, that whereas three hospitals preferred home dialysis over hospital/center dialysis by 4 or 5 to 1, eleven offered no home dialysis at all. Similarly, three hospitals relied on CAPD for 53 to 71 percent of their ESRD patients, while two other hospitals made no use of it and another used it for only one patient.

Certainly, part of the regional differences can be explained by differences in regional age profiles, urbanization rates, and incidences of ESRD. Yet it is hard to believe that such conceptually benign variables can account for discrepancies so numerous and of so great a magnitude (*Lancet,* 1981, p. 596).

Table 14. *UK medical staff in nephrology, 1982 (PMP)*

	Senior staff	Junior staff	Total staff
Northern	3.2	5.5	3.7
Yorkshire	1.4	3.6	5.0
Trent	1.8	3.6	5.4
East Anglia	1.6	3.2	4.8
NW Thames	2.9	3.4	6.3
NE Thames	3.0	5.1	8.1
SE Thames	3.7	6.9	10.6
SW Thames	.7	1.3	2.0
Wessex	1.1	1.9	3.0
Oxford	.9	2.6	3.5
South Western	1.3	3.7	5.0
West Midlands	1.9	2.7	4.6
Mersey	1.3	2.1	3.4
North Western	2.0	4.5	6.5
Scotland	3.3	4.4	7.7
Wales	1.4	3.2	4.6
Northern Ireland	2.7	1.3	4.0

Source: Royal College of Physicians of London.

Regional differences, moreover, appear to be not only quantitative, but qualitative as well; for significant differences in graft survival rates have been found among the various transplant centers (Taylor et al., 1985).

Staffing patterns reveal comparable discrepancies (Table 14). Again, regional differences are marked. Staffing in the Northern region is nearly three times the level in Wessex, with Mersey and Oxford faring little better. Similarly, there are almost four times the level of senior staff in Scotland and the Northern region as in Oxford. Some regions, like Oxford, Yorkshire, and South Western, have high ratios of junior to senior staff, and others, like Northern Ireland, North West Thames, and Scotland, have very low ones.

CONCLUSIONS

Since the late 1970s, the dominant motif in the UK's ESRD treatment pattern has been transplantation, the therapy that is most cost efficient and promises the best quality of life. Until surgery is appropriate or if the graft fails, CAPD or home dialysis will in all likelihood be used. CAPD or home dialysis will also be used in some cases in which transplantation is not a real option. In this context, the emphasis on non-hospital-based therapies, as one American analyst put it, "is simultaneously an escape from the few number of dialysis centers and also a rationing mechanism, since only the 'best' of the terminally ill ESRD patients do well at home."

Hospital/center dialysis, by far the most costly treatment, is reserved for patients who have experienced temporary difficulty with home dialysis or CAPD and for a fairly small number of others. "Selecting patients according to their suitability for home dialysis and transplantation," the *British Medical Journal* (1978) observed, "must clearly be more restrictive than selecting them for longterm hospital treatment" (p. 1449). And so those classes of patients who are believed not to respond as well to non-hospital-based therapies – patients over the age of fifty-five, with complicating diseases, or with certain kinds of psychosocial or domestic problems – will probably be given no treatment at all. Some regions treat more patients than do others, and some districts treat more patients than do others, but the broad pattern prevails pretty much throughout the country.

The general picture of ESRD treatment in the United Kingdom, then, is decidedly mixed. In transplantation, CAPD, and home dialysis, the United Kingdom is a leader and has maintained this position for many years. The United Kingdom's utilization of hospital/center dialysis, however, is so low that it brings down the rate of total patients treated and new patients admitted to treatment to levels considerably below those prevailing in comparable nations, even poorer Italy and Spain. Nor is the distribution of treatment in the United Kingdom itself without its own serious inequities, particularly with regard to age and region.

2. Macroallocation

Virtually all patients in the United Kingdom suffering from ESRD are wholly dependent on the National Health Service (NHS), a comprehensive, centrally financed health care system that provides for the entire population with little or no charge at the point of service.[1] What follows is a case study of the policy-making process within the NHS.[2]

NHS resources are strictly limited. Demand for services greatly exceeds supply. No set of principles that would dictate specific allocative decisions commands universal support. Every choice produces winners and losers; every choice is presumed by all concerned to be merely temporary and always subject to review; and every choice is made by individuals buffeted by personal, institutional, ideological, and a dozen other considerations. The process is not neat, rational, and indisputable, like a bright child's book of sums, but instead exhibits the less orderly qualities of a vigorous schoolyard football match.

The NHS is a "heterogeneous conglomerate" (Klein, 1981, p. 161), employing more than 800,000 people, spending nearly 20

---

[1] Of the NHS budget, approximately 86% is financed out of general taxation, 11% out of social insurance contributions, and only 3% out of user charges (and these mostly for prescriptions and dental work).

[2] In discussing UK policy regarding ESRD, it may be useful to distinguish between the macroallocative and the microallocative levels, where "macroallocation" refers to the way health resources are divided and "microallocation" to the way persons are selected for treatment (see Calabresi and Bobbitt, 1978, pp. 17–20; Beauchamp, 1978; but cf. Basson, 1979, p. 313).

billion pounds annually, and occupying a position of immense practical and ideological importance. Since its creation in 1948, it has been reorganized twice, in 1974 and 1982, but from the outset subnational structures have been granted considerable authority in such areas as spending, planning, and managing. The pertinent portions of the current structure for England – it is somewhat different in Scotland, Wales, and Northern Ireland – can be quickly sketched:[3]

Secretary of state for social services

|

Department of Health and Social Security

|

National Health Service

|

Regional Health Authorities (14)

|

District Health Authorities (192)
and regional specialties (including renal units)

The secretary of state for social services is responsible, via the Cabinet, to Parliament and ultimately to the electorate.

How, then, is ESRD policy made? As if reading from a common script, all those who were interviewed chuckled and gave the same response: "What policy?" Indeed, neither the secretary of state nor the higher civil servants nor anyone else at the Elephant and Castle headquarters has formulated and published a comprehensive statement of means and ends that could be recognized as an ESRD policy. Among nephrologists, in fact, the complaint "of being controlled by events rather than of being in control" has become a sad cliché (Hamilton and Briggs, 1978, p. 36),[4] though ESRD is certainly not unique in this regard.[5]

---

[3] Structures not significantly involved in the macroallocative process (e.g., Community Health Councils) are omitted.

[4] This remark was directed at transplantation, but could as easily have described reactions to the panoply of ESRD therapies.

[5] Can there be a national policy if there is no national policy maker? The query calls to mind the famous scholastic argument for the existence of God: The laws of na-

There is, in truth, a sense in which the refusal to put policies on paper sounds hierarchical, antirational, even premodern echoes, whose very mystery appears to add to the power and authority of decision makers. If there are problems with all of this, the assumption seems to be, they derive not from the sophisticated bureaucracy but rather from the vulgarly narrow preoccupation of critics with precision.

Yet critics, of course, recoil from the language of omission, of ritual, of gesture, of hyphenated jargon. It all seems a half-secret code aimed less at facilitating mutual communication than at bureaucratic manipulation and control. "Specialists without spirit, sensualists without heart," Weber (1958) called the bureaucracy; "this nullity imagines that it has attained a level of civilization never before achieved" (p. 182). Individual bureaucrats, of course, are human beings, but the deliberately impersonal character of their roles and relationships, critics maintain, may dehumanize them, leaving them as two dimensional as the lines and boxes on an organization chart (Hummel, 1982; but cf. Hartwig, 1987).

---

ture imply a supreme law giver. Lasswell and Kaplan (1950) would seem to adopt this perspective, defining policy as a "projected program of goals, values, and practices" (p. 71). "Projected" suggests some intention that can come only from a policy maker. Similarly, Thompson's (1981) view of policy as hypothesis – "if a, b, c, . . . are done at time one, then x, y, z, . . . will result at time two" (p. 8) – clearly implies a hypothesis formulator.

Yet Adam Smith demonstrated more than two centuries ago that coordination of human efforts need not require a coordinator, but merely the impersonal market forces of supply and demand (Smith, 1937 [1776]). Elaborating upon that notion, a leading modern political scientist produced an entire book on the theme "that people can coordinate with each other without anyone's coordinating them, without a dominant common purpose, and without rules that fully prescribe their relations to each other." From this vantage, a policy may sometimes be "a resultant . . . of conflicting or at least diverse decisions" (Lindblom 1965, pp. 3, 11), and thus would not seem to presuppose a policy maker. Moreover, it has become commonplace to observe that actors may work to keep threatening issues off the public agenda, thus exerting influence not by decision making but by non–decision making (Bachrach and Baratz, 1963) – and that a "policy, like a decision, can consist of what is not being done" (Heclo, 1972, p. 85).

ESRD POLICY: THE FORMATIVE YEARS

How, then, to repeat, is ESRD policy made? One way to answer this question is to examine the official response to the stunning technological innovations of the 1950s and 1960s that seemed to promise so much to those suffering from ESRD.

Certainly, the Ministry of Health was well aware of these epic developments. Indeed, as the then chief medical officer later recalled, "Even before the breakthrough, we had kept in touch with work in the United States and Britain." In 1963 an acute renal failure center of the Royal Free Hospital in London began to dialyze ESRD patients. Later that year, a second hospital joined it, and in 1964 the first purpose-built ESRD dialysis center was established at Charing Cross Hospital, also in London. The Charing Cross center, however, was built not with government funds but with charitable contributions, and though maintained by the ministry, the funding may have been accomplished without the ministry's knowledge. "Funds get lost," a nephrologist who was present at the creation said with a wink, adding that NHS facilities and personnel were utilized and other expenses met in more ingenious ways (see Stocking, 1986, p. 21).

Although these costs were small, the nephrologists' goal was substantial: to demonstrate and publicize the feasibility of the new technology and thereby create a demand for it to which the NHS would feel compelled to respond. One nephrologist called such an approach the "common back door" means of introducing expensive innovations. By 1966, similar small centers started by local initiative had been set up in a dozen cities throughout the United Kingdom.

In 1965 the Ministry of Health turned to Max L. Rosenheim, soon to be elected president of the Royal College of Physicians, to convene a conference of hospital consultants, which in turn set up a working party headed by Hugh E. de Wardener of Charing Cross to consider details of how to proceed. The working party's recommendations, subsequently accepted by the conference, were that at least one dialysis center be established in each health region, preferably at a teaching hospital, and that widespread use of home dialysis be put off until it could be adequately evaluated. In addition, it suggested specific numbers of beds and nurses per unit, equipment-purchasing practices, and equipment safety standards. The committee did not, however, consider setting down rules as to the kinds of patients to be accepted or rejected for treatment, leaving that to the clinical judgment of the doctors involved.

Subsequently, the committee issued recommendations on home dialysis as well. In addition, it suggested that the dialysis units be expanded to full-fledged renal units, arguing that this would offer more comprehensive care to patients and a better setting for training and research. Although the committee stressed that its recommended treatment network was meant to serve only as a basis for later growth, when de Wardener told the ministry that his committee should move on to consider the next phase, he recalled, the committee was disbanded.

The ministry, however, not only accepted most of the recommendations, but also took the unusual step of providing money to establish the dialysis centers, the minister for health, Kenneth Robinson, even securing an extra allotment of funds for the purpose. It was an impressive beginning, most nephrologists felt, and optimism was everywhere. As a prominent renal physician from Newcastle expressed it, "Great Britain should be an ideal situation for the development of intermittent haemodialysis." The compactness of the country meant that "a relatively small number of centers" would be required, and it was plainly a comfort to believe that the Rosenheim group "decides broad policy. . . . Considerable priority," he concluded, "was given to the development of a national intermittent haemodialysis system" (Kerr, 1966, p. 153).

Meanwhile, in 1967 the Medical Research Council, a nonprofit agency that commissions research, often in response to government funding, had advised the ministry that transplantation was no longer merely experimental. In response, the ministry set up an Advisory Committee on Renal Transplantation under the eminent Sir Hedley Atkins to provide expert advice. The committee recommended that the number of renal centers be increased to about twenty and set a thousand transplants per year as a goal. Again, the ministry accepted these recommendations and earmarked funds for these purposes.

The role of the Royal College of Physicians and that of its president, Rosenheim, were particularly important during these early years. Unlike the British Medical Association, which is open to all physicians, the Royal College is extremely selective, admitting new members only by election and not by mere application. It represents, in other words, the elite of the profession and, as such, has tended to be viewed by policy makers as the natural place to look for high-quality professional advice. "The department will go where the expertise is," a former chief medical officer confirmed, "to the Royal College." Thus, just before his election as president of the Royal College, Rosenheim chaired the first advisory committee on dialysis; in 1970 he chaired another committee dealing with the dangers of viral hepatitis to ESRD patients and staff; and in 1972, a few months before his death, he chaired yet another committee, this on both dialysis and transplantation.

There is some question, however, as to the extent that Rosenheim dominated these committees. For one thing, he was, as one of his colleagues rather delicately put it, "a very old fashioned nephrologist." He had done some research as a young man (indeed, he had made a useful discovery related to the treatment of kidney infections when a medical student in 1930), but had long since moved to administrative work and had acquired a reputation as "an expert committee-man" (London *Times*, 1972). In fact, during the period in which he headed the ESRD advisory committees, he also headed other advisory committees on clinical pharmacology, heat-sterilized fluids, thoracic medicine, geriatrics, cardiology, and the prevention of microbial contamination of medical products. Why was Rosenheim called on to head so many committees, many of which were quite outside his area of expertise? As president of the Royal College, he may have seemed the obvious person, and because each report seemed satisfactory – that is, because each addressed narrow problems and did not challenge the department's broad allocative assumptions – one assignment naturally led to another. By the end, within six years, Rosenheim had moved from professor to knight to baron.

Meanwhile, the spectacular development of dialysis in the early 1960s had created, as one Ministry of Health official who observed matters firsthand noted, "intense pressure to provide this life-saving measure" (Dennis, 1971, p. 144). At the same time, however, the ministry saw that if not carefully controlled, dialysis (and transplantation) could become a bureaucrat's nightmare. For it was immediately apparent to the ministry's sophisticated civil servants that the new technologies combined three incendiary ingredients: They were fairly reliable, they were lifesaving, and they were expensive. If they had incorporated only two of these, no great problem would have been posed. If, for example, they had been reliable and lifesaving but not expensive (like, say, the polio vaccine), they might have been adopted without frightening allocative consequences. Or if they had been lifesaving and expensive but not reliable (like pancreas transplants), they might have been assigned a low priority. Or if they had been reliable and expensive but not lifesaving (like cosmetic face lifts), they might simply have been put aside as a luxury (but cf. MacGreggor, 1979). But each of the techniques, dialysis and transplantation, had all three qualities.

It was equally obvious to the ministry that in an era of rapid advances in medical technology that tend to generate a "technological imperative" to use them (Mechanic, 1979), dialysis and transplantation would before long be joined by other therapies that would also be reliable, lifesaving, and expensive and would have their own articulate advocates (see, e.g., Sherlock, 1983; Bailey, in Timmins, 1983). The new renal technologies, therefore, could not be viewed in isolation, but rather had to be seen as prototypes of a new kind of treatment that would threaten existing financial patterns, even as it provided hope to patients and their families.[6]

How was the Ministry of Health to respond? The new technologies seemed both too valuable to ignore and too costly to embrace.

---

[6] Indeed, nearly all medical progress has the effect of increasing medical costs, for even curative therapies can be viewed as providing patients with an added increment of life during which they will likely incur medical costs that exceed those that would have been spent on the older therapies that would have failed to save them. This, of course, is hardly an argument against medical progress, even on economic grounds, since the patient (at least, the nonelderly patient) may well earn enough during this added increment of life to more than pay for his added medical costs (cf. McPherson, 1985, p. 1679).

The answer plainly was to adopt a policy lying somewhere between these two poles. Since the ministry was perennially short of funds, was at this time dominated by "an ideology of efficiency" (Klein, 1983b, p. 64), and could hardly have welcomed the prospect of reallocation that a major ESRD effort would involve, the policy it chose did not lie exactly halfway between the two extremes. Instead, the decision was to make an understandably rather cautious beginning, coupled with no firm commitments about the future.

Talk of cost effectiveness, however, would not suffice to sell such a limited program to the medical community or to deflect any outrage that might later come from the media, members of Parliament, or others. What was required was medical legitimation of the program. It was at this point that the physicians' committees were activated. Pragmatic types socialized into understanding NHS reality and eager to get the program going, the committees' members shared the ministry's assumption of a modest beginning and gave most of their attention to practical suggestions. Cumulatively, they knew, these suggestions could help to determine the success of the program, and if the committees did not focus upon such matters, they would be left with mere trial and error, and all the possibilities of needless death and suffering and avoidable budgetary retaliation that that might entail.

But because these physicians tended to view their task in such narrow terms, to see themselves as team players, and to be preoccupied with quality to the virtual exclusion of quantity, they were easy for ministry bureaucrats to use: The physicians did not have to be manipulated; it was enough to appeal to their highest sentiments. Less eminent or more egalitarian physicians might have been more concerned with the eventual size of the program, it is true. Yet it is impossible to fault the physicians' integrity and even difficult to quarrel with the assertion that no ironclad bureaucratic commitments on expansion would have been forthcoming in any case – nor would they necessarily have been kept, if made. In any event, it must have been entirely predictable that distinguished physician committees (i.e., committees drawn from physicians at teaching hospitals) would be far more sensitive to the creation of renal units at centers of excellence (i.e., at teaching hospitals) than the expansion of treatment patterns to cover underserved portions of the population. Certainly, the relatively few teaching hospitals had become accustomed to a status even more favorable than that enjoyed by their counterparts in the United States. It was this limited approach that was initially recommended.

Once its macroallocative decision had received the imprimatur of the medical elite, the ministry assented to what it had helped bring about. Implementation, which in other contexts is often problematical (Pressman and Wildavsky, 1973), raised no difficulties here; for in the name of spurring the establishment of the centers, the ministry retained control over renal unit financing during the initial stage. In 1971 the ministry (now reorganized into the Department of Health and Social Security [DHSS]) turned over the funding of renal units to the Regional Health Authorities, which subsumed it in their regular budgets. After a period of special treatment, in short, renal unit funding was put on essentially the same footing as other ordinary claimants.

ESRD POLICY: SINCE THE FORMATIVE YEARS

What has been most striking about ESRD policy in the United Kingdom is how gradual its evolution has been. While nearly all the rest of the Western world bounded ahead like a hare, at least until 1986 the United Kingdom proceeded at a more tortoise-like pace.

How to explain ESRD policy since the early, formative years? To a large extent, the answer must be sought among the various bureaucratic strata of the DHSS and their relations one with another. At the top in the central office is the paper-thin crust of political appointees: the secretary of state for social services, the minister for health, and a few others. Theoretically, these appointees are in control, though it is generally taken for granted that as a practical matter, political appointees are crucially dependent upon their career civil service subordinates, the administrative class. These subordinates, knowledgeable and experienced, fluent and self-confident, are believed to educate the appointees about what the department has done and is committed to doing and what its potentialities and limitations are, and to encourage the appointees' adoption of the department's traditional perspective and modes of operations. The career civil servants are also thought to be vital for identifying problems, formulating solutions, and monitoring their execution. As one former minister for health recalled:

> I felt like somebody floating on the most comfortable support. The whole department is there to support the minister. Into his in-tray came, by and by, notes with suggestions as to what he should do. Everything is done to sustain him in the line officials think he should take. . . . Each ministry has its own departmental policy and this policy goes on while ministers come and go. (Crossman, 1975)

Hence, the inadequacy of the traditional view of the civil servant as having "just one loyalty – to the public, which in practice means to the democratically elected representatives of the public" (Chapman, 1978, p. 7; see also Wheare, 1955, p. 17; Hayes, in Young and Sloman, 1982, p. 26). Though far less partisan than civil servants in France or Germany (Suleiman, 1985), British officials are hardly mere neutral implementers of politicians' policies. Of course, this is not to deny that political appointees can make a difference, but they must choose their areas of concern carefully and proceed with vigor, tenacity, and skill – and even then, they may not prevail.

In its relations with the lower levels, the central office can draw on a series of major power resources that the other levels simply cannot claim (see Rhodes, 1979). Hierarchically, the DHSS is supreme. It must approve regional and district plans, and through the secretary of state it appoints members and chairs of Regional Health Authorities (RHAs) and chairs of District Health Authorities (DHAs). Neither elected nor by convention necessarily representative of local organizations, these officials, for the most part, lack a power base in the community; they are accountable not to the community downward, but to the secretary upward (Hunter, 1984, p. 43; Steel, 1984, p. 39). Formally, if not always factually, as a minister for health expressed it, "All members are appointed for their personal qualities and the contribution that they can make to the work of the authority corporately. They are not to be mandated to represent any sectional or particular interest" (Clark, in Timmins, 1985). Politically, the DHSS has close proximity and ready access to dominant elective leaders. Legally and constitutionally, the DHSS can ask (and has asked) the secretary of state to suspend lower-level officers when it has found it necessary. Indeed, in a unitary system, in which all legitimate power derives from parliamentary legislation, regional and district authorities are utterly without independent constitutional foundation.

Most important, financially, the DHSS issues a general budget, allocates money to regions, and enforces compliance through a number of formal and informal means, including an implied threat to trim the following year's allowance. "Legislation, Departmental circulars, and cash limits," one district board member admitted, "provide the framework within which authorities operate" (Steel, 1984, p. 37). The assumption is, as one analyst put it, that the "*national* health service should be under national control" (Hunter, 1984, p. 44). It is hardly surprising, therefore, that a minister for health in the early 1960s concluded that the central office was all powerful (Powell, 1976) or that a secretary of state in the mid-1970s dismissed the RHAs as "necessarily pretty subservient" (Castle, 1980, p. 315).

Further facilitating central control was the creation in 1982 of a system of performance indicators – average cost per patient, average number of outpatients per clinic session, and so on. These have been used by regions to assess the performance of districts and by the central office to assess the performance of regions, all on a comparative basis. The indicators have been widely criticized as crude and inflexible measures of performance that are insensitive to the quality of care delivered, and efforts have been made to modify them to take these objections into account. The indicators have also been said to stifle local initiative and innovation and to impose perhaps inappropriate administrative targets in the name of accountability (Allen et al., 1987). For their part, however, defenders of the system view it as a useful device for pruning inefficiencies from the NHS and insist that it is merely one of the many starting points for performance evaluation. Often, defenders add that any system, no matter how skillfully drawn up, would probably agitate lower-level officials, who are seen as inherently resistant to change.

As a consequence of all this, physicians' attitudes toward the central office fall short of affection. One nephrologist who was interviewed, for example, said repeatedly that "the department is interested in money; we are interested in patients." Another complained that the career officials at the central office tended to be "leftists who loathe doctors" as members of a prototypical elitist group. And two others charged that the department followed a divide-and-rule strategy, playing specialties off against each other, general practitioners off against hospital consultants, and regions off against regions. Sometimes these remarks were accompanied by unconcealed bitterness.

Yet it must be said that there is less to this central dominance than meets the eye. For one thing, the NHS is simply too big to permit a small group in London to maintain effective control over all its services throughout the entire nation. It is not uncommon, for instance, for RHA plans to ignore relevant DHSS directives (Elcock and Haywood, 1980, p. 74) or for plans to be filed late or even not at all.

For another thing, when it comes to information and experience, the lower-level bureaucrats are quite well situated. Their day-to-day contacts with patients and line staff, particularly at the district and regional specialty level, give them a knowledge and perspective that the DHSS cannot duplicate. And this knowledge and perspective, as the DHSS well knows, must be skillfully utilized if its goals are to be met. It must be acknowledged, though, that lower-level bureaucrats often "have found it difficult to collect the information they need" (Elcock, 1979, p. 17) and do not always possess much technological sophistication.

Most important, the general principle is that although the central office allocates funds to the regions, it leaves the task of determining how these funds are to be spent – in a word, policy making – to the regions and districts.[7] Thus, a Cabinet health care spokesperson could say of ESRD, "The provision of facilities for the treatment of

---

[7] Bulpitt (1983) maintains that Whitehall traditionally distinguishes between "high politics" (e.g., foreign and defense policy, the courts) and "low politics" (e.g., health, welfare, education); the former are highly centralized in administration, he believes, and the latter much less so.

kidney patients is a health authority responsibility" (Whitney, in *Parliamentary Debates*, 1986b). Tight control is exercised over total expenditure, where limits are rigidly fixed, but the DHSS does not frequently earmark funds for specific purposes (as initially occurred with ESRD), and only major capital projects costing more than 2 million pounds are actually reviewed by the central office. Some regional authorities have even drawn up their own allocation formulas (Butts et al., 1981). Since the mid-1970s, moreover, the regions have explicitly been granted further budgetary discretion. Within limits, they can now carry money forward from one year to the next, for example, and can transfer funds from one functional category to another.

Much regional variation in program support, it must also be said, does not reflect gross differences in available resources but merely alternative views on where resources ought to be allocated. Thus, Wessex, which admits relatively few ESRD patients for treatment, also admits a relatively large number of osteoarthritis patients for arthroplasty of the hip, where East Anglia, which admits a relatively large number of ESRD patients, admits relatively few patients for arthroplasty (Laing and Taylor, 1982, p. 11).

Delegation of authority to the regions, however, is not invariant. As a former chief medical officer noted, "The decision to organize a national program for haemodialysis was an example of specific central action" (Godber, 1975, p. 94). It was the central office that until 1971 allotted funds for this purpose; it was the central office that established a pair of structures to facilitate transplantation, the National Tissue Typing Reference Laboratory in 1969 and the National Organ Matching and Distributing Service in 1972; it was the central office that supplied money for dialysis machines for children in 1977; in response to growing public attention, it was the central office that informally advised the regions in 1983 to strengthen their budgets for renal services in 1984; it was the central office that in 1985 provided half a million pounds "to ensure that treatment is available to all children . . . who would benefit from treatment" (Patten, in Hamilton, 1985); and most important (as we shall see), it was the central office that instructed the regions in 1984 to aim for an intake rate of forty PMP by 1987.

Notwithstanding these and other departures from regional delegation, however, it is fair to say, as one regional officer put it, that the DHSS confines itself to "setting a broad framework," within which what the regions do "is up to them, within broad tolerances." Shifting metaphors, he described the DHSS's attitude as a "threshold approach – the regions must meet minimum levels but after that are basically on their own." In sum, although it may be an error to contend that the lower levels are dominant (Crossman, 1972), they are clearly not without real impact.

In truth, the relationship between center and periphery is a dynamic one, which is to say that it is always changing, or at least subject to change. Different reorganization plans, different administrators at the central and lower levels, different regions with different problems and different styles and mixes of medical resources, different eras of relative prosperity or recession, different issues involving different magnitudes of political and health costs and benefits – these and other variables may affect the relationship. What prevails regarding ESRD in the 1980s, therefore, cannot be regarded as a model of NHS policy making fixed forever, like an insect in amber.

THE REGIONS

Below the central office are fourteen Regional Health Authorities, each with overtly political and administrative components. The political component ostensibly sits atop each structure and includes about twenty members, all named by the secretary of state, normally after consultation with appropriate interests. It is hard to make general statements about the RHAs, partly because variation among regions is striking and partly because the available data are neither representative nor recent. Yet it appears that a typical RHA member is a businessman in his fifties, who belongs to many organizations and does not regard the "RHA as playing a major part" in his life. He attends the monthly RHA meetings, yet with twenty to thirty-five items packing the agenda, there is usually not much time for debate. Probably, he feels, this is just as well, since making broad policy decisions or preparing plans do not interest him much. Even conscientious members are likely to be ineffective. As one Trent RHA member expressed it:

> The administration of the NHS . . . leaves no easily discernible role for an amateur, part-time, inexperienced, volunteer member. The strategy of the use of resources is well beyond the comprehension of most members and therefore on major issues they face recommendations which are well argued and proven; they do not have to deal with the options . . . because the selection of the preferred option has already been carried out before the matter comes to the authority. What is left for members to consider are items of no real importance. (Spungrin, 1985)

The RHA chairman, a "first among equals," handles communications with the media and the secretary of state and receives a part-time salary (ordinary members receive only expenses). Although he may act as a chief executive at RHA meetings, decisions there have traditionally been reached by consensus (Elcock, 1978). In all likelihood, he attends working management meetings only "occasionally" (Chaplin, 1982, p. 109), though he is the only board member who attends annual review meetings with the DHSS and the districts. If vigorous RHA leadership does at times emerge, this could hardly be called an optimal setting for it.

As a practical matter, therefore, it is the career officials – the regional teams of officers (RTOs) – who ordinarily dominate regional decision making. The RTO includes the regional administrator, treasurer, medical officer, and works officer. Supporting the RTO is a diverse staff of administrators, statisticians, engineers, and others.

It is the RTO that every four years revises the authority's ten-year strategic plan; it annually develops the required three-year operating plan; it handles most communications with the DHSS; it draws up the action plans for the districts at the annual review meetings; and, most important, it formulates budgetary requests and makes budgetary allocations. All of this, of course, is done under the RHA's name.

Like the RHAs, the RTOs have been confined to decision making by consensus, an approach that has generated considerable controversy. One regional administrator, for example, praised it as "very effective." Although it led to "a certain amount of horse trading" and may overload officers with trivial items, its great strength was in its "insuring commitment" of the entire team, enhancing harmony, and improving functional integration. Others, however, complained that the necessity of reaching a consensus slows the process of decision making, discourages departures from settled policies, and inhibits strong leadership and personal accountability.

THE DISTRICTS

The 192 District Health Authorities resemble the RHAs in general outline, each being headed by an unpaid sixteen- to nineteen-member board and served by a district management team (DMT). The DMT consists of the district administrator, treasurer, medical officer, and nursing officer, plus a hospital consultant and general practitioner, each elected by his respective colleagues.

There are two major differences, however, between DHAs and RHAs. One involves competence. Frequently, DHA board members are, as one observer put it, "parish pump politicians," and the impression that they tend to be even more lacking in sophistication and commitment than RHA members appears to be widely held. DHA members receive almost no training or preparation before assuming their positions (Steel, 1984, p. 37), and it is said that the more able DHA members tend to be graduated to a position on an RHA. More important, the generally lower level of competence is also believed to extend to the district staff. Not only are districts often lacking in needed technical capacity, for example, but sometimes they seem to lack interest in even acquiring that capacity. Thus, only a third of the districts expressed an interest in joining a computerized system for compiling and comparing tender costs, though required to do so by law (Jones, 1983).

The second main difference is that the districts are responsible for actual service delivery. As a result, even more than RTOs, DMTs tend to focus on specifics rather than abstractions, to see themselves as enablers, organizers, or coordinators rather than grand policy makers, in short, as doers rather than thinkers (Stewart et al., 1980, esp. ch. 6).[8] Historically constrained by consensus decision making, receiving advice that is "overwhelmingly medical" (Council for Science and Society, 1982, p. 18), and beset by myriad requests from their constituents – staffs, department heads, professional advisory committees, and so on – they generally feel too pressured by the hurly-burly of daily events to pause for strategic contemplation. Calls to them for budgets and plans, therefore, tend to be greeted merely as opportunities to bid for more resources. Lacking criteria that would enable them to choose among these bids, the district's role, as one member from a London area cynically stated, is "to provide psychological comfort for those unwilling to pronounce on medical trade-offs" (Beesley, 1985, p. 148). Critics have complained that DHAs "appear not to be accountable to anyone and float in organizational space" (Hunter, 1984, p. 44), but the demands from their administrative subordinates are so insistent that "autonomous" is almost the last word that DHA members would use to describe their role.

DHAs are widely believed to be dominated by their ostensibly subordinate DMTs, and the reasons usually given are obvious: DHA members tend to be part-time amateurs with modest relevant expertise; DHA members are frequently confused in their loyalties (appointed by RHAs, they probably were nominated by an interest group or local governmental unit and may also feel committed to the welfare of the medical staff or the ordinary patient [Ranadé, 1985, p. 185]); and DHA members cannot call on the legitimacy that popular elections can confer (Regen and Stewart, 1982). As a consequence, their reputations have never been high.

REGIONAL SPECIALTIES

Regional specialties (like renal units), though possessing far narrower jurisdictions, appear to exhibit an even more oppressive

---

[8] This study was conducted before the latest NHS reorganization, but RHA administrators continue to echo its conclusions.

orientation to the here and now. With fewer personnel and sub-divisions, they have scant opportunity for internal shuffling and maneuvering and little bureaucratic fat that can be trimmed away. Thus, even more than district managers, heads of regional specialties are, as one RHA administrator put it, "forced to be entrepreneuers" and heavily reliant on "the ad hoc." Predictably, this response some-times manifests itself as empire building. Regional specialties, as another regional officer observed, often "attract powerful people and high technology" and can act as "magnets for funds." Yet specialties may also sometimes be satisfied merely with fighting a holding operation. Another regional officer noted, for instance, that the renal specialists in his region, far from pressing for funds for ex-pansion, seemed to feel that a "steady state was adequate."

In any case, at least as far as ESRD is concerned, it is the renal unit that constitutes the basic budgetary unit. Clinicians, though the ul-timate resource allocators, have tended to shy away from budgetary concerns, feeling that their involvement would be "a waste of con-sultants' valuable skills and patient care attributes" (Poynton, 1983, p. 23). It is the renal units, therefore – along with other regional specialties and the DHAs – that press the RHAs for money.

As a consequence of the activities of this gaggle of claimants, RHA career officers frequently complain that they feel like "men in the middle." From below, they are beseiged with requests from dis-tricts and regional specialties to remedy long lists of deficiencies. Nearly always, of course, the extent of the deficiencies is ex-aggerated, and yet the existence of serious deficiencies is beyond question. Some of these items raise issues of life or death; others pose major questions about the quality of life. As a spokesperson for the West Midlands RHA, in replying to nephrologists' calls for more money, commented:

> Other branches beside the treatment of end-stage renal failure are also life-saving. Others offer comfort and the relief of pain to both the chronically ill and the elderly ill, and some try to help those who are mentally ill or handicapped. Some are con-cerned with preserving the life of the newborn, for which the West Midlands also has a poor record. Some are concerned with the promotion of practices which will help people to

avoid ill health, such as the addition of fluoride to drinking
water and a reduction in smoking. (Quoted in Butcher,
1982)

Plainly, there is no shortage of meritorious requests. And no wonder
that as early as 1956, official reports were expressing concern about
projected health costs (Guillebaud, 1956).[9]

Exacerbating the problem has been a chronic shortage of funds.
To what extent, if at all, the NHS has suffered under Tory
stewardship has been a topic of sharp dispute. Conservatives have
tended to argue that from 1979 to 1986 real per capita spending on
health care grew by 24 percent, that health care's share of the gross
domestic product increased from 4.8 to 5.5 percent, and that efficiency savings made more of the budget available for useful purposes. Labour critics have often replied that nearly all these apparent
gains either were required by demographic changes (chiefly, an
aging society) or were consumed by higher prices and pay for the
same levels of services. Thus, when the government points to a 10
percent increase in the number of doctors, dentists, nurses, and mid-
wives, the opposition is liable to focus on a 10 percent decline in
hospital beds and a loss of 434 medical academic posts. But however
one resolves the debate, it is hard to argue with a DHA treasurer
who grumbled, "Gone are the days when the main argument used to
be, 'who has the additional money?' Now it is, 'how can a development be justified if it can only take place at the expense of curtailing
another service?'" (Poynton, 1983, p. 23).

How, then, is the RHA to choose among all the requests it
receives? The shopping-list approach generally adopted by districts
and regional specialties is not of much help because it does not confront the problem of scarcity with the weapon of priorities. And yet
it is clearly unrealistic to expect long-range proposals from routin-
izers and problem solvers or negative decisions from administrators
who must work closest with those who would feel most aggrieved
by rejection.

---

[9] Meanwhile, from 1950 to 1955 the percentage of the United Kingdom's gross
national product devoted to health care actually declined by 0.5 percent (Maxwell, 1981).

If those below the RHAs are a greater source of pressure than of help, those above are perceived as supplying precious little support. Even where DHSS preferences are well known, the department may offer only inconsequential assistance. Transplantation, for example, is clearly the department's treatment of choice for ESRD, and yet for years its efforts were pretty much confined to a series of ineffectual publicity campaigns for donor cards, none of which was even formally evaluated (Lewis, 1979, p. 6). Not until 1984 was the nation's first major public campaign mounted, as twelve and a half million donor cards were distributed. Though the government repeatedly attributed the record organ harvest that year to the campaign and a London transplant surgeon loudly dismissed it as "just a load of rubbish" (Williams, in Timmins, 1986b), no formal evaluations exist to substantiate either conclusion (Patten, in *Parliamentary Debates*, 1985a).

Nor has the government adopted an "opt out" policy that would mandate cadaver organ donation unless the patient or the patient's family expressly demurred[10] or even a "required request" policy that would compel physicians to ask the deceased's relatives to donate his organs. Instead, officials have simply expressed the hope that doctors would bind themselves to making the request through a voluntary code of practice (Timmins, 1986c).

Nor has the government moved aggressively to facilitate transplants. Only in 1984, after years of discussion, was a pilot project begun with "the appointment of a number of consultants to act as part-time advisors with the job of improving hospital liaison procedures" (Patten, in *Parliamentary Debates*, 1983). Even this aimed only at educating hospital staff and appealing to their sense of duty; they still had considerable time-consuming work – chiefly, applying the criteria for brain death – for which they received no special compensation (Grist, 1981).[11] And a proposal to establish a free-

---

[10] France's "opt out" law, however, has proved rather disappointing, for physicians have continued to request permission from the potential donor's family. Switzerland and Austria have also found that many of the expected gains have failed to materialize.

[11] Until recently, the United States was so lacking in national coordinating machinery that no central body monitored supply and demand and no criteria

standing national computer registry of potential organ donors was only reluctantly considered by the government, which publicly expressed doubt that the program's benefits would exceed its costs (Whitney, in *Parliamentary Debates*, 1986a).

As for home dialysis, for many years the second most favored treatment, no consideration apparently has been given to utilizing a simplified system, which, when tried on an unselected patient population in Australia, proved workable in nearly 90 percent of the cases (George, 1983; Lynn et al., 1984). Although somewhat more costly than the United Kingdom's current home-dialysis procedure, it is much less expensive than hospital dialysis. Not even a pilot project in the United Kingdom has been discussed. A health ministry committed to transplantation or home dialysis might be expected to consider these (or similar measures), for if they were to succeed, the entire nationwide system would benefit. It has not proved realistic to expect individual regions to fund such efforts, however, for the improvements would constitute public goods that would benefit the entire community, including even those members who bore no costs

for allocating the organs were devised. One consequence was a heavy reliance on informal physician networks; another was that many donated kidneys simply went unused. At first, reformers aimed not at centralizing the system, but rather at inducing states to require hospitals to ask relatives of patients who died to donate their organs. In 1985, four states adopted such laws, and in 1986 "required request" bills were introduced in twenty-one other states; compliance, however, has been spotty. All states, though, allow applicants for driver's licenses to register as organ donors (Malcolm, 1986b; Merritt and Toff, 1986). In 1987, as a little noted part of the 205-page Omnibus Budget Reconciliation Act (PL-509), Congress extended the required request principle to all hospitals receiving Medicare or Medicaid funds and ordered all transplanting hospitals to join and abide by the rules of the federally funded, private non-profit Organ Procurement and Transplantation Network. The required request law in the United States has not met its sponsors' hopes, mainly because many physicians do not like to become involved in brain death decisions or contact donors' families; many physicians also fear legal liabilities from the organ procurement process (Annas, 1988; Prottas and Batten, 1988). Late in 1987, the DHSS announced that it had dropped plans for required request procedures for NHS doctors; disappointment with the results of the American experience (which at the national level was only a few months old) was cited by the department. A few months later, in early 1988, the government announced that it would reconsider the required request system in 1990.

or risks in developing them. What is evident here is the "free-rider" phenomenon (see Olson, 1965), where self-interest leads each region to avoid the burden in the hope that it can profit from another's efforts, with the result that very little gets done. Only a collective approach, in other words, can save the rationality of individual regions from stifling the pursuit of the common goal.

Even more distressing to the regions, the DHSS ordinarily withholds the most useful tool for enforcing policy on subordinates: explicit guidance from the central office. In its place is occasional advice and, more often, simply silence. The regions, as a consequence, are left to confront the cacophony of demands from districts and regional specialties with little to protect themselves. They cannot easily shift the blame for unpleasant decisions to their superiors – and, traditionally, blame-taking is one of the superiors' main functions – but must shoulder it themselves. Of course, some regional officers welcome this. "The buck comes to us," one said forcefully. "We are the resource allocators." What he viewed as an opportunity, however, others see as merely a problem. The DHSS, meanwhile, in complete harmony with its parliamentary mandate, justifies its abdication by reference to maximizing responsiveness to regions and districts.

THE GRIFFITHS REPORT

The 1982 NHS reorganization had scarcely been put in place when Roy Griffiths, managing director of Sainsbury's, a large supermarket chain and one of Britain's most prominent commercial successes, was asked to head a management inquiry team. In 1983 the team issued its report, a compilation of management recommendations intended to infuse the NHS with dynamic, private-sector-type executive leadership, particularly from those outside the organization. "If Florence Nightingale were carrying her lamp through the corridors of the health service today," the report declared acidly, "she would almost certainly be looking for the people in charge" (DHSS, 1983). The aim of the report, as one supporter explained, was to make the central office more important in setting targets and ensuring that they are met and less important in the actual day-to-day management of operations (Edwards, 1984).

The report's most significant recommendation was that the secretary of state name general managers at all levels of the bureaucracy, including a general manager for each region, district, and unit and a general manager of an NHS Management Board to provide management leadership for the entire organization. Although the report also called for greater clinician involvement in management, it was the physicians and nurses who opposed the recommendations most vigorously. They believed – correctly, as the early evidence suggests – that clinicians either would not be interested in management or would find the pay and terms of employment unattractive, that relatively few clinicians would therefore become general managers, and that the influence of clinicians would be displaced by that of the new managers. Typical perhaps was the comment of the chairman of the Royal Commission on the NHS, who, finding insufficient evidence that the changes were needed, concluded, "The NHS has in the last ten years had far too much administrative reform" (Merrison, in Timmins, 1984a).

Other early losers included the district management teams and, to a lesser degree, the regional teams of officers, both of which now had to contend with potent competitors for power in the form of centrally appointed general managers. In an obvious effort to mollify the district and regional teams, the report carefully emphasized its intention to retain the "good features" of consensus decision making; the general managers were to work with the preexisting management teams to try to produce a consensus, and only if this failed were the managers supposed to impose their own solution.

How all this will work in practice is not easy to predict, for neither the general managers' roles nor their formal relationships with other structures and officers are clearly spelled out, and leadership and consensus are in many plain and practical ways incompatible goals. Nor is it clear, despite assurances that the changes will not simply mean "jobs for the boys," that many outsiders will be recruited for the new managerial positions; the overwhelming number of new appointments initially went to existing NHS staff members. One pair of observers called the introduction of general managers "probably the most radical change in NHS administration since 1948" (Grimes and Allen, 1985, p. 1368), but others were dubious that its effects would be all that great.

ESRD'S PECULIAR DISADVANTAGES

To this situation of institutionalized, almost genetically based caution, ESRD brings several important disadvantages. First, relative to the treatment modalities of most other diseases – more than 70 percent of NHS spending goes to wages and salaries (Gray, 1984) – ESRD has a rather unusual mix of capital and labor costs. The widely used home-based therapies in effect enroll the patient and the patient's family as unpaid employees of the NHS and therefore entail only modest staffing. One result is that there are fewer personnel to press for expansion or to oppose retrenchment. Another is that funding restraints would produce only a small number of layoffs, a situation administrators greatly prefer. The temptation for policy makers to resist increased ESRD funding, as a consequence, is ever present and must go far to explain the long-standing practice of so understaffing renal units that they operate at only about half their capacity (Davison et al., 1984).

Second, in recent years, the general thrust of DHSS efforts has been to shift "expenditures away from hospitals and toward general medicine and community health activities" (Ham, 1982, p. 29). On one side, bureaucrats and reformers have argued that greater funding for prevention (DHSS, 1976b) and the so-called Cinderella services for the mentally ill, the handicapped, and the aged is required both by cost effectiveness and by simple justice (DHSS, 1976c). Resisting this trend have been hospital consultants, skeptical about health education, dubious that public health measures have much more to offer, and engaged by the intellectual challenge of acute care (Jennett, 1984). Despite the consultants' efforts, however, a change in emphasis has clearly taken place.

This newer emphasis can only buttress ongoing ESRD treatment patterns, which have stressed less expensive, non-hospital-based therapies for many years. Any effort to expand treatment patterns significantly by increasing the number of patients dialyzed in hospitals or centers must collide with this more fashionable approach, perhaps appearing hopelessly out of date.

A third disadvantage attaching to ESRD is that the expensiveness of ESRD treatment raises questions about the individual's right to health care that do not emerge with comparable impact in most other conditions. This is not the place to rehearse the familiar ethical arguments, pro and con. They have been addressed at great length in appropriate forums (e.g., Rescher, 1969; Katz and Capron, 1975; Almeder, 1979; Winslow, 1982) and will be discussed in more detail in the concluding chapter of this book.

It is enough to say here that in the United Kingdom it has traditionally been accepted that, in the words of a DHSS senior medical advisor, "there is no right to treatment" (Pincherle, in Parson and Ogg, 1983, p. 113).[12] Thus, the relevant portion of the National Health Service Act of 1977 reads, "It is the Secretary of State's duty to provide throughout England and Wales to such an extent as he considers necessary to meet all reasonable requirements . . . medical . . . services." It is certainly clear that the statute was not intended to give all the secretary's unsupported subjective judgments the force of law; a full evaluation of relevant factors may be required. But it is even clearer that such a statute can hardly be the product of legislators intent upon creating a right to treatment (but cf. Morris, 1983). Indeed, in *Regina* v. *Secretary of State for Social Services, ex parte Hincks et al.* (1980), the Court of Appeal declared, "It cannot be supposed that the Secretary of State has to supply all the latest equipment [or] to provide all the kidney machines which are asked for, or . . . all the new developments, such as heart transplants, in every case where people would benefit from them." Far from imposing an absolute duty to provide care, the law grants discretion to the secretary, who may take financial restraints into account. The alternative view, that there exists an absolute duty to provide care, would entail clear breaches of duty by prior secretaries, none of which was so much as noted by Parliament, and

---

[12] In the United States, there is no constitutional right to health care (*Maher* v. *Roe*, 1977, p. 469; *Harris* v. *McRae*, 1980, p. 318) either, though there are a host of statutory rights, many deriving from Medicare or Medicaid legislation (e.g., *Elder* v. *Beal*, 1979; *Schweiker* v. *Gray Panthers*, 1981).

this was hardly plausible (Brahams, 1984).[13] Similarly, in *re Walker's application* (London *Times*, 1987), concerning surgery to relieve congenital heart disease in an infant, the Court of Appeal ruled that courts should not countermand the government's allocation decisions unless they were "unreasonable" or constituted breaches of duty under public law. And even in these few circumstances, courts were instructed to exercise discretion and take account of all circumstances (Brahams, 1987). In the United Kingdom, in short, policy considerations, apparently a rough utilitarian view of the public interest, trump the entitlement principle (cf. Dworkin, 1985, ch. 3).

Hence, although there has been talk of a lawsuit endeavoring to enforce a duty to provide treatment to all ESRD patients, it is generally viewed as merely another means of generating publicity to pressure the government to provide more funds. Were such a suit to prevail, funding patterns throughout the Health Service would be threatened, its long-standing role as medical rationer as well as provider would be abandoned, and patient demands would burst budget levels with the force of a ruptured aneurysm. All this may, of course, be desirable, but it is not the sort of change that is likely to be brought about and sustained by a lawsuit.

By contrast, in West Germany, France, Spain, and, until recently, Italy, ESRD treatment is funded through insurance schemes, and so the ruling assumption is that the patient is entitled to whatever treatment is medically indicated on the ground that he has paid his "premiums." (That insurance is merely a camouflage for transfer payments is immaterial, since the fiction is so widely accepted as fact.) The United States, which funds ESRD treatment under Medicare, has taken essentially the same view.[14]

---

[13] The case, however, involved a failure to provide nonurgent orthopedic services, not dialysis. Thus, the remarks on kidney machines are nonbinding *obiter dicta*.

[14] In the United States, however, a number of significant costs are not covered by Medicare: The patient must pay the first $520 of any hospital visit; in general, Medicare coverage does not begin until the third month after dialysis treatments begin; Medicare pays only 80% of the approved dialysis facility or surgeon's fee and other covered medical services; and Medicare does not cover transportation

The notion that ESRD patients ought legally to be entitled to treatment, however, is regarded by United Kingdom policy makers with a mixture of contempt and horror. Indeed, the American experience is looked to as the chief cautionary example (but cf. Neu and Kjellstrand, 1986). From 10,000 patients in 1973, the United States increased the number of patients treated in 1986 to 87,000 at a cost of about 2 billion dollars. In interview after interview, UK administrators and physicians decried the American policy as medically absurd – recounting tales of the dialyzing of senile patients with metastatic cancer – and financially "out of control," attributing it to naively idealistic congressmen and greedy proprietary dialysis center owners. America, it was always pointed out, was wealthy enough to afford such foolish extravagance; the United Kingdom was not. The fear of treating too many, in short, inspired much more passion than the fear of treating too few.[15]

Plainly, much of the difference between British and American ESRD treatment patterns can be attributed simply to America's greater wealth. In general terms, it is widely accepted that more than 90 percent of the observed variation in health care spending among different countries is associated with income levels. Not only do wealthier countries spend more on health care, but they spend

costs to a dialysis facility, dialysis aides' services for home dialysis, and so forth (Health Care Financing Administration, 1987). For a moving account of the costs (financial, as well as social and psychological) borne by the patient on home dialysis, see Campbell and Campbell (1978). As a result of legislation adopted in 1978, the Medicare bias against home dialysis has been reduced, though the skillful efforts of proprietary dialysis interests succeeded in killing most of the major financial incentives for home dialysis (Greenberg, 1978). In 1981, however, Congress required the Department of Health and Human Services to develop a prospective payment system for outpatient dialysis services that would further promote home dialysis, and in 1983 a monthly capitation payment system was instituted. Although it has been argued that home dialysis is not cheaper than center dialysis (Stason and Barnes, 1985), by the end of 1985, 19.6% of American ESRD patients were dialyzing at home. By 1986, general pressures for health care cost containment produced a reduction in physician reimbursements for dialysis from 3.8 to 5.5% (Durenberger, 1985).

[15] In the United States, too, the ESRD program is increasingly being raised as a point against the creation of an end-stage cardiac disease program and similar programs (Evans et al., 1986, p. 1896).

higher proportions of their gross national product on health care (Kleiman, 1974; Newhouse, 1977).

It would be too facile, however, to credit the difference entirely to this factor. Also involved are Britain's low expectations about its economic future. As late as 1951, though still reeling from the effects of World War II, Britain could boast a per capita income exceeding that of any European member of the Atlantic Alliance and an industrial production greater than that of France and Germany combined. Notwithstanding Wilson's talk of faster economic growth and Thatcher's of revitalization, nor the emergence of "swinging London," nor the exploitation of North Sea oil, nearly everyone acknowledges that the nation has until recently steadily lost ground to its Western neighbors. Alone in the industrialized world, Britain's manufacturing output actually declined from 1973 to 1983, by which time it became a net importer of manufactured goods for the first time since the onset of the industrial revolution in the eighteenth century. The first Thatcher term was a difficult period, as the government attacked paternalism and inefficiency with what seemed to many Britons to be an icy harshness. Even as prosperity picked up in the mid 1980s, however, unemployment remained at or near double-digit figures. Thus, if the United Kingdom's employment growth from 1982 to 1987 (second quarter) of 2.8 percent clearly bettered that of West Germany, France, Italy, or Spain, its modesty was revealed by the vastly greater 12.5 percent of the United States. During much of this time, the real rate of growth of Britain's gross domestic product was higher than that of any other nation in Europe or North America; yet long-standing defeatism persisted like a child's runny nose. Thus, a Gallup poll (1985, p. 28) revealed that in terms of taxes, prices, unemployment, or general economic difficulties, public expectations of conditions in the year ahead have been almost uniformly negative since 1957. Such an attitude is hardly conducive to open-ended entitlement programs.

Also involved are certain pertinent choices made by the United Kingdom. If the British have been rather parsimonious with the NHS, in other words, this partially reflects decisions taken after the war to allocate large sums to schools, housing, and social services.

Thus, compared with the developed world as represented by the Organization for Economic Cooperation and Development, the United Kingdom has spent a below-average portion of its gross domestic product on health care since 1960 – and the gap has steadily widened. Comparisons with the United States reveal still greater disparities, again reflecting differences in priorities as well as in wealth; even as Tocqueville (1961, Vol. 2, pp. 153–5) noted, Americans place an unusual value on physical well-being.

Equally, perhaps, the UK practice may stem from an almost reflexive horror of welfare-state extravagance. "Value for money" is a phrase a visitor soon learns, and "value" here implies a reasonable return not only to the patient but also to the public. This attitude, engrafted long ago in the notorious Elizabethan Poor Laws, lies near the core of the benevolent NHS as well. An outsider becomes accustomed to hearing that the NHS is "without fear of challenge . . . the best-buy model of health care in the world" (Klein, 1985, p. 42). Though what the DHSS spends on health care per capita is less than a third of what the United States spends, less than half of what the FRG spends, and barely half of what France spends, UK life expectancy and infant mortality rates are remarkably similar to those of the three other nations. Of course, by themselves these hardly suffice as societal measures of health; morbidity must be considered, too. Still, the inference that an additional expenditure on health care may well generate only a disproportionately small improvement in health is rather widely held among UK health administrators. Thus, the long-standing reluctance to dialyze older ESRD patients finds a clear parallel in the late 1950s, when full rehabilitation services were offered pretty much only to those under the age of sixty-five (first priority being given to those under fifty or fifty-five), to those with a history of gainful employment, and to those for whom reemployment appeared certain. Similarly, cataract surgery for a while was also restricted to patients under sixty-five. Given this tradition and what was until recently an almost universal pessimism regarding a near-term end to significant scarcity in Britain, the ESRD budgetary restraints must have seemed not only sensible but necessary – and in a patently obvious way.

A fourth disadvantage peculiar to ESRD is that it is not a curative, "one off" affair, but instead involves a heavy, continuing commitment for the rest of the patient's life, often for well over a decade (cf. Festenstein et al., 1986, p. 8). Hospital dialysis, of course, is especially costly, but even a successful transplant is not cheap. Each ESRD patient, therefore, must be viewed financially as a potential consumer of tens of thousands of pounds, not to mention the time and energy of innumerable physicians, nurses, counselors, and other staff. Thus, unlike, say, the polio vaccine, ESRD treatments do not relieve the health system, but rather add to its cumulative burden.

What this means for ESRD patients collectively is that each year's budget allocations must not only cover the costs of adding new patients, presumably at least at the ongoing rate; the money must also pay for the continuing costs of the patients already receiving treatment, less those of the relatively small number who have died during the past year.[16] Thus, even if there were no inflation, the costs of maintaining the program at a constant level would entail significant annual increases. When inflation and a desire to expand the program are added, the annual increases become even greater.

Of course, technical cost-cutting breakthroughs are always possible. Indeed, in the early 1970s in the United States it was widely believed that such breakthroughs would soon render transplantation both much less costly and much less risky, thereby permitting virtually all persons who required ESRD therapies to be treated at an only moderate aggregate cost (Scribner, 1971). The breakthroughs, however, never fully materialized, and the cost of the American program now approaches 2 billion dollars per year; that is, in 1983 about 0.25 percent of the total Medicare part B beneficiaries accounted for about 8.5 percent of part B costs (General Accounting Office, 1985, p. 1). What had initially seemed merely optimistic is, in hindsight, revealed as wishful thinking.

Unlike many other high-technology innovations, ESRD treatments still involve high marginal costs. An antibiotic drug may be expensive to develop, for example, but once this has been accomplished, each additional patient can benefit at only a very small ad-

---

[16] On the average, in a given year, new patients outnumber those who die by somewhat more than 2 to 1.

ditional cost. In contrast, not only were dialysis and transplantation expensive to develop, but each new patient is expensive to treat; marginal costs, far from becoming trivial, have remained significant.

Fifth, the very uncommonness of ESRD hampers attempts to increase funding, and not simply because it limits the political attractiveness of the effort. For the chief goal of the NHS, equity in health care distribution, in practice has really meant a commitment to providing minimum adequate levels of care, "minimum" being defined as the "services that most people use most of the time" (Abel-Smith, 1978, p. 19). ESRD, of course, does not fit comfortably in such an approach: It afflicts far too few people, and its costliness is seen as an intrusion upon the resource base required to fund minimum care levels for far larger populations. ESRD demands that will seem barely adequate to some, therefore, will always appear clearly excessive to others.

Sixth (though the implications of this point are disputed), ESRD treatment has been more thoroughly quantified demographically and "costed out" financially than treatment for almost any other condition in the United Kingdom (Laing, 1979 p. 113), allegedly to the disadvantage of ESRD treatment advocates. The initiative for this quantification came from renal physicians themselves, who established the European Dialysis and Transplant Association in 1964, an organization that has generated and published impressive amounts of data on a wide range of topics concerning ESRD. As one nephrologist explained, it was believed that masses of information would not only improve patient care but also strengthen bureaucratic arguments for greater funding, thereby expanding treatment patterns. "Undoubtedly," concluded another nephrologist, "it has helped in preparing 'ammunition' to fire at governments for requesting more resources" (Parson, 1982, p. 22). Accompanying these efforts have been a number of governmental and private cost studies.

Most ESRD treatment advocates appear to believe, however, that all this has proved counterproductive. When they decry physicians' spending of large sums on hopeless cancer patients (Wing, in London *Times*, 1981a; Cattell, in Parson and Ogg, 1983, pp. 53–4), for example, these advocates are fully aware that their evidence is almost entirely anecdotal and thus that their assertions that ESRD treatment deserves priority over these procedures may have a self-serving, unpersuasive ring. As one physician put it regarding these cancer patients, "How much money are we really talking about? We really don't know." With ESRD, however, advocates believe that "we do know" and find it far more difficult to construct their arguments from the low estimates that other claimants may find so useful. "The very accurate costing of our therapies when compared with the ignorance about costing in so many other fields of medicine," one nephrologist typically maintained, "is an undoubted disadvantage" (Robinson, 1978, p. 17).

Yet it must be noted that ESRD treatments have not been costed out all that well. Estimates have varied widely, apparently reflecting differences not only in expenses but also in methods of calculation. There is no consensus, for example, on how to deal financially with patients who move from one therapy to another or with medical complications that may accompany treatment or whether transplantation should be discounted by a "quality of life" factor (and if so, by how much). Nor has a nationwide analysis been performed. Indeed, a 1976 DHSS study was based on experience at a single hospital – and that one was considered by many nephrologists to be highly atypical. A 1981 DHSS study represented a substantial improvement, though its sample of only twenty-four patients each from three renal centers necessarily rendered extrapolation hazardous. A 1984 estimate based on the 1981 study produced lower figures (Mancini, 1984) (Table 15).[17] Certain other treatment strategies (e.g., minimum care "satellite" or "subsatellite" dialysis centers or simplified home-dialysis systems) have not been costed out at all.

Despite these problems, the impression persists among all interested individuals who were interviewed that ESRD treatment is well costed out. The consensus among sophisticated observers regarding the entire health system appears to be that cost and utilization data are generally poor (Maynard, 1986, p. 333), that "often there is very

[17] By way of comparison, in the United States the average first-year cost of a kidney transplant in 1985 was about $35,000 and the average lifetime cost of providing dialysis and associated medical care was about $158,000.

Table 15. *Average annual cost of ESRD treatment, 1984 estimates*

Treatment	Cost (pounds)
Hospital dialysis	12,300–10,650
Home dialysis	7,850–7,250
CAPD	6,950–6,050
Successful transplant	
First year	6,400–5,600
Subsequent years	1,850–1,600

Source: European Dialysis and Transplant Association.

limited evaluative information about medical technology," and that "there is no one body that makes sure that the necessary research is done, pulled together, and disseminated throughout the NHS" (Stocking, 1986, p. 21). Acknowledging the problems, one regional administrator declared, "The NHS costing system is primitive in the extreme, but it is better for renal services than for nearly any other area." The contrast to coronary artery bypass graft surgery, for which comparable data were said to be simply unavailable, was often noted.

The same regional administrator went on to say, however, that ESRD treatment advocates were quite mistaken if they imagined that their costing data weakened them in the scramble for resources. On the contrary, he argued, "if you can quantify something, you're king. The act of putting figures on a proposal gives it power." Regional officers, particularly treasurers, tend to be very suspicious of vague and unsubstantiated claims.

Taking the United Kingdom as a whole, however, it is impossible to say whether ESRD costing data harm treatment advocates (as they contend) or help them (as the regional administrator believes). The answer may even vary from region to region and from time to time.

In their favor, ESRD treatment advocates can in the last analysis point only to a single factor, though in a society ostensibly committed to increasing social welfare it is one of considerable potency: The treatments can reliably extend useful life for thousands of people. Obviously, this does not guarantee treatment advocates budgetary success, but it does assure them of a hearing and makes the issue impossible to ignore completely.

AN INCREMENTALIST RESPONSE

Given the regional policy makers' bureaucratic position and the peculiar problems attaching to ESRD treatments, comprehensive decision making involving a consideration of "all" alternatives over the long term appears to strike most actors as patently irrational. The costs of such a process seem high – diverting policy makers from more pressing concerns, consuming scarce administrative time and manpower, alienating long-term losers – and the risks of a decision's being undone – by actions at the DHSS, district, or regional specialty levels – are ever present. In contrast, the gains of even wise and prescient comprehensive decision making are likely not to appear for some years and may be too remote in time or place to be of much help to the regional actors.

NHS planning systems with their formal five-step approach, therefore, must not be taken too seriously (DHSS, 1976a); for although it is certainly true that the "rational model is overwhelmingly the most widely articulated approach to planning in the service" (Stoten, 1982, p. 234), articulation need not imply practice. Everyone supports rationality – perhaps on the theory that the alternative is to support irrationality – but few let it intrude unduly into their serious work. One reason for this is that planning systems can serve a number of frequently incompatible goals (e.g., maximizing service delivery, efficiency, political support). Arguably, NHS planning has evolved from overtly stressing service delivery to emphasizing efficiency, while covertly pursuing political support above all else (Lee and Mills, 1982, pp. 33–5; Klein 1983b).

In such a context, the only approach that seems to make sense is one that "takes existing reality as one alternative and compares the probable gains and losses of closely related alternatives by making relatively small adjustments in existing reality" (Dahl and Lindblom, 1953, p. 82)[18] or, in a word, incrementalism.

---

[18] This is the original formulation of the concept.

Thus, for many years the regions by and large accepted current levels of ESRD treatment as a given. They could not be lowered, it was recognized, except by denying care to some of those then receiving treatment or by rejecting the kind of applicants who in the past had been accepted. Either way, settled expectations and arrangements would have come under serious challenge, thereby adding to the stress under which the regions must act. "New policies," in Schattschneider's (1963 p. 288) phrase, "create new politics"; policy makers wanting to avoid dealing with a new political situation, therefore, were not eager to advance new policies, for "the more different an alternative is from past policies, the more difficult it is to predict its consequences" (Dror, 1968, p. 144).

By the same token, though, treatment patterns could have been greatly expanded only at the expense of some other claimant, or as the *Lancet* (1984) put it, by "paying Paul at the expense of robbing Peter," for budget allocations, once fixed, are rarely expanded.[19] The same fear of upsetting a livable routine that protects ESRD against cutbacks also protects its rivals. Expansion of ESRD treatment, therefore, was only gradual. The UK did not reach its outmoded target of forty new patients per million population until nearly a decade and a half after the goal had been informally adopted. Meanwhile, tens of thousands of "prematurely ill" patients died.

There is, of course, nothing unusual about bureaucratic incrementalism. Indeed, though the label is only thirty years old, the phenomenon itself probably dates back to the first bureaucracy. Its persistance and prevalence, presumably, are testaments to its advantages: It cuts decision-making costs and does not make unrealistic demands on decision makers, it promotes predictability and continuity, it minimizes the risk of error, and, most important, it protects the decision maker and eases his task. As its best known inter-

---

19 In the United States, by contrast, budget allotments tend to be mere projections, which all interested parties recognize will be supplemented when they are exhausted. Whereas U.S. policy makers know only in hindsight what they have spent, therefore, UK officials have a clear idea before the fact.

preter has argued, incrementalism "is not only in fact a common method of policy formulation"; it is also "superior to any other decision making method available for complex problems in many circumstances, certainly superior to a futile attempt at superhuman comprehensiveness" (Lindblom, 1959).

It is also true, however, that incrementalism is deeply hostile to the new – in fact, hostile on principle. With incrementalism, next year's projections are based on this year's levels, which in turn are based on last year's levels, and so on. Regularity is the key (Dempster and Wildavsky, 1979, p. 374), for only proposed increments receive real scrutiny. Elements in the environment that may justify substantial departures are not easily incorporated into this way of thinking. In fact, an exasperated Orwell (1968) declared, "All the bosh that is talked about our national genius for 'muddling through' . . . means *au fond* that it is *safer not to think*" (p. 8). In "Yes Minister," "novel," "imaginative," and "courageous" are terms of abuse.

Clearly, though, incrementalism has not precluded change. More ESRD patients are treated today in the United Kingdom than ever before. But equally clearly, "change" has not meant "something new"; it has meant "a little more." In a medical, scientific setting, such an outlook may well strike the observer as jarring, for science suggests a willingness to alter direction that the incrementalist can scarcely imagine. Some scientific advances can be accommodated by incrementalism, of course, as the forearm catheter or CAPD were. But that is not merely because they were improvements on existing technology; it is also because their acceptance involved no departure from incrementalist resource growth. Other scientific findings – that, for example, home dialysis may be workable for nearly 90 percent of all patients (George, 1983) – have been essentially ignored. This is not because they conflict with earlier normative assumptions about patient quality of life, but instead because their adoption would entail at least a temporary rejection of incrementalism. It is this incrementalism, sustained by vast bureaucratic momentum and undeniable bureaucratic rationality, that those seeking major departures in ESRD treatment patterns have had to confront and conquer.

Incrementalism not only explains long years of slowly changing ESRD treatment policy, but also helps one to understand the pronounced discrepancies among the fourteen regions, discrepancies that have partially survived two major NHS reorganizations and persistent and widespread criticism. As we have seen, until 1971, renal unit financing was handled not by the regions but by the Ministry of Health, which thus was able to impose its own schema upon the entire system. Specifically, it decided to concentrate resources in centers of excellence based in teaching hospitals, mostly in London, and not to fund all areas of the country more or less equally. Whatever the merits of this approach, it meant gross inequalities of funding from one region to the next, and once the pattern was set, subsequent allocations served only to reinforce it.

These regional discrepancies did not apply to ESRD exclusively; indeed, similar discrepancies pervaded all of the NHS. Complaints, of course, came from disadvantaged regions, and later from academics and even a minister for health, Richard Crossman. As a result, a revenue allocation formula was introduced in 1971, and when that proved inadequate, a Resource Allocation Working Party (RAWP) was created to "reduce progressively, and as far as is feasible, the disparities between the different parts of the country in terms of opportunity for access to health care for people at equal risk, taking into account measures of health needs, and social and environmental factors which may affect the need for health care" (DHSS, 1975).

A 1976 RAWP report provided targets for capital and operating allocations toward which current allocations were expected to move in order to redress the regional imbalances. The targets consisted of estimates of how much each region would receive if it used resources at the same rate as the national average. Efforts were made to control for age, sex, and certain other medically relevant factors. Standardized mortality ratios were used as a measure of need – the higher the ratio, the greater the need – and joined to population size in the RAWP formula.

Implementation of the RAWP guidelines began at the regional level in 1977, but it has long since been apparent that they have shaken the prevailing incrementalism much less than might have been predicted. For from the outset, the DHSS made it clear that it supported "leveling up," not "leveling down." In other words, "overfunded" regions would not be cut, but would merely receive smaller increases than "underfunded" regions. Regional redistribution, therefore, was made to depend on a growing resource base. When with the economic stagnation of the late 1970s and early 1980s, sufficient growth did not take place, redistribution became modest indeed. As a consequence, it was a decade before observers could count the RAWP regional targets as having been substantially met (Holland, 1986; Maynard, 1986); the difference between the best and worst funded regions had declined from 26 percent in 1977 to 11 percent in 1986 (NHS Management Board, 1986, p. 5). Even now, moreover, many commentators believe that RAWP's central redistributive goal has been frustrated. As one critic commented, "RAWP is a method of taking money from the poor in rich areas and giving it to the rich in poor areas" (Davies, 1985, p. 608).

AN END TO INCREMENTALISM?

There is a venerable tradition in Britain of berating what Mrs. Castle called the "entrenched lethargy" of the administrative class. Still, the fact remains that in the brief two-year period, 1985 and 1986, the United Kingdom's ESRD intake rate increased by more than 38 percent. This is not the kind of increment that incrementalists normally have in mind.

How is this to be explained? The answer, it appears, relates only secondarily to ESRD and its familiar political/bureaucratic context, for ESRD had become a piece in a much larger game: the Thatcher government's struggle for enhanced productivity. In the context of health policy, the government made clear its belief that the old system was hobbled by a pair of seriously flawed assumptions. The first was the political assumption that commitment to the Health Service could be satisfactorily measured by annual budgetary increases; the bigger the commitment, the bigger the increase. To this, the government declared that performance was a matter of output, not input, and that the old approach of simply counting pounds sterling was wasteful, inefficient, and illogical. The second assumption, which had been part of the basic understanding surrounding the birth of the NHS itself, was that clinical autonomy effectively protected physicians against government productivity pressures. Instead, the Thatcher government, which had earlier attacked the productivity of miners and teachers, moved further up the socioeconomic status scale and took on the doctors. Variations in medical treatment patterns and tales of indolence (particularly regarding hospital consultants) were used to bolster a determination to tighten up what the government took to be laxities enshrined by tradition. There was even talk of issuing performance-related contracts to consultants.

What has this to do with ESRD? One way the government's managerial commitment to productivity was manifested – in addition to such creations as the general manager – was in the setting of targets for the regions. These were not input targets requiring the regions to expend certain levels of funds, but rather output targets requiring certain levels of performance. Not all medical areas were selected for targeting; that would be impractical. But on what basis should the targeted areas be chosen? Obviously, the selection would have to be intellectually justifiable, and reaching the target would have to be feasible. In addition, it should also rebut the antipatient charges emanating from the by now inflamed medical community, which regarded the government's attack on long-standing rights and privileges as an ungrateful betrayal of trust, a renunciation of institutionalized compassion, and a move against the NHS itself.

In all three respects, ESRD fit the government's needs perfectly. Intake rates in the United Kingdom trailed those in comparable nations by such margins that targeting it would be unassailable intellectually. Facilities and personnel were frequently underutilized, making quickly meeting the target practicable. And the ESRD situation was so well known that targeting would seem, far from a mean-spirited intrusion into clinical autonomy, an unanswerable act from the heart.

Hence, the government determined that ESRD was to be selected for targeting, announcing in 1984 that all regions would be expected to reach the traditional benchmark patient intake level of forty PMP by 1987. By 1986, this was accomplished.

It would be rash to conclude, however, that incrementalism is dead. Instead, as one observer noted, "It will need a silver stake through its heart." The advantages of incrementalism are so numerous and pervasive, that is, that they can be counted on to reassert themselves once the managerial enthusiasm has faded. In the meanwhile, though, ESRD patients must be rated as one of the major winners in the combat.

THE EXTRABUREAUCRATIC ACTORS

It is possible, of course, to focus too narrowly upon the bureaucracy and, like a Hardy with his Wessex, to create from the tangled and changing structures and relationships a self-contained little world. Creating little worlds, however, may distract our attention from the big one around us. And the NHS, far from existing in isolation, is a visible and important institution in a vigorously pluralistic society. As such, it not only exerts influence but is the object of others' efforts to exert influence.

How significant, then, have such extrabureaucratic elements as interest groups, politicians, the media, and public opinion actually been? Many academic analysts, it must be said, have tended to stress these elements. Lifting the veil of official authority, these analysts have tended to argue that real power resides elsewhere, normally hidden from view but no less potent for its public invisibility.

INTEREST GROUPS

"Now whatever else we may say about England," an astute observer once wryly reported, "it has certainly been a paradise of groups" (Barker, 1938, p. 175). Though not all his successors have likened groups to cherubim and seraphim, few have failed to comment on their vitality and fecundity. For generations, indeed, it has been commonplace to observe that British politics is unusually accommodationist and nonideological, concerned with placating interests, constructing coalitions, and making do with piecemeal, ad hoc solutions. Some have applauded the evident distaste for comprehensiveness and principle; others have disparaged it; but few have denied it. In fact, in a widely discussed essay on the rise and decline of nations, one commentator argued, "[W]ith age British society has acquired so many strong organizations and collusions that it suffers from an institutional sclerosis that slows its adaptation to changing circumstances and technologies" (Olson, 1982, p. 78; but cf. Fitzgerald, 1988). The very "immunity from dictatorship, invasion, and revolution" (Olson, 1982, p. 77) of which Britons are so proud also gave the past as represented by organized interests immense power over the present. Like forest fires, social cataclysms, in addition to generating short-term pain and destruction, can also have cleansing, invigorating effects.

Particularly influential in postwar efforts to understand British policy making have been the writings of Samuel Beer (1956, 1982a, 1982b), who with great skill and impact has stressed the primacy of interest groups, especially producer groups. According to this view, as the British government extended its authority over the private sector after World War II, it paradoxically found itself becoming ever more dependent upon the very interests it sought to control; for it recognized that its policies could not succeed without the information and the acquiescence (and sometimes the support) that only the groups involved could provide. As Beer (1982b) expressed it, "In a free country, the enormous new powers that government exercises over producer and consumer groups at the same time puts these groups in a position to frustrate these powers by refusing their cooperation and consent" (p. 14). Intimate, interdependent group-bureaucracy relationships developed, it was said, typically behind the scenes, as "producers influenced policy largely through direct contact with the executive in what may be called a system of functional representation" (Beer, 1982a, p. 319). What was thought to have made all this possible was an unspoken agreement on centrist policies that directed groups to the bureaucracy for the resolution of disputes on detail, rather than to elections, parties, or even Westminster, where such technical and mundane matters were ordinarily ignored. Thus emerges a picture in which "all . . . factors pull in a single direction toward the concentration of pressure group activities on the administrative departments" (Eckstein, 1960, p. 17), and coherent overviews are defaced by the shards of pluralism (Beer, 1982b, p. 4).

For their part, British analysts have generally echoed this American conclusion that UK policies represent the result of a process of adjustment among bureaucracies and groups. If anything, indeed, British analysts have tended to assign groups an even greater importance, sometimes adding, "No longer do the assets of government markedly outweigh the assets of any given group or set of groups in a bargaining situation" (Richardson and Jordan, 1979, p. 172). Or as Mackenzie (1976) rather flamboyantly claimed, "The state is submerged by the interests; it continues, but only as a form of contest. The so-called government is like a medieval king amid the barons' wars; his body is a symbol and a prize that the factions strive to possess" (p. 12).

Perhaps the best known testing ground of Beer's group-oriented approach has been health policy, most influentially in two thoughtful and provocative works by a former student of his at Harvard, Harry Eckstein, entitled *The English Health Service* (1958) and *Pressure Group Politics* (1960). Both books, which deservedly won high praise, emphasize the key role of the British Medical Association (BMA) in the creation of the NHS and the formulation and implementation of its policies. The BMA, in fact, was portrayed as the prototype of the dominant producer group.[20]

Later health policy analysts have redrawn the picture with only subtle refinements. Haywood and Hunter, for example, though reporting that physician groups have been joined by trades unions, other professional groups, and voluntary bodies, continue to underline the importance of personalized, stable group–bureaucratic interrelationships, especially in the inner circle, where ideas are said to develop (Haywood and Hunter, 1982, pp. 157, 161; Rose, 1986, p. 339). Hood and Dunshire (1981) highlight this proliferation of groups, identifying no less than 108 that focus their attention on the DHSS; only two other departments out of a total of sixty-nine attract more groups. And Klein (1983b) notes how "a stage where once the leaders of the medical profession had been able to solilo-

---

[20] The view bears some resemblance to Alford's (1975) well-known typology of structural interests: dominant (physicians), challenging (health bureaucrats), and repressed (lower middle class, poor, blacks).

quise with little interruption had now become crowded with actors all clamouring to be heard" (p. 105). The old consensus, particularly the faith in rational planning, has become "changed, battered and motheaten," he contends, discerning a drive "to decentralize responsibility" in order "to disclaim blame" (p. 140). The impact of groups upon policy, as a result, has inescapably been magnified (Klein, 1983b; see also Elcock and Haywood, 1980, p. 100).

How well does this group-dominated vision describe ESRD macroallocative policy making? The short answer is: with one important exception, not very well. Consider, first, the producer groups. Three are concerned principally with nephrology: the Renal Association, the British Association of Paediatric Nephrology, and the National Kidney Research Fund.

PRODUCER GROUPS

The most important producer group is the "clubbish" (Rennie et al., 1985, p. 324) Renal Association, an organization of renal physicians that is considered the voice of the profession. As such, it has been represented on virtually every advisory committee that has studied any aspect of ESRD, sometimes assuming a major role. Viewing this assignment as scientific rather than political, however, a past president maintained that its most noteworthy political victory was its successful opposition to a DHSS move to cut back physician staffing standards for renal units.

It would be quite inaccurate, therefore, to characterize the Renal Association, as did the past president, as "totally nonpolitical"; it would be equally inaccurate, however, to depict it as an association aggressively committed to achieving fundamental changes in treatment patterns. Instead, it has taken a long series of discrete actions intended to improve the quality of service and broaden treatment as a consequence of the accretion of small, rather technical alterations.

Several factors appear to have conspired to narrow the association's ends and confine its choice of means: It is quite small; most of its members have professional responsibilities that are so time-consuming and vital that they can give little of themselves to political activity; group cohesion has been impeded by divisions in the profession between physicians more involved in dialysis and those more involved in transplantation,[21] between those favoring greatly expanding treatment patterns and those basically satisfied with current trends, and between ESRD-oriented physicians and other nephrologists who tend to view dialysis and transplantation as "really for the non-scientific, the non-academic, not the true blue university type consultant" (Cattell, in Parson and Ogg, 1983, p. 240). Also, though individual nephrologists are occasionally quite militant, most seem reluctant to exchange even a part of the physician's self-image of healer for that of political activist.

The British Association of Paediatric Nephrology, a body of sub-specialists concerned with ESRD among children, also is often included in advisory committees. More important, it produced a pair of influential reports, one in 1974 and one in 1979, on the organization of pediatric nephrology services. But though the reports' basic structural recommendations for "supraregions" was followed, the association still found that the number of children receiving treatment was "disappointing." In fact, in its second report, the association admitted that the very structure it had suggested may have contributed to this result, observing that the administrative and financial arrangements for such atypical structures were "poorly developed" (Houston et al., 1979, p. 1).[22]

Whatever the association's contribution to higher rates of treatment for children – and these rates have risen over the years – its impact on overall ESRD treatment patterns has necessarily been quite small; for childhood is by far the least likely time for kidneys to fail.

As for the National Kidney Research Fund, its interest lies in supporting "research which aims to prevent and cure kidney failure, or to improve treatment of the established condition," on which it "has spent many millions of pounds" (National Kidney Research Fund, 1982, p. 1). Altering prevailing treatment patterns has not generally

---

[21] One dialysis specialist, for example, complained that transplant specialists had called him a "plumber."

[22] Despite this – or, perhaps, because of it – the government recently announced that liver transplants for children will also be organized on a supraregional basis (Hamilton, 1985).

been the organization's concern. And on those few occasions when it has, the fund has not always acted in concert with other relevant groups. For example, while the president of one patient group greeted a government announcement that four hundred more kidney dialysis machines would be provided as "the most spendid news we've had for years" (Ward, in Roper, 1978), the National Kidney Research Fund declared that the real need was for staff and space, not equipment (London *Times*, 1978).

On an individual basis, a small number of nephrologists have been very active in trying to change policy. Most of this activity, it appears, consists of efforts to draw attention of the plight of ESRD patients to the medical community and the general public. Numerous editorials have been written in medical journals (e.g., *Lancet*, 1981), for example, and dramatic announcements and proposals made to the media (e.g., Cameron, in Gillie, 1983; Mallick et al., 1983; Moorhead, in London *Hampstead and Highgate Express*, 1983; Ogg, in Prentice, 1983; Bewick, in Timmins, 1986a). "We are camping out on their doorstep," one prominent nephrologist declared, "and we will not go away."

There can be no doubt that this has helped to sensitize health policy makers, physicians generally, and even the mass public to the issue. As a consequence, it has certainly become easier for sympathetic policy makers to support broadening ESRD treatment patterns and harder for hostile policy makers to oppose all change. And sporadically since 1983 there has been some evidence that the nephrologists' outcries have contributed to the issue's becoming a minor embarrassment for the government and this may have helped persuade the government eventually to target ESRD for enhanced treatment rates. More, though, would be difficult to claim. Nor have the nephrologists' meetings with DHSS officials had much impact. As probably the most militant of the UK nephrologists conceded, "Despite lobbying, renal physicians have achieved little through the usual channel of communication or protest" (Cameron, 1983a, p. 2). Their rhetoric, both public and private, often reflects this frustration (e.g., Parson, in Parson and Ogg, 1983, p. 110).

Despite their profound commitment, however, nephrologists do not always confront their resource problem with great sophistication. One persistent difficulty, for instance, has been a marked shortage of cadaveric donor kidneys. It has become obvious that much of the responsibility for this situation rests with physicians in charge of patients dying from traumas, who are deterred from pursuing the donation by cumbersome new brain-death criteria, the awkwardness of requesting permission from the grieving family to remove the kidneys, the stress on nurses from placing moribund patients on respirators, and attending physicians' lack of interest in transplantation. As one transplant surgeon complained, "We ask doctors if they will refer patients as possible donors and they say they never get anybody suitable to be a donor. We know damn well that they do" (Williams, in Timmins, 1986b). "Emergency room doctors feel like vultures or ghouls," one observer reported. And as the director of UK transplants put it, "It's an awful lot of trouble to refer a donor. It's at least a day's work for someone" (Bradley, in Grist, 1981). Clearly, the only way these obstacles can be overcome is to make donor referral worth the physician's while through some system of compensation, financial or otherwise. Yet nephrologists have for the most part failed to face the congeries of disincentives for referral, disdaining material rewards (Macpherson, 1986, p. 503) and instead simply exhorting their fellow physicians to virtue and urging ordinary citizens to carry donor cards. (Ironically, a 1981 Gallup survey disclosed that only 27 percent of physicians themselves carried donor cards [Social Surveys, 1981, table 5].) Indeed, more than one nephrologist commented that "doctors are expected to do *more* than their duty," virtually glorying in the martyrdom of their perceived exploitation.[23]

In addition to the physician groups dominated by kidney concerns, two larger associations deserve attention. The better known is the British Medical Association, though despite Eckstein's (1960) famous portrayal of its dominating UK medical policy, it seems basically to have ignored ESRD. There is no BMA renal physician's committee; and there is, in the words of one BMA spokesperson, "no particular policy" on ESRD, apart from the association's

---

[23] From this perspective, altering the incentive structure to encourage donations may appear ineffective, if not actually counterproductive.

general commitment to the physician's clinical autonomy. Occasionally, editorials critical of ESRD treatment patterns appear in the independently edited *British Medical Journal*, but both BMA spokespersons and nephrologists maintain that nothing concrete has been done. Nephrologists, in particular, seem prone to dismissing the BMA altogether, terming it "right wing," "a trade union," or "only representative of GPs." Clearly, nephrologists have never expected it to influence ESRD policy in any major way and would be astonished if it did in the future. As a former chief medical officer at the Ministry of Health commented, "The BMA doesn't play any part in this."

The other general purpose physicians group, the Royal College of Physicians, played a vital, if subordinate, role during the early years of ESRD treatment.[24] More recently, however, its advisory – or legitimating – activities have diminished, principally perhaps as a reflection of the department's understandable reluctance to reopen long-settled questions. In addition, however, an episode in the early 1980s demonstrated that the College's legitimating powers are not unlimited and that when these boundaries are crossed, the cost to the organization is apt to be rather high. Specifically, in 1981 a report of the College's medical services study group on physicians' refusal to treat renal failure among patients under the age of fifty led to a condemnation by nephrologists that was uncommon in its breadth and vigor. The report, published in the *British Medical Journal*, purported to find that no patient had inappropriately been denied treatment (Medical Services Study Group, 1981). So outrageous did this conclusion seem that the same issue of the journal featured an editorial disputing it (*British Medical Journal*, 1981), and in subsequent issues many of the profession's prominent figures followed suit (Cameron et al., 1981; Large and Ahmed, 1981; Michael and Adu, 1981; Parsons and Lock, 1981; Verwilgher, 1981). Years later, moreover, the report invariably was the first thing mentioned by nephrologists when asked about the College. For an organization claiming deference by dint of expertise, such an embarrassment is neither

[24] Though more circumspect today, the Royal College sought to advance the status and pay of physicians in the Victorian era with great effect (Waddington, 1985).

quickly forgotten nor easily forgiven. In the near term, at least, it appears unlikely that the College will be called on again to legitimate any controversial ESRD policy; its eagerness to collaborate with the department was, as one observer said, "just too unseemly."

In reviewing the efforts of producer groups, then, what is most striking is the modesty of their impact. With some exceptions, the groups have tended to be such models of propriety and decorum that their opposition to prevailing policies has tended to be undercut by their fear of making a scene. As a practical matter, this diffidence virtually invites cooptation and the striking of an unspoken bargain: The department agrees to call on the groups for advice on technical matters, and the groups in turn agree to accept the larger macroallocative decisions.

Beer's strictures to the contrary notwithstanding, the groups simply are not very favorably situated. They can disavow discretion and cause a fuss, but in a society where this is frowned upon, they are unlikely to benefit much from this approach. Nor are they in a position to refuse to implement the policies with which they differ. For if they withdraw their services or otherwise undermine established procedures, the first and heaviest losers will be the very clientele they seek to protect, their patients, and the losses will be counted as deaths. The nephrologists know this; the DHSS knows this; and each knows that the other knows this. In such a setting, the producers' options are severely limited.

CONSUMER GROUPS

What, then, of those interests most significantly affected by ESRD treatment patterns, the patients (or, to adopt group theory usage, the consumers)? Though group analysts are careful to stress the primacy of producer groups, they have also come to argue that consumer groups "loomed large" (Beer, 1982b, p. 13) and are notable for their "growing assertiveness" (Klein, 1983b, p. 116).

In the case of ESRD, however, only two consumer groups have exhibited any activity worth noting. The first is the British Kidney Patient Association (BKPA), established in 1975 on a two thousand

pound grant from a pharmaceutical company and still very much the
creature of its extraordinary founder and president, Elizabeth Ward,
the wealthy mother of a son who underwent dialysis for twelve years
and has received three transplants (see Ward, 1986). Running the
organization from her home outside a small Hampshire town, she
not only has raised more than 9 million pounds to improve patients'
quality of life,[25] but also has labored to try to alter policy so that
"everyone requiring treatment will receive it." With boundless energy, commitment, and optimism, the formidable Mrs. Ward has
cultivated media contacts, aired her views on television and radio
and in newspapers and magazines, and discussed ESRD policy with
pertinent civil servants on a regular basis. In this, Mrs. Ward has dis-
played not only enormous drive, but also the grit to say the unsay-
able (e.g., to criticize physicians for what she takes to be their
arrogance and indifference) and the gift of coining memorable
phrases ("My God is the sort who would say at the doors of Heaven:
'What are you doing coming up here with your kidneys?' " [Ward,
quoted in Davenport, 1986]).

In dealing with decision makers, Mrs. Ward has not exhibited the
mixture of caution, deference, and stoicism that is often expected of
supplicants in the United Kingdom, but instead has frequently been
quite forceful, sometimes apparently abrasively so. Indeed, one of
the main thrusts of her efforts has been to publicize her belief that
ESRD is too important to be left quietly to the medical establishment's good offices. There is no question that this has earned
her a certain amount of notoriety and alienated some actors (see,
e.g., Giles and Davison, 1985, pp. 547–8), who perhaps find her
strength a reproach to their own acquiescence. "She is really more in
the American style," as one physician administrator commented.

The second consumer group, the National Federation of Kidney
Patients Associations (NFKPA), is a loose collection of about
thirty-five autonomous branches, each connected with a hospital
renal unit and having at least 60 percent of its members as kidney

---

[25] In 1986 the BKPA had £531,140 in commitments that included operating
holiday dialysis centers, providing financial aid to individual patients, supporting pediatric renal units, funding renal social workers, and providing other
services.

patients. The NFKPA's central office helps to coordinate actions and share information among the branches, acts "as a well-informed national voice for all kidney patients," and seeks to influence policy. Most of its work has been carried out behind the scenes in meetings with the minister for health, DHSS officials, and RHA officers. The press has provided limited coverage of the NFKPA's requests for more funds for CAPD and transplants, but though a spokeswoman conceded that the media were important, they seem far more interested in Mrs. Ward, who clearly has emerged as the kidney patient's most visible advocate.

When asked to discuss the NFKPA's successes, the spokeswoman began candidly, "I don't know," and then mentioned its support of CAPD, which she felt may have helped encourage its use, and a series of "little tiny things," which eased the patient's situation financially and in other ways. By its own lights, in short, the NFKPA seems the archetypal British interest group that "is more concerned with the politics of detail than the politics of issues" (Stewart, 1958, p. 29).

Compounding the BKPA and NFKPA's problems is a general lack of interest or willingness to cooperate on the part of the ostensibly allied groups. To begin with, the two consumer groups go their own separate ways. In its literature, in fact, the BKPA refers to itself as "the only national association concerned with the welfare of kidney patients" and, according to the NFKPA, rebuffed an offer to join them and work together. Relations between the two appear chilly.

Perhaps reflecting its higher expectations, the BKPA voices less satisfaction with the contributions of nephrologists and corporations than does the NFKPA. Physicians have not always been forthcoming for fear of alienating their bureaucratic superiors or relinquishing some of their clinical autonomy, the BKPA believes, and even now none has stepped forward to aid Mrs. Ward in her effort to have a lawsuit brought establishing the NHS's legal duty to treat ESRD patients. Also, she maintains, corporations that stand to gain from broader treatment patterns feel constrained by considerations of propriety to do little but sponsor publications and conferences. The NFKPA, for its part, points to its forty-member renal physician advisory panel, which acts "very sympathetically" and "with great seriousness," and to financial grants and seminar invitations from corporations in the renal field.[26] Even these contributions, however, must be rated as quite minor.

Nor have other relevant interest groups made an active attempt to influence ESRD policy. Although the United Kingdom's ESRD policy is severely biased against the elderly, for example, Age Concern, the principal organization representing the aged in health matters, conceded, "We haven't taken the issue up." A spokeswoman said that there was no point in trying to influence policy, since "consultants control everything" and, when reminded that they are restrained by the limited facilities and staff available, retorted that the government "obviously wasn't interested in doing anything" to help. Private charities, she indicated, might provide the funds, but she had never heard of any such offers, not even the well-publicized offers of the BKPA. The cost of significantly broadening the availability of dialysis and transplantation, in any case, is so far beyond the capacity of private charities that the remark served merely to underline Age Concern's essential ignorance of the problem. The United Kingdom's other major organization for the elderly, Help the Aged, concentrates its efforts on housing and was unacquainted with the issue. For their part, neither the BKPA nor the NFKPA had sought these organizations out. Mrs. Ward attributed this to the natural tendency "to live in our own little worlds," and Ruth Lupton, the late honorary secretary of the NFKPA, said simply that her organization "hadn't thought of it."

The macroallocative bias against the elderly, in short, has not come under serious challenge even from the organized elderly themselves. Indeed, the acquiescence may reflect what one DHSS official described as a consensus within society at large and the medical community as well that treating such patients must be re-

---

[26] Travenol, for instance, publishes *Diabetic Nephropathy*, sponsored a 1983 conference bringing together renal physicians and leaders of the British Diabetic Association with a view to improving the likelihood of dialyzing diabetics with renal failure, and has given money to the NFKPA to help cover office expenses.

garded as a low priority. They are more difficult and expensive to treat, their prognosis for success is poorer than that of younger patients, and they have already lived many years.

Similarly, though diabetics have suffered heavily from the United Kingdom's ESRD policy, the British Diabetic Association until recently has given little time to the issue. An effort by the NFKPA to contact the association was turned aside, a spokeswoman for the diabetic group later admitting in 1983 that it had just become aware of the long-standing, general reluctance to treat diabetics. Finally, in 1985 it joined the Renal Association and the Royal College of Physicians to conduct a survey of diabetic renal failure in six regions to gather rather basic data. Preoccupied with other political battles, it is only now beginning to turn its attention to ESRD diabetics.

Another problem is the severe fragmentation characterizing the government's ESRD policy-making process. Such fragmentation works a special hardship on small groups, which tend to lack the resources needed to identify the real power wielders or, having identified them, to influence the pockets of policy makers distributed throughout the nation. A prominent London elite may be easier to deal with than a plethora of provincial structures.

An even larger difficulty, however, confronts both the BKPA and the NFKAP: There is little either organization can do to or for policy makers. The organizations themselves are so peripheral that a threat to withhold their cooperation from the health system would have no appreciable impact, for its working hardly depends upon them. Any curtailment of BKPA or NFKPA activities, in fact, would hurt only the groups' own members. Nor does it seem likely that the organizations could persuade patients to withdraw their cooperation. It is true, of course, that the United Kingdom's stress on non-hospital-based therapies relies heavily on patient cooperation. Yet as vital as this cooperation is for the system, it is far more vital for the patients themselves; if they withhold it, they die. Any threat in that direction, therefore, would be instantly dismissed as reflecting juvenile frustration and being utterly empty.

Nor can patient groups help policy makers much. They possess no information critical to bureaucrats, and their members are too few and too diffuse geographically to constitute an electoral factor worth the parties' concern. Nor can they draw upon the resources of the truly dissatisfied consumers, namely, those denied treatment, for they quickly die.

What is left? Until recently, the answer seemed to be: principally, appeals to guilt or shame, made either in person or through the media. "If you do not help us," they essentially say, "we shall die, and our blood will be on your hands and everyone will know it." Even appeals such as this, however, proved only sporadically effective. Occasionally, that is, they prodded the government of the DHSS to single out ESRD for special favors, but the favors were not large, the singling out did not last long, and the preexisting pattern basically endured.

Shame, in any case, was far more potent than guilt; for shame involves the DHSS's or the government's public reputation, in which it invariably has a large investment, whereas guilt is seen to be too personal and sentimental, too disdainful of economic considerations, too lacking in the unemotional societal perspective that is the essence of the bureaucrat's and the politician's vision.[27]

Notwithstanding the long stretch of poky incrementalism, Mrs. Ward persisted in assessing the BKPA's impact as "enormous." For many years, it was difficult to share her evaluation completely. Indeed, through 1984 one finds a pattern of increases in the ESRD patient intake rate that seem quite unaffected by the group's ac-

---

[27] Thus, Mrs. Ward's confidence that all ESRD patients could be treated for an additional £50 million per year and that the funds could be found without their being taken from other claimants plainly put her poles apart from policy makers. Whereas she stressed how few resources there were to go round among all the medically worthy ESRD patients, policy makers tended to emphasize how few there were to go round for the entire NHS. It was therefore not merely finding a little more money for ERSD – though another estimate was well over four times that of Mrs. Ward (Laing, 1980, p. 6). Instead, conceding that ESRD merited the funds entailed either conceding the validity of dozens of other worthy causes that could pose similar demands or demonstrating that ESRD patients deserved preferential treatment. The first alternative was viewed as too costly and the second as untenable. Thus, the BKPA's arguments did not generate much guilt. Nor were the deaths from treatable ESRD visible enough to the public, despite all the media coverage, to generate more than episodic shame.

tivities. During this period, the internal dynamics within the NHS seemed overwhelmingly the determinative factor, so much so that an outsider might well have mistaken Mrs. Ward's unending efforts at molding public opinion as either hopelessly quixotic or a mere function of her ebullient indefatigability.

Instead, however, the cumulative effect of the public opinion labors was decisive, for when the Thatcher government decided to target the performance of the regions in certain medical areas, it saw ESRD as a dramatic example of its major points. That is, the government believed that a public consensus existed to the effect that current ESRD treatment patterns were indefensible and that a radical departure would be welcomed as sensible, decent, and compassionate. In fact, Mrs. Ward had helped to transform ESRD into a symbol that came to stand for the indifference to suffering and death that critics claimed to find in the NHS. To those not conversant with the complex reality of government goals, the easily personalized stories of ESRD helped provide a sense of comprehension and a basis for judgment. And so when the government moved to enhance NHS productivity, it naturally selected ESRD as a recognized failure to be made into a success.

Governments, of course, have always known that the manipulation of symbols is essential not only for achieving their purposes, but even for maintaining their power. But what Mrs. Ward seems to have grasped is the often overlooked point that whatever the motives for raising ESRD to symbolic status, that status could confer very major practical benefits. And so she nurtured the public image of ESRD, apparently fully understanding that the cause could not prove useful to the government without at the same time proving still more useful to ESRD's victims. It is hard to believe that the government would have chosen ESRD as a performance target had it not been for the exertions of Mrs. Ward.

PARLIAMENT

If the influence of interest groups on ESRD policy, apart from that of the BKPA, has been modest, the influence of other nonbureaucratic actors has by and large been weaker still. Parliament, for instance, though ostensibly sovereign, lost its effective legislative role years ago. Parliamentary questions may embarrass a minister or occasionally produce "a ripple across the serene waters of government and administration" (Ingle and Tether, 1981, p. 149);[28] adjournment debates may compel an official reply to a local administrator's problem; select committees may pry information from Whitehall or publicize administrative abuses and thus contribute to scrutiny and accountability (Drewry, 1985);[29] policy details may be altered as a result of amendments, Public Accounts Committee recommendations, or private members' bills; All Party Groups can provide a forum where members can exchange information and opinions, attract media attention, work with interest groups, and "help fill in the detail of proposed policy" (Morgan, 1979, p. 63). But none of these changes can be effected without the government's consent, and their total impact, even when members have truly exerted themselves, has nearly always been quite small. In the case of ESRD policy, where MPs have pretty well confined themselves to questions and speeches on improving the kidney donor program or to attending All Party Disablement Group meetings, not even the pretense of influence can be discerned.

Of course, MPs are not well equipped to affect policy anyway. A member of Labour's Shadow Cabinet, for example, complained that the entire body was "accommodated in a single corridor" (Cook, 1983) and that Opposition spokespersons are allotted only one desk for both their secretary and research assistant. Backbenchers, of course, are given even less (but cf. Review Body of Top Salaries, 1983, section 1, tables 16 and 17).

This modest provision of resources is no accident. It is universally acknowledged that it is the job of the government, not of Parliament, to govern. Straitjacketed by a tight party discipline that virtually eliminates their policy-making role, MPs have had to focus their attention on constituency service or scoring debating points.

[28] The DHSS is the subject of more parliamentary questions and adjournment debates than any other department, presumably reflecting the MPs' commitment to constituency service (Norton, 1981, pp. 171–2).

[29] The performance of the social services committee, however, is not ranked highly by other MPs (O'Higgins, 1984; but cf. Johnston, 1986).

But though some members may confuse success here with the exercise of power, it is hard to quarrel with the conclusion of a meticulous inquiry into the role of Parliament as a health policy maker during the years 1970–5: "Parliament's ability to influence the policies of the government was minimal" (Ingle and Tether, 1981, p. 153). Even an analyst prone to giving Parliament the benefit of the doubt admits that "it is difficult to document specific instances where MPs have directly shaped policy or determined Ministers' decisions" (Klein, 1978, p. 1498). The formative ESRD policy decisions did not even require formal parliamentary acquiescence.

THE CABINET

As for the Cabinet, it is certainly true that under the principle of ministerial responsibility, the secretary of state for health and social services (through his junior minister for health) can be held to account for the workings of his department, and that under the principle of Cabinet responsibility, the entire Cabinet can be held to account for Cabinet decisions and actions taken to carry them out.

Perhaps as important as the Ministry of Health is the Treasury, which reviews the annual budget requests of the other ministries and addresses the cost of each new measure before the Cabinet can consider it. In this, the Treasury is guided not only by its beliefs in the cost–benefit merits of the specific programs, but also by larger macroeconomic considerations, which are read to dictate increases or decreases in public spending generally. More mundane political considerations – electoral calculations, interest group pressures, and so forth – are also too predictable to be written off as mere intruders.

Prior to the Thatcher years, the Treasury civil servants, particularly the economists, were widely feared by even prominent politicians. As one secretary of state for health and social services in the mid–1970s complained, "None of us are equipped with the sort of economic advice that enables us to stand up to the dubious expertise of the Treasury" (Castle, 1980). Under the Thatcher team, strong in its economic views and until 1987 relentlessly dominated by the prime minister, the impact of the Treasury as an independent force has appeared to wane.

In any case, the implications of many constitutional abstractions for ESRD policy have been difficult to chart; for although ministers can be of importance in making issues salient and drawing up policy agendas (Banting, 1979), they have until recently rarely found their interest engaged by ESRD: Kenneth Robinson got an extra allocation of funds to help RHAs establish their own renal units; in 1977 funds were provided for dialysis machines for children; and in 1978 the Treasury purchased four hundred dialysis machines (an act of generosity that even some ESRD reformers believed was misplaced [e.g., Cattell, 1979]). For the most part, though, as a former chief medical officer observed, "Ministers don't get involved in technicalities like this."

Yet in 1984, the government began to involve itself with ESRD in a very significant way, not only allotting an additional 310,000 pounds to eight hospitals to expand treatment facilities but, more important, selecting ESRD as a performance target area for the regions. This was decisive in altering the modest incrementalism that had clung to ESRD like a shabby shawl on a winter's night.

Certainly, there had been no question that the Cabinet was aware of the issue. A letter from Prime Minister Thatcher, for example, adorns the BKPA's *Silver Lining Appeal*, and years earlier a former secretary of state for social services had written, "Either a man is given renal dialysis or he is not. If he's not, he dies" (Crossman, 1972, p. 27). Yet for many years, it had not seemed politically useful for governments to seize the initiative, and so, apart from a few isolated gestures, little was tried. By 1984, this had changed. Now the sad ESRD treatment patterns seemed to symbolize the failure of the status quo and to provide an opportunity to dramatize the need for change. And at this juncture, government action made an important difference.

PARTIES

Until 1984, political parties had not proved influential on ESRD policy either. At first glance, this may seem odd, for conventional rhetoric describes Labour as soft-headed and Conservatives as hard-hearted, stereotypes suggesting obvious implications for health care. In fact, however, so popular is the NHS as the "centerpiece of Great Britain's welfare state" that "politicians of every persuasion . . . seem duty bound not to be seen as attacking it" (Iglehart, 1983, pp. 1264, 1265).[30]

Similarly, although in opposition Labour has often cited government policy on ESRD as an illustration of Tory heartlessness (e.g., Johnson, 1983; London *Times*, 1983b, c), in office Labour has in fact tended to be less generous than the Conservatives. From 1973 through 1986, the number of new ESRD patients PMP under Labour budgets increased on average 7.4 percent per year, whereas under Conservative budgets the average increase was 11.9 percent per year.

Until ESRD was targeted in 1984, however, it was probably a mistake to attribute these differences to the parties. For one thing, except as a rhetorical opportunity (or problem), the parties hardly seemed aware of ESRD's existence. Focusing almost entirely on nomination and election – and only at the Cabinet level are national health policy makers elected – parties could not reasonably be expected to concern themselves with such a technical issue touching so few voters. It is true that new governments normally try to follow through on proposals in their election manifestoes, but ESRD has never been included in any party platform.

For another thing, until the targeting the real allocative decisions took place at the regional level, where policy makers are technocrats, not partisans. So little, indeed, does party count at this level that the chairpersons of the RHAs, ostensibly the most important political figures in health policy at the regional level, are not appointed on the basis of party allegiance (Chaplin, 1982, p. 108; but cf. Smith et al., 1985). Nor are the new regional general managers, whatever else their faults, simply party hacks.

Still, when ESRD permitted the Conservatives to make a point about the way the NHS had been run and should be run, Mrs.

---

[30] Thus, one reason ESRD was selected by the Thatcher government for special attention was to counter charges of hostility to the Health Service.

Thatcher did not hesitate to grasp the opportunity. The result was a significant broadening of treatment patterns.

MASS MEDIA

The awesome power of the mass media – television, radio, newspapers, magazines – to manipulate the unsuspecting average person is one of the governing clichés of the last quarter century. And it is certainly clear that the media have had a major impact on public opinion. For one thing, they are a key source of information about the world, even if they often seem content with presenting a mere recital of headlines. The media teach us about circumstances we rarely encounter firsthand – like anxiously awaiting a transplant – though these images may be dramatized and oversimplified to the point of being misleading. The media supply information to politicians and officials and give them means for mobilizing public support for their decisions. And the media are courted or feared by officeholders, who view them as the "voice of the people" or worry that hostile coverage may dash ambitions and ruin careers.

Given all this, it is not surprising that "by and large, those wishing to complain [about health policy] turned to the media and not to Parliament for redress," believing that a parliamentary question "cannot be compared with the effect of a report in the [weekly tabloid] *News of the World*" (Ingle and Tether, 1981, pp. 148, 149). Thus, from time to time, the press, radio, or television has addressed ESRD treatment policy, almost invariably treating it as scandalous, iniquitous, and tragic (Ferriman, 1982a,b; Harding, 1982; Veitch, 1982; Honigsbaum, 1983, p. 12). Moreover, London's famous bulletin board for opinion leaders, the *Times* editorial and letters page, has also devoted significant space to the issue (e.g., Cameron, 1983b; London *Times*, 1983d, 1985).

Yet the media are limited, too. In the first place, they are forced to accept their audience as a given. That is, the basic attitudes and beliefs of the viewers or readers have already been formed by family, peers, and other influences, and so the mind of the audience hardly constitutes a blank slate on which the media can write. Moreover, much of the information disseminated by the media follows a two-step flow, traveling first from the media to opinion leaders within social groups and then from the opinion leaders to their followers. Trusted and knowledgeable about their groups, the opinion leaders can translate the media's message into language their listeners can understand. But in the process, the message is frequently altered, sometimes decisively so.

In the second place, the media exist in a world of many other competing influences. Different television and radio stations, newspapers, and magazines offer different points of views, stress different facts, and make different arguments. Nor do we simply watch, listen, or read; we also work, play, shop, eat, and engage in dozens of other activities that may effectively shut the media off from our consciousness. As a consequence, the impact of the media has often been less than one might suppose. This is particularly true when the subject of the media's story has little apparent direct relevance to the audience's experience, like ESRD.

Thus, the unavoidable impression left by the ESRD media exposés is of so many (to use the British term) "nine-day wonders." That is, the issue surfaces noisily, generates some heated public discussion, and rapidly sinks back into oblivion.

In August 1983, for example, ITV's "First Tuesday" featured a powerful documentary on ESRD in Britain, "A Lottery for Life," which highlighted underfunding and regional variations in images that a prosecutor might well have envied. Even a sympathetic nephrologist was moved to declare, "The program was clearly designed to shock, to provoke discussion, to produce political pressure, and to influence decisions about allocating resources" (Wing, 1983). Did it, in fact, accomplish these goals? Plainly, it did not. The government, evidently on the theory that it took two to make a controversy, refused to be drawn into the matter. Indeed, it refused offers to send the secretary of state for social services or the minister for health to defend ESRD treatment patterns, according to the program's producer, from "an obvious desire to let things blow over." And though mail and press reactions to the program were overwhelmingly positive, its effects did, in fact, "blow over." By the end of the week, they were nowhere to be seen.

A 1985 controversy precipitated by routine news coverage rather than investigative reporting was also notable for its brevity and lack of consequences. The story concerned a former psychiatric patient suffering from ESRD and the head of the local renal unit, who had decided to terminate dialysis treatments. Mrs. Ward, terming the decision "sinister," "horrendous," and "terrifying," called for a governmental investigation of the action and, as if seeking to shame the authorities into expanding services, announced that her organization would pay to have the patient (who was a member of the BKPA) dialyzed at a private nursing home (Hughes, 1985a).

According to Mrs. Ward, a Labour MP, and the warden of the hostel for homeless men where the patient had been residing, doctors had simply concluded that "he is not worth keeping alive" (Hall, in Hughes, 1985a; Ward and Carter-Jones, in Hughes, 1985b). All this received considerable attention in both the broadcast and print media.

The health authority's response, characteristically, was firm but very low key. The general manager noted that the patient's mental condition had deteriorated since brain tumor surgery two years earlier, that he had refused to take his blood pressure medication, and that he would die within weeks or months from hypertension in any case. "I suppose you could say that discontinuing his treatment is letting nature take its course," he declared (Paine, in Hughes, 1985b).

By the fourth day, the *Times* gave only a paragraph to a National Council for Civil Liberties story on the subject. Subsequently, two other brief items appeared, and then after a ten-week interval, it was announced that following a stroke the patient had died. By this time media interest was almost nil, and the tangible impact of the events was hard to find.

Probably the only media effort of which this could not be said was an October 1980 BBC I "Panorama" story entitled, "Transplants: Are the Donors Really Dead?" The answer, predictably, was: sometimes not. And the consequences of this suggestion that physicians had taken organs from their patients, rather than revive them, in the words of a Manchester nephrologist, were "like the Wall Street crash" (Johnson, in London *Times*, 1981a). Relatives refused to permit comatose patients to donate their kidneys, doctors became reluctant even to discuss the procedure, and the number of transplants performed in the following year fell about 10 percent. This was only the second time that the number of transplants performed in one year was less than it had been in the preceding year.

A possible second instance of media influence on ESRD occurred in 1984, when "That's Life" acquainted millions of television viewers with a lovable two-year-old boy who required a liver transplant (Rantzen and Woodward, 1985). Eventually, the boy died, but some nephrologists attributed the record-breaking harvest of kidneys that year to an aroused public interest in organ donations generated by the boy's closely followed and deeply moving story – and a falloff in donations the following year was attributed partly to the absence of a similar, widely publicized case (Timmins, 1986a). The government, for its part, credited the record 1984 harvest to its own donor campaign (Patten, in Timmins, 1984).

Often, however, the media have simply missed the point. Repeatedly, in editorials and articles, for example, the *Times* has bemoaned the United Kingdom's ESRD record – but has never failed to attribute it to a shortage of kidneys for transplantation, rather than to funding too inadequate to service all medically suitable patients (London *Times*, 1975, 1981b; Ferriman, 1982a; cf. Sells et al., 1985, p. 195).

Have the media had an impact on policy? All the actors seem to assume that the media are weighty, though for many years the evidence was hardly overwhelming; for approximately the same incremental funding changes seemed to recur, regardless of the nature and extent of the media coverage given to ESRD. Perhaps the fear of even more hostile coverage helped to prevent any backsliding; but no policy maker could be found to argue for reducing the number of patients treated anyway. Certainly, absent media coverage, persons outside the medical community would have been quite unaware of the situation; yet, again, what awareness that existed hardly seemed to make a difference in the pattern of treatment. Further, by contributing to the public belief that health problems have high-technology solutions (Best et al., 1977, p. 25), the media may have helped to "create expectations and demands" (Council for Science and Society, 1982, p. 25) that ESRD advocates might find useful, though widespread satisfaction with the low-technology medicine currently practiced in the United Kingdom suggests that public fascination with high technology may not go very deep.

Yet in a more subtle way, the media have indeed had an impact on ESRD policy. But to understand it, one must first consider the role of the public.

THE PUBLIC

Ordinary citizens, it would appear, have a highly ambivalent role. On the one hand, as taxpayers, they presumably want to minimize costs, particularly those involving expensive, lifesaving technology that aids only a small number of people and consumes a highly disproportionate share of available resources. Efficiency (or "value for money"), they cannot avoid noting, is widely prized, and they probably see the NHS as an organization designed to provide basic services for all, rather than exotic services for a few. Treating those patients likely to make a social contribution – chiefly, the younger and healthier ones – may seem justified, therefore, but anything beyond this may seem wasteful and extravagant. A rather restrictive view of ESRD patient selection, in other words, would seem to be implied. On the other hand, as potential patients or as members of a patient's family, citizens presumably would want to be assured that persons requiring treatment would receive whatever was indicated. After all, the treatment is far too costly for typical patients to provide it for themselves. This would seem to entail an expansive view of patient selection.

Complicating matters further, the actual process of supplying medical care is handled directly by physicians and indirectly by bureaucrats and politicians, about whom citizens doubtlessly know very little. And the subject itself is so technically intimidating that few lay people are likely to understand much about it or even to try to learn. Moreover, internalized values – such as the belief that one has a duty to help one's unfortunate neighbor, that it is bad form to complain, or that life with a disability is worth less than a healthy life or perhaps is not worth living at all – may also interfere with rational, goal-maximizing drives.

All this suggests that ordinary citizens might be expected to react to ESRD claimants with hesitancy, confusion, and reservation. Cross-pressured in various directions on the conscious and subconscious levels, they would seem likely to withdraw uninformed from the arena, so lacking in convictions that they may simply never have made up their minds at all. To the extent that they reach any conclusion, they might be expected to favor narrow treatment patterns, inasmuch as they must certainly be aware that the probability of their paying taxes is nearly as large as the probability of their receiving ESRD treatment is small.

The facts are entirely the reverse.

For one thing, far from being uninformed, the public is quite well aware of dialysis and transplantation. A decade ago when ESRD was far less visible than it is today, three-quarters of a national sample spontaneously mentioned each as a treatment and, when the interviewees were prompted, the responses leaped to 98 and 97 percent, respectively. More than four-fifths, moreover, reported that transplantation was generally preferred by patients and was less costly than dialysis and that "very [many]" fewer dialysis machines and donor kidneys were available than were needed (Marplan, Ltd., 1979, pp. 46–9, 54). Though the public scored much poorer on more technical questions, its knowledge of a rather uncommon medical condition must be counted suprisingly high. Television and radio, apparently, deserve the credit. Though the citizen is a taxpayer continuously and a health consumer only occasionally, the role of the consumer, risk averse and preoccupied with security, seems far more salient.

Second, the public – perhaps reflecting the media's obvious sympathies – supports expanded ESRD treatment patterns by overwhelming margins, as Table 16 indicates. Remarkably, almost no one believes that too much is spent on ESRD treatment, notwithstanding the recognition that dialysis and transplantation are expensive therapies that benefit relatively few persons. On the contrary, a large majority feels that too little is being spent, usually "a great deal" too little.

Table 16. *Public attitudes on funds spent for dialysis and transplantation, 1978*

Amount spent is:	Dialysis (%)	Transplantation (%)
Too much		
(a great deal)	1	—
(a bit)	1	—
The right amount	8	14
Too little		
(a bit)	17	16
(a great deal)	64	48
Don't know	11	21

Source: Marplan, Ltd. (1979).

Reinforcing this broad support for ESRD treatment is the widespread public approval of the NHS and the backing for greater health funding. Indeed, it is almost universally acknowledged by politicians, bureaucrats, and media observers that the public views the NHS as the nation's greatest domestic achievement in the twentieth century. (What makes popular support for the NHS even more impressive is the British public's profound skepticism as to government's capacity to improve their lives. One survey disclosed, for example, that barely a third of Britons believed that government had either a positive or a mixed impact upon them; the majority said the government's impact had been trivial or negative [Moss, 1982, p. 23].)

This generalized support, furthermore, seems to carry over into support for funding increases. One poll found, for example, that only 4 percent of the public favored NHS cuts, whereas 59 percent favored increases. None of the ten other areas of public spending on which the sample was queried received nearly so favorable a set of responses (Lipsey, 1983).

In short, public opinion on ESRD can be characterized as a permissive consensus (cf. Key, 1961, pp. 32–5), supporting but not demanding broadened treatment. And in the development of this, the media clearly played a central role, time and again returning to the personal drama of specific ESRD patients.

Those laboring under a simplistic populism may have been disappointed that the overwhelming majority opinion was not promptly translated into public policy. But it is the nature of modern politics that governments ordinarily retain the initiative to act and, indeed, the entire system of representative government is constructed on this premise. Policy change, therefore, can hardly come from the unorganized public. The people can applaud – or even reward – the victor, but they cannot run the race. Yet if a permissive consensus is not sufficient to produce policy change, it may very often appear necessary.

CONCLUSIONS

Until the government intervened in 1984 and required the regions to admit at least forty PMP for treatment by 1987, extrabureaucratic actors did not impress much with their influence. Those possessing an intense commitment – the patient groups and the nephrologists – lacked the power bases to convert their demands into policy. They could help to "constantly define opinion for government" (Eckstein, 1960, p. 162) by labeling the expansion of treatment services good and retrenchment bad. They could appeal to the media and meet with officials to try, as one put it, "to keep the pressure on." Through these efforts, they could win small gains and make it easier for policy makers to continue to enlarge the program and more difficult to cut it back. But despite often heroic exertions, these committed actors do not appear to have been particularly significant.

In addition to these actors with great intensity but weak power bases were those with weak intensity but great power bases – the relevant Cabinet ministers – and with weak intensity and weak power bases – like the MPs. Until recently the contribution of these groups of actors to the formulation and execution of ESRD policy was, with a few isolated exceptions, practically nil.

Hence, over the years, it proved difficult for extrabureaucratic elements – whether politicians, physician or patient groups, the media, or public opinion – to force the bureaucracy to do anything that it did not want to do regarding ESRD treatment. It is true that the bureaucracy did not bring the new technologies into being (nor could it have wished them away, even if it had so desired). Yet it is also true that the bureaucracy orchestrated their introduction and has effectively controlled their growth. What this suggests is that absent a strong initiative from their superiors, the policy makers' own values, goals, and beliefs are probably of central importance in understanding their behavior. The analyst must proceed with caution here, of course, for hard data are absent, impressions can mislead, and speculation can be treacherous.

Nevertheless, the observer is left feeling that bureaucratic policy makers are of two minds on the question of ESRD treatment (see Downs, 1967, ch. 8). First, as officers in the proudest institution of the British welfare state, they appear to be driven, at least in part, by compassionate concerns. This is one reason they entered the Health Service to begin with, and not some other line of work. Time and again, policy makers volunteered that the NHS was not doing enough for ESRD patients, and though efforts were made to stress long-term improvements or to blame shortfalls on others, no one indicated that he or she considered the policies adequate. Typical, perhaps, was the remark of a DHSS official who, on hearing the cost effectiveness of ESRD treatment patterns praised, remarked with heavy irony, "Death is cheap."

The sense of compassion, perhaps in truth an amalgam of guilt and shame, is reinforced by a number of extrabureaucratic actors: patients' groups, renal physicians, the media, and so on. Given the kinds of people the Health Service recruits, these feelings would probably be present anyway. Still, outside actors collectively may be significant in strengthening these feelings or at least in preventing their erosion.

Second, as officers in an institution the policy makers are, above all, bureaucrats. As such, they are driven by bureaucratic ideals (like efficiency), they think in bureaucratic terms (focusing on abstract collectivities rather than on suffering individuals), and they respond to bureaucratic imperatives (such as avoiding upsetting settled relationships and standard operating procedures).

In this regard, it is important to note that despite its compassionate rationale, the NHS was not a product of a paroxysm of altruism, political radicalism, or working-class struggle. Instead, as a Marxist critic acknowledged, "the state was responding to the organizational and fiscal problems within the health sector and . . . was seeking to create a rational, efficient, nationally coordinated health service" (Walters, 1980, p. 156). As early as the 1920s, health professionals were disturbed by an increasingly serious chorus of problems: maldistribution and lack of coordination of facilities and personnel that produced both duplications and shortages, chronic financial crises facing the voluntary hospitals, national health insurance that provided inadequate coverage, and so forth. Matters worsened during the Great Depression, and wartime imposed still greater stresses. By the end of the war, almost no one believed that the jerry-built system should be left unchanged to confront the next rush of problems. It was this conviction that led to the creation of the NHS, a creation brought about by what one analyst aptly called the "paternalistic rationalists within the civil service and the medical technocrats who sought to maximize the opportunities to deploy the tools of medical science" (Klein, 1983b, p. 25; 1984, pp. 84–7). Ideologues and politicians played a relatively minor role.

How is the dissonance struck by the compassionate and bureaucratic themes to be resolved? For many years incrementalism provided a workable response, for it obviated the need to make difficult choices. Instead, all that was required was to continue on the path others had earlier marked out. Of course, initially a choice had had to be made – with ESRD as with so many other diseases, it was an obvious compromise between competing approaches – but that was long ago. Once made, it did not have to be reexamined but merely (with gradual alterations) repeated; for if incrementalism did not exactly eliminate conflict, it did minimize its pain and discomfort. The question really was not whether policy makers were captives of incrementalism or whether they could have burst its restraints through an immense act of will, but why they should have been presumed to regard such a comforting routine as their enemy.

Even as incrementalism proceeded, however, the consensus of the 1960s and early 1970s fell apart. Partly, this may simply have resulted from the growing number of people who sought to involve themselves in ESRD policy making. Initially, relatively few had been interested, and nearly all of these had been physicians. Exhilarated by the prospects afforded by the new technology, sharing similar backgrounds, values, and commitments, they constituted a relatively homogenous community of essentially like-minded individuals. As time passed, however, others, often "outsiders" like Mrs. Ward or media reporters, joined the fray, leaving the participants too numerous and diverse for the old sense of community to survive.

Meanwhile, as virtually all of Western Europe began to surpass the United Kingdom in patient intake rates, the initial optimism was irretrievably destroyed. Often in its place grew frustration, a feeling of betrayal, even bitterness. By 1981 and with the storm over the Royal College's report on the refusal to treat patients over the age of fifty, the consensus had vanished like Alice's Cheshire cat; only ritualistically uttered hopes for the future, like the cat's bizzare grin, remained.

The same consensus buckling that had generated problems for the older and still dominant forces, however, created opportunites for the new, who for the first time in years were able to contemplate the future in terms of expanding possibilities. Believing that the collapse of the consensus was a necessary precondition for significant change, they strove to view the period as a transition to broader treatment patterns to come.

It was at this point that the Thatcher government, impatient with business as usual at the NHS and determined to impose its own managerial philosophy, chose ESRD as a vehicle for making its point. Targeted for special attention by the regions, the ESRD intake rate jumped 38 percent in two years and by 1987 had achieved respectability. To some, it may seem ironic that help, when it finally arrived, appears to have been motivated by considerations so remote from ESRD itself. But to others, ESRD was not in the right place at the right time because of random chance or the workings of a benign universe, but rather because patient advocates had labored long to ensure that someday the ESRD problem would constitute a government opportunity. They had not labored in vain.

3. Microallocation

The importance of microallocation is directly attributable to the macroallocative patterns that have emerged. If sufficient resources had been provided to treat virtually all ESRD patients, as in the United States, the microallocative decision as to whether to treat would have long since faded away, like the background of an old snapshot. Because such resources have not been made available – because, indeed, a condition of hyperscarcity has prevailed from the outset –the microallocative decision has retained immense significance and continues to raise a number of rather disturbing issues.

In the microallocative decision as to which ESRD patients are to receive treatment, the key players are the patient, the general practitioner and general medicine hospital consultant, and the nephrologist. The players proceed with great seriousness, for the stakes are nothing less than life and death. Yet the rules seem only vaguely defined and are understood by different players in radically different ways. And those willing to make the microallocative decision need not have thought much about decision criteria or even systematically considered the decision criteria applied by others. It is a game played with courage, skill, and tenacity, and with deception, detachment, and arrogance. And mottling the field, like large patches of scorched grass, is a stubborn and awful sadness.

THE ROLE OF THE PATIENT

The patient's importance, it must be said at the outset, lies almost entirely in his condition and rarely is a function of efforts on his part to influence outcomes. As one distinguished renal physician put it, "There is a tradition for far more acceptance by our patients of the view of their primary care doctor or the first doctor they meet at the hospital. They will take it literally lying down and say, 'Thank you doctor, I know you know best' " (Wing, 1985a, p. 273).

Partly, this may simply be a function of the nature of most health care in advanced societies. Health care, of course, is unusual in that after the patient's initial decision to see a physician, it is the producer who determines demand far more than the patient-consumer. In the first place, that is, it is normally the physician, not the patient, who determines whether and what tests, drugs, surgery, and so forth are required by the patient.

More than that, it is a producer's elite that helps to shape the working physicians' demands: Scribner and his associates, who made dialysis a viable treatment for ESRD (Quinton et al., 1960); Cimino and Brescia, whose forearm fistula made the procedure capable of many more repetitions (Brescia et al., 1966); Tenckhoff, whose improved catheter made CAPD feasible (Tenckhoff and Schecter, 1968); and so on. The patient's inarticulate pleas for help, in other words, would remain mere pitiful noise without those who create technological innovations and without physicians to utilize that technology. The innovators saw a need and responded to it, and so did the physicians; patients benefit from technology but did not bring it into being or apply it to individuals, though their compliance with physician's instructions (particularly if they dialyze at home) does, in a sense, make them junior partners in the treatment.

Partly, also, the patient's relative unimportance may reflect the physician's natural dominance, commonly attributed to his specialized knowledge, skills, and experience and to the potent scientific and life-or-death mystique surrounding his role. Most patients still call their doctors "sir," one physician observed, and a nephrologist maintained that in terms of public perceptions, the physician's position could be compared to that of the old English squire or even the colonial administrator.

There is some evidence that the traditionally passive British patient is more assertive and knowledgeable today than in the past – malpractice insurance premiums, for example, have increased dramatically in the 1980s – but passivity remains the rule, and since the hospital specialist may be the most prestigious of professions, patients' deference is likely to be very great indeed (Cartwright and Anderson, 1981; Schwartz and Aaron, 1984, p. 56). ESRD patients, often fatigued, confused, and vulnerable, may seem particularly helpless and aware of their dependency and limitations.

For the most part, however, physicians who were interviewed explained the passivity of the typical patient in terms of venerable stereotypes of the British national character. One physician administrator, for example, referring to a queuing mentality, declared, "People put up with things. People accept that's the way things are. . . . If you get an itch in America, you scratch it; here, you just hope it will go away."

Similarly, one consultant remarked that "the English tend to be rather docile," and another spoke of the "British quality of 'up-puttingness'" (i.e., the predilection for putting up with adversity and viewing complaining as bad form). This, he felt, was reinforced by a "rather stratified class structure," which in the medical context encourages the belief that the "doctor knows best."[1] Therefore, it is hardly surprising, the other doctors interviewed observed, that although a decision not to treat was sometimes reversed when a patient complained, the overwhelming proportion of patients denied treatment simply acquiesced without protest (see Schwartz and Aaron, 1984, p. 56).

Clearly, however, it would be a mistake to exaggerate the extent of this docility. The United Kingdom is a nation not only of considerable class deference but also of class conflict; and its modern history could not be told without reference to the rise of the Labour party, the actions of militant trades unions, the intellectual generation of *Look Back in Anger,* the persistent disaffection of significant strata of youth, and so on (Hart, 1978, pp. 193–202; Kavanaugh, 1980, pp. 156–8; Beer, 1982a, ch. 4). Nor can it be ignored that the physicians' stress upon patient docility, though clearly uttered with

[1] Proceeding from a different angle, a leading British health policy analyst has reached the same conclusion. "Britain," he writes, "is an original sin society in which illness and debility are seen as part of the natural order of things and patients tend to be deferential" (Klein, 1984b, p. 144).

sincere exasperation, has its own self-serving ring, for it lays the problem entirely on the patient or the vast, impersonal forces that are said to have shaped him, and leaves the physician as blameless as a benevolent father cursed with a rather doltish child. In the American context, for example, one psychoanalyst has suggested that the authoritarianism of physicians may derive partly from insecurity: Physicians are trained to project (and patients are apt to demand) a confidence that clashes with normal medical uncertainty and self-doubt, and this is expressed as a paternalistic refusal to view patients as adults capable of understanding their situation and making choices (Katz, 1984).

Yet the sheer, almost overwhelming stability of the United Kingdom certainly points to respect for authority as a long-potent factor.[2] And even if the stolid national character may be mostly mythical, it need not on that account be unimportant. As Orwell put it:

> Myths which are believed tend to become true, because they set up a type or a person which the average person will do his best to resemble. . . . Traditionally the Englishman is phlegmatic, unimaginative, not easily rattled; and since that is what he thinks he ought to be, that is what he tends to become. Dislike of hysteria and "fuss," admiration for stubbornness, are all but universal, shared by everyone except the intelligentsia. Millions of English people willingly accept as their national emblem the bulldog, an animal noted for its obstinacy, ugliness and impenetrable stupidity. (In Richards, 1985, p. 61)

---

[2] An impressionistic argument has been made for the medical value of encouraging this docility, one physician defending it as a bias in favor of "fighters," who "really want to live." Such persons, other things being equal, typically cope better with the rigors of treatment, he noted. And even if the "fighting" is carried on not by the patient but by his family – as is usually the case – this is indicative of the support he can expect, an important consideration in the United Kingdom, given the dominance of home-based treatments. Yet under this system "fighters" may be preferred even when other things are not equal, and this may not be medically justified. It may be, then, that some physicians prefer patient docility simply because by minimizing resistance, it makes their job much easier and less stressful.

Thus, the docility of the British patient is not simply a function of widespread popular ignorance and apathy regarding ESRD; in fact, as we have seen, the public is surprisingly knowledgeable about dialysis and transplantation, believes that treatment patterns are far too narrow, and supports efforts to expand these patterns. Although data on the attitudes of ESRD patients and their families to these questions are not available, these people can hardly be more uninformed and restrictive than the disinterested society at large. Notwithstanding all this, British patients generally remain reluctant to protest what must appear to some to be sentences of death.

The relative passivity of the British patient may also be traced to a marked capacity to endure pain and discomfort. In this regard, many of those interviewed spontaneously pointed to the formative influence of the war years, with its unrelieved scarcity of public and private goods and services and its pall of anxiety brought on by bombings at home and the fighting of loved ones abroad. The point was not simply to educate a visiting American about a period he had not experienced firsthand, but more tellingly to explain why so many Britons, particularly those in late middle age or older (the high-risk medical years), appear to have rather meager expectations as to what their society can do for them.

Also, on an everyday level, as more than one physician who was interviewed observed, the average Briton seems willing to tolerate numerous daily discomforts – poorly heated homes, scratchy woolen clothing, and so on – that most other Western Europeans have evidently placed a far higher priority on reducing. Less likely to complain, the British patient may be more likely to accept both his illness and his physician's decision as to what ought to be done about it (though not focusig on ESRD, see Zborowski, 1952; Zola, 1966; but cf. Koopman et al., 1984).

The character of the doctor–patient relationship may have other explanations as well. Although the British academic literature remains rather scanty, in the United States numerous studies and analyses have focused on the relationship, and they may be of some heuristic value here. As early as 1935, Henderson described the doctor–patient relationship as a social system within which medical decisions are made. But the truly seminal writer here, as in so many other areas, was Talcott Parsons (1951), who stressed the asymmetry of active, dominant physicians relating to passive, dependent patients, whose very illness labels them as deviant. Subsequent observers have tended to confirm or reinforce the picture of the "good" patient as trusting and obedient and the "bad" patient as the reverse. Everyone who was interviewed for the present study agreed that this phenomenon is even more pronounced in the United Kingdom.

All this, of course, has an impact upon doctor–patient communications, the inequality of which has in any case long been evident (Szasz and Hollender, 1956). The nature of these communications – what is said, how it is said, what is left unsaid – can help to determine whether a patient is labeled "good" or "bad," an act with potentially momentuous consequences.

The physician, for his part, generally tends to be wary about passing on much information to the patient or his family. If the physician's own uncertainties or the patient's poor prognosis were made known to him, his faith in his doctor would be undermined and with it, it is believed, his capacity to treat his patient successfully. This capacity, in turn, is seen as dependent on the physician's authority and autonomy, which are justified not only by his specialized knowledge and experience, but also by his presumed altruistic commitment to placing his patient's interests before any other. It is more than traditional British reserve, for example, that explains that about a quarter of all those who suffer from multiple sclerosis are never officially informed of the fact, and that many who do learn of their affliction learn from someone other than a physician (Elian and Dean, 1985).

That a presumption of altruism has so long endured, even as a sometimes wobbly ideal, is itself a most remarkable fact, for the usual presumption regarding the basis of relationships outside the family or friendship circle is self-interest. Thus, although there is frequent criticism of America's fee-for-service system because it provides incentives to overtreat, it is rarely noted that the United Kingdom's capitation (general practitioner) or salary (hospital consultants) system provides an incentive to undertreat.

And what makes the British presumption of altruism all the more noteworthy is that beyond assuming that the patient wishes to avoid pain and death – and even these two assumptions may on occasion conflict – the doctor is unlikely to know much about the way the patient sees his own interests. This is particularly true of general practitioners, whose average patient list in 1985 was 2,068, but it applies to consultants, as well. The neurologists who withheld information on multiple sclerosis from their patients, for instance, were quite confident that this was in their patients' interests, but very few of the patients themselves preferred not to know the diagnosis, and some admitted that they would have reached different conclusions about certain vital life decisions had they known. Similarly, American researchers have shown that objective and subjective evaluations of ESRD patients' quality of life may yield substantially different results. As measured by functional impairment and ability to work, the patients' quality of life was rather poor, but as measured by answers to indices of psychological affect, overall life satisfaction, and well-being, the quality of life was only slightly lower than that of the general population (Evans et al., 1985; see also Najam and Levine, 1981).

Yet the presumption of altruism serves not to motivate physicians to inquire into patient interests, but rather to make such inquiry appear superfluous; for the corollary presumption seems to be that the doctor knows best, perhaps even that the patient should be treated as a child, unaware of (if not actually incapable of knowing) his true interests.

Meanwhile, patients – vulnerable, needy, and anxious – may be unwilling to push for much information either. In this regard, a prominent American physician and psychoanalyst has suggested that many patients transfer to their physicians the key qualities of their earliest caretakers. The result of this transference he sees as a basically irrational amalgam of past and present, fantasy and reality, as patients crave a comforting parent/caretaker and physicians seek a compliant child/patient. Too often, though, these naive hopes are soured by events. And as doctors retreat to silence or patronizing efforts at reassurance, patients may feel abandoned and either angry at their physician or guilty over the childlike behavior they fear may have driven him away (Katz, 1984, pp. 142–7, 208–12). It is hardly

surprising, then, that among British hospital patients' chief dissatis-
factions are the paucity of information given them about their condition and treatment (Royal Commission on the National Health
Service, 1979).

The physician's perspective, of course, is quite different. As one
general practitioner explained:

> I find the older working classes and generally the lower mid-
> dle classes of all ages easier to deal with than my own sort. My
> own sort ask complicated questions and are often dissatisfied
> with the answers. And want long discussions in the middle of a
> busy surgery. The others simply listen and do more what you
> ask. (Gathorne-Hardy, 1984)

Additionally, the patient's passivity appears to be accentuated by
certain structural constraints built into the NHS; for he cannot con-
sult a specialist on his own, but only upon a specific referral from his
general practitioner. And if the general practitioner concludes that a
specialist is required, it is the general practitioner who selects the
specialist (see General Medical Council, 1987, pp. 22–3).

In such a context, the patient's passivity can be said to be one of
the system's ruling assumptions, for if dissatisfied, the patient may
perceive his options to be exceedingly limited. He can accept his lot,
perhaps grumbling to himself about his bad luck. Or he can complain to his general practitioner, at the risk of alienating him during
this time of crisis. Or he can try to replace his general practitioner, a
task that entails obtaining permission from his local Family Practitioner Committee and then finding a new general practitioner who
will accept him. But though Family Practitioner Committees usually
grant permission, their involvement ordinarily is so intimidating and
time-consuming that most patients are deterred from following this
option – and for those patients not so deterred, the prospect of
securing another, more compliant general practitioner seems sufficiently difficult to discourage most from doing so. The "shopping
around" for physicians that is so widespread in the United States is
far less common in the United Kingdom, where convenience and
tradition rather than medical evaluation tend to determine the
patient's choice of general practitioner. Usually, in fact, the British

patient does not even perceive a choice to be made: Either he knows no other doctor or has no reason to believe that a change would bring improvement. It is hardly surprising, then, that only 4 percent of patients surveyed in 1977 had changed general practitioners as a result of dissatisfaction (Cartwright and Anderson, 1981, p. 8).

THE ROLE OF THE GENERAL PRACTITIONER

Far more important than the patient as a microallocative actor is the general practitioner. It is his responsibility to reach a preliminary diagnosis and to decide whether the patient should be sent either to a nephrologist or, as is more often the case, to a general medicine department at a local hospital, which may then refer the patient to a renal unit.

The general practitioner's significance, therefore, is more commonly negative than positive: By misdiagnosing or deciding against referral, he effectively closes the door to treatment, and by sending the patient to a nephrologist or a general medicine department, he merely passes the decision on to a higher level. His relative inexperience with ESRD, however, may hamper his efforts, for many general practitioners identify only a single case every two (Beven et al., 1980, p. 169) or perhaps every ten years (Parson, in Parson and Ogg, 1983, p. 245), and most lack ties with nephrologists as well as personal access to the biochemical facilities that ESRD diagnosis requires. General practitioners may also be quite unacquainted with prevailing treatment patterns and fail to refer patients for reasons that have long since become obsolete. Thus, one general practitioner, when presented with sixteen hypothetical cases, observed ruefully that "under present circumstances probably none would be accepted" for treatment (Challah et al., 1984, p. 1122), though such extreme resource scarcity had not existed for many years.

A nephrologist who was interviewed also suggested that patients' attitudes may partly be to blame for the failure to refer. The deference granted doctors, he suggested, may be taken as implying a duty "to know everything," which can easily be translated into a face-saving reluctance to seek second opinions: "If a doctor has to ask for a second opinion," the nephrologist said, "he may be seen as a little low in quality. It is necessary to be good enough and secure enough to be humble, and that is not always the case. . . . General practitioners tend to practice paternalistic medicine. This can be very comforting for patients, but can also remove opportunities for the application of modern medicine." As one physician commented, "There is not as much request for a second opinion as you would suppose, and this is probably accentuated by my profession itself almost appearing to be offended when such a request is made" (Wing, 1985b, p. 273). No wonder that among nephrologists, the apathy and ignorance of general practitioners concerning ESRD are proverbial (e.g., Little et al., in Parson and Ogg, 1983, pp. 242–3).

However, one general practitioner who was interviewed retorted "Of course nephrologists want to treat. That's their job, isn't it? That's what they're trained to do. Sometimes, they tend to go a bit overboard, though." What appears as an opportunity to the nephrologist, in short, may seem merely a problem to the general practitioner.

Exacerbating difficulties of communication and coordination is the traditional antagonism between hospital and community-based physicians. One of the chief pioneers in home dialysis sought to minimize these problems by trying to demonstrate that general practitioners can and should arrange stable home dialysis for patients (Shaldon, 1968a). The Ministry of Health, however, concluded that general practitioners tended to lack the time and inclination to take on that task, which in any case was often not routine and raised problems beyond their training or expertise. Thus, very early on, the chief medical officer took the position that dialysis was "primarily a hospital-based service [with] limited clinical responsibility" residing with the "medical staff of the main approved centres" (Godber, 1968, p. 1). Subsequent efforts to bridge the gap that this division of labor had widened have by all accounts been ineffective.

THE ROLE OF THE GENERAL MEDICINE CONSULTANT

Although the general practitioner may reject treatment for some ESRD patients, this negative decision is more likely to be made by a general medicine consultant from a nearby hospital (Challah et al., 1984, p. 1120). The consultant, however, typically has "limited experience in renal medicine" (Gabriel, 1983, p. 36) and may be prone to making referral decisions on moral or other nonmedical grounds. "I have always referred on merit," one consultant reported, "but I have made the value judgment as to who is meritorious myself" (Challah et al., 1984, p. 1122). There is also reason to believe that out-of-date clinical selection criteria may sometimes be used. As one nephrologist put it, "New developments have not really percolated to the consultant level," and so their practice tends to reflect what they learned a decade or more earlier.

Moreover, as one nephrologist explained, with a nephrologist in only every fifth district hospital, the general medicine consultant may feel that referral involves "admitting that they can't do it. They must eat humble pie." That is, he suggested, they may feel that they would be conceding not only a personal but an institutional inadequacy. The general medicine consultant, in other words, appears far more aggressively restrictive in his views toward treatment than does the kidney specialist. And since the patient cannot ordinarily see the nephrologist on his own, it is frequently the view of the general medicine consultant that prevails (cf. Chantler, paraphrased in Lupton, 1979, pp. 3–4).

Both the general practitioner and the general medicine consultant, then, play the so-called gatekeeper role, selectively screening out patients who will be denied access to medically higher levels and admitting only a relatively small number.

One reason that the general practitioner and the general medicine consultant can play this role so effectively is that both are free of financial incentives to treat. Most of the general practitioner's earnings consist of fixed amounts paid him for each person on his list; the treatments he prescribes make little difference. As for the consultants, as hospital physicians they simply receive salaries. By contrast, in West Germany, France, Italy, and Spain, general practitioners are paid on a fee-for-service basis, as are the many internists who practice outside hospital settings. This provides a tangible reward for treatment – particularly with easily documented treatments like dialysis and transplantation – that does not exist to this extent in the United Kingdom, where restraint may be almost equally rewarded. This may help to explain the much greater willingness of doctors in these other countries to treat.

The screening activity of the general practitioner and the general medicine consultant illustrates some of the strengths and weaknesses of the gatekeeper approach. On the one hand, minimizing the role of the specialist curtails the more expansive styles of practicing medicine. Costs, as a result, are certainly kept down. Hence, the consensus, in the words of one acute observer, that "general practice is stronger in the United Kingdom than elsewhere. It provides a flexible, relatively inexpensive, first level of medical contact" (Maxwell, 1984, p. 37; cf. Hiatt, 1987).

On the other hand, some medical decisions that might be better made by specialists are left to physicians with less relevant expertise and experience. The problem, of course, is aggravated if the physician is overloaded with patients or is the kind of doctor who requires external stimulation (competition, colleague pressure, etc.) to force him to keep current and provide personalized service. For a comprehensive, taxpayer-supported system like the NHS, the cost containment imperative probably will always dominate. Nonetheless, as the case of ESRD demonstrates, there are medical costs involved in ascribing the gatekeeper role to nonspecialists, and these costs are borne primarily by the patient.

THE ROLE OF THE NEPHROLOGIST

The first thing to note about United Kingdom nephrologists is how few of them there are – only 117 senior and 207 junior staff (Royal College of Physicians of London, 1983, tables 1, 2). (In Italy, by contrast, there are about 2,500.) Partially, these small numbers may reflect the terrible and persistent frustrations brought on by budgetary and referral problems. That nephrology does not appear to be an attractive speciality is indicated by the fact that among new physicians only 0.1 percent list nephrology as their first choice and only 0.2 percent as their second or third choice (Parkhouse et al., 1983).

But as one distinguished nephrologist emphasized, the paucity of renal physicians also stems from a deliberate policy of the NHS. Administrators control the creation of consultant positions and, in order to control ESRD costs, he contended, have set the UK level at a fifth to a tenth of that obtaining in other Western European countries or in the United States. With four out of five district general hospitals lacking even a single renal physician, many general practitioners and general medicine consultants will not even consider conferring with a nephrologist, and talk of proliferating renal units throughout the nation must invariably come to naught. Limiting the number of nephrologists, then, becomes an indispensable tool for limiting the number of ESRD patients to be treated (Wing, 1985a, p. 54).

It is with the nephrologist, nevertheless, that the most carefully considered microallocative decision ordinarily rests. The context in which he makes his decision, to be sure, may be far from ideal. The nature of renal failure is such that symptoms usually are not reported until the disease has progressed quite far, and referral procedures may sometimes add to the delay. As a consequence, by the time the nephrologist sees the patient, it may be "too late . . . for a carefully considered plan of investigation leading to a carefully constructed strategy for treatment" (Knapp, 1982, p. 848). It may even in some rare cases be "too late to treat the patient at all" (*British Medical Journal,* 1978, p. 1449).

THE DECISION TO TREAT

Whether confronted in an optimal context or not, the decision whether and how to treat must be made. How is it reached? The usual answer given by physicians – general practitioners, general medicine consultants, or nephrologists – is that it is a clinical judgment found by applying sound medical criteria to the individual patient's case. These criteria are not always clearly spelled out, but generally seem to entail at least an implicit calculation of the probability that the treatment will succeed and, if successful, that the patient can then expect a satisfactory quality of life. Thus, the physician asks, for example, whether the patient is otherwise healthy or suffers from a complicating illness; or whether he is psychologically able to cope with the stress the treatment will impose or is likely to fail to comply adequately with the prescribed regimen or even to drop out of the treatment program entirely.

Despite the apparent reasonableness of such questions, however, the exclusive emphasis on the medical character of patient selection appears undermined by several major problems. The first is that physicians' clinical judgments need not agree with one another. Partly, this reflects disagreement as to the proper meaning of medical need. When asked what criteria should determine who receives a transplant, for example, two American surgeons answered, medical need. One, however, took this to mean selecting the "individual who has the best chance for survival" (Najarian, in *Dialysis and Transplantation*, 1986, p. 305), whereas the other construed it as choosing the patient whose life would be most endangered if denied the transplant (Peters, in *Dialysis and Transplantation*, 1986, p. 305). Although a persuasive case might be made for each answer, clearly they may entail different patient selections; a patient responding poorly to dialysis might well meet the second definition but not the first.

In addition to conceptual differences as to what constitutes medical need are errors and disagreements regarding observations and evaluations. These, of course, are hardly unique to ESRD (see, e.g., Graham et al., 1971; Bennett, 1979, pp. 165–79). Yet in ESRD cases there is evidence that the extent of the disagreement can be astonishing. In one study, for example, twenty-five British nephrologists were asked to reject ten out of forty hypothetical ESRD "patients." Only thirteen "patients" received unanimous judgments – all acceptances – and six of the "patients" most frequently rejected were actually modeled after real patients who had been successfully treated (Taylor et al., 1975). Similarly, in a more recent study, eight Glasgow clinicians in a renal unit were asked to classify the suitability of one hundred hypothetical ESRD "patients" for treatment; in only thirty-two cases did all of the physicians agree either to treat or not to treat the patients (Parsons and Lock, 1980).

Moreover, different physicians apparently rely upon different key indicators to aid their judgments. Some physicians, for instance, may predict medical outcomes on the basis of early patient reactions to dietary restrictions (Czackes and Kaplan De-Nour, 1978, pp. 154–6); others report this to be of little help (Robinson, 1978, p. 16). Some may tend to turn away diabetics (Medical Services Study Group, 1981, p. 285); others may accept them (Berger et al., 1983; Legrain, 1983). Some may be dubious about treating children under five; others may treat infants (Hodson et al., 1978; Trompeter et al., 1983). Some may automatically reject patients over the age of sixty-five; others may treat those in their eighties (Chester et al., 1979) or even a senile patient of ninety (Gurland, in *Controversies in Nephrology*, 1979, p. 133). Certainty of death in the absence of treatment is countered by the uncertainty of the efficacy of treatment in specific cases. As one prominent nephrologist concluded, "When treatment is provided for patients with an apparently poor prognosis, surprisingly often those expected to fare badly may do well. There are, in fact, few objective measurements to predict the response to treatment" (Knapp, 1982, p. 848).

To some extent, these differences among physicians may reflect differences in ability and conscientiousness. And as one analyst argued, "Although UK consultants have more freedom than most specialists in other countries, they also are more isolated and have fewer means of knowing how their performance compares with others. . . . Consultants may be appointed at thirty-five and for the next thirty years have no real scrutiny of their work" (Dick, 1983, p. 899).

More than this, however, differences in medical judgments also flow from what one physician who was interviewed called the "inherent subjectivity" of the process. Though some patients clearly have excellent prognoses and others poor ones, a number of patients fall in the grey area in between. Whether they will be assigned to the "accept" or "reject" track is a difficult, complex, problematic question. In answering it, physicians naturally proceed analogically. "The apparent diagnostic acumen of the senior clinician," as one Dublin physician wryly put it, "may be nothing more than déjà vu; having seen it before he can now recognize it" (McCormick, 1986, p. 1734). The physician, that is, compares the patient before him with similar patients he has treated, observed, or otherwise learned about through the literature or from colleagues. The physician assumes that identical patients with identical diseases will respond identically to identical therapies. But he knows, too, that in the real world, "identical" is merely an analytical construct and that in the real world he must content himself with "similar." This realization, however, necessarily generates uncertainty: Is the patient seated before me, he must ask, so like another patient I am familiar with that I should treat him in the same way or so different that I should treat him in a different way – or not at all? To such questions there may be several answers, for a single response is compelled neither by science nor by logic. Instead, reasonable, thoroughly competent physicians will differ, some stressing the similarities, others the differences. No unambiguous, objective methodology can be relied on to yield infallible answers.[3]

Lacking such a methodology, physicians must be presumed to be influenced by their knowledge, experience, and training, and probably also by the prevailing practices at their hospitals, their own personalities, pressures from the patient's family, and any number of other factors that will be unique to each physician. Whatever the explanation, though, the data on physicians' disagreements about ESRD patients would seem to leave in tatters any pretense that the uttering of "clinical judgment" can banish doubts behind a curtain of consensus.

Is "clinical judgment," then, uniquely subjective in cases of ESRD? Clearly not. All clinical judgments are, after all, *judgments,* a word that implies recourse to a subjective best estimate. Moreover, since untreated chronic renal failure almost uniformly results in death, the consequences of a decision not to treat are quite predictable. This element of virtual certainty, however distressing, is lack-

---

[3] Eddy (1982) contends that clinical decisions are significantly influenced by "clinical policies – guidelines that tell one what to do when certain situations occur: If A, then do B." These guidelines may appear in books or regulations, although most develop from the literature and from countless formal and informal discussions. But however it develops, the "distinguishing feature of a clinical policy is that it makes an unambiguous recommendation about the management of a specific clinical problem in a specific class of patients" (p. 343). Inasmuch as there is no universal consensus as to the content of such policies nor any certainty that a given patient will not trigger the implementation of more than one such policy, discretion and disagreement would persist under Eddy's analysis as well.

ing in the vast majority of other diseases. Furthermore, inasmuch as the UK nephrologist is not employed on a fee-for-service basis, he lacks the "personal financial incentive to treat more patients" (*British Medical Journal*, 1978, p. 1449; Schwartz and Aaron, 1984, p. 54), and thus may work with greater detachment than his colleagues in other countries.[4]

By the same token, however, it may be more difficult to forecast patient response to ESRD treatment than that to many other diseases (Shapiro and Umen, 1983); for to an uncommon degree, success depends not only on physiological factors, but also on psychological and even domestic factors. The physician's ability to predict the effects of these variables, let alone to influence them, may be much less than he would desire. As one renal unit nurse said, "So often patients will adapt much better than has been perhaps forecast for them" (Stephens, in Gaze, 1985, p. 17).

A second problem with an exclusive reliance on clinical judgment is that many pertinent medical criteria have not been systematically tested empirically. One pioneering figure in the development of home dialysis, for example, stressed the importance of the patient's being of average intelligence (Shaldon, 1968a, p. 522): If he were below average, it was argued, he might be unable to learn and perform all his tasks; and if he were above average, he might have difficulty accepting his role and become extremely anxious. Presumably, some patients considered to be outside the intelligence limits were denied treatment on that account and consequently died. But was the hypothesis ever tested? Was the intelligence of the patients precisely determined? Was intelligence itself, notoriously an ambiguous and vague concept, satisfactorily defined? The record is barren of answers. (Indeed, subsequent research indicates that barring the retarded and confused, there is no correlation between intelligence and compliance [Winoker et al., 1973].)

Of course, the intelligence hypothesis seems plausible, but plausibility cannot be confused with confirmation, particularly when life or death decisions are being taken. A modicum of psy-

---

[4] It is easy to exaggerate the significance of this point; the financial is only one of a vast tangle of incentives and disincentives (see, e.g., Grist, 1981).

chological denial, for example, may not at first glance seem a good predictor of successful patient adjustment to home dialysis. But by suppressing somatic preoccupation and depression and by inducing patients to see themselves as only marginally ill and thus quite able to resume their normal roles, denial can indeed be functional (Short and Wilson, 1969; Glassman and Siegel, 1970; Ziarnik et al., 1977; Richmond et al., 1982; but cf. Kaplan De-Nour and Czaczkes, 1972). Similarly, although it has generally been assumed that marriage, social support, absence of psychiatric illness, and greater education were all associated with dialysis patients' survival, a decade-long study of black patients in New York found none of these relationships statistically significant (Friend et al., 1986); a study of home- and center-dialysis patients in St. Louis also confounded expectations that an adequate system of social support was essential for success (Smith et al., 1985), and another study of dialysis patients identified the hypertensive as among the most compliant (Ferraro et al., 1986).

Some hypotheses, though, lack even surface plausibility. In the early years of dialysis, for example, one of the most widely respected UK nephrologists assured his colleagues that "gainful employment in a well chosen occupation is necessary to achieve the best results" in hemodialysis, since "only the minority wish to live on charity" (Parson, 1967, p. 623). This extraordinary proposition – that the unemployed make poor patients because most would literally rather die than become public charges – was simply announced, as if it were too self-evident to require further explanation, let alone rigorous investigation. Never was it even mentioned that large numbers of dialysis patients have always found the treatment too debilitating or time-consuming to permit them to work. Similarly, Katz reports a French nephrologist who, upon examining a peasant suffering from ESRD, told him that no medical treatment could help him. "To say more would have been cruel," he explained. "Peasants do not adjust well to a permanent move to a large city." Dialysis would have required a permanent move to Paris, some forty miles away (Katz, 1984, p. 5).

A third problem is that agreement among physicians as to clinical facts need not entail agreement as to clinical inferences. A pair of physicians examining a pair of patients may be united as to what they see, but divided as to what they want to do about it. One physician, for instance, might favor a transplant for the healthier patient, in order to maximize the likely benefit from the donated organ. Meanwhile, the second physician might argue for a transplant for the sicker patient, emphasizing that his need is more urgent. Both physicians, grounding their inferences in clinical facts, may profess their genuine commitment to applying only medical criteria, but this hardly solves their problem.

Indeed, far from solving such problems, a clinical emphasis may disguise their true nature – even from the participants themselves – and make them that much more intractable. Thus, the conflict over whether the healthier or the sicker patient should be treated is fundamentally not a clinical conflict at all, but rather a value conflict between efficiency and need; talk of clinical judgment is irrelevant, if not actually a hindrance.

What this suggests is that medical criteria incorporated into the judgment process often become entangled with clearly nonmedical considerations. One major pioneering nephrologist, for instance, declared that in selecting patients for dialysis, preference would be given not only to those with "the qualities of reliability, common sense, and stoicism" – all of which arguably would increase the likelihood of successful treatment – but also to patients with young children (Ogg, 1970, p. 412; see also London *Times,* 1985). (American physicians appear equally prone to resort to nonmedical considerations. Thus, a recent survey of 453 medical directors of dialysis and transplantation facilities revealed that from 69 to 56 percent would consider whether other persons are dependent on the prospective recipient, whether his treatment would consume a disproportionate share of resources, and how much society would benefit from his being treated [Kilner, 1988, p. 145].) These considerations bear on the worthiness of the patient to receive treatment, and are not medical in character at all. Although physicians may for good and obvious reasons claim authority to devise and apply medical criteria, however, their nonmedical judgments would not appear to deserve special weight. Indeed, given what one philosopher of medicine who was interviewed characterized as the average physician's "rather shallow" acquaintance with systematic work in medical ethics, his implicit assumption of competence in this area must strike some observers as deeply disturbing.

A fourth problem with exclusive reliance on clinical judgment is that even if the first three problems were to vanish, the number of patients deemed medically suitable for treatment would substantially exceed the number the system could accommodate (but cf. Abram and Wadlington, 1968; Medical Services Study Group, 1981). In such a situation, what should the physician do? The platitudinous reply (drawn here from a non-ESRD context) is that the "individual physician in his effort to save the individual patient, cannot, and cannot be expected to, consider the allocation of resources" (Fried, 1975a; Hiatt, 1975, pp. 235–41; Bendixen, 1977, p. 383; Caplan, 1984, p. 129). "The selection process ought to be directed toward choosing the most appropriate modality of therapy for an individual rather than determining whether or not to treat him" (Hampers et al., 1973, p. 65).

But if this represents the ideal, the real world extorts precisely the opposite answer: "What constitutes 'good' medical practice and 'right' clinical decision will be determined by cost effective analysis as well as by scientific correctness and by humanitarian content" (Wing, 1979, p. 152). With this in mind, two doctors deplored "the extent to which physicians' professional expertise and position of trust is being used to translate economic and political decisions into the selection of patients, without those presenting with renal disease, their relatives or the public necessarily being aware of the process" (Parsons and Lock, 1980, p. 175). The *Lancet* (1981) echoed this conclusion, editorializing, "Economic necessity dictates clinical decisions but is not always seen to do so" (p. 595).

Indeed, there is some evidence that the rhetoric of physicians on clinical judgment has misled even some physicians themselves. Thus, at a time when the UK patient intake rate barely exceeded half its modest target, five of nine renal unit directors who were interviewed reported that they rejected no patients who could be considered medically suitable for treatment and three that they turned away only "some" good cases (Laing, 1980, p. 5).[5]

---

[5] Others have attributed this kind of denial to "defensive postures in the guise of scientific analysis" (Delano et al., 1982, p. 193).

SHOULD MEDICAL CRITERIA ALONE DETERMINE
PATIENT SELECTION?

Even if, for the sake of argument, we assume that wholly objective medical criteria simply await the physician's automatic application, a larger question persists: Ought medical criteria to be the only legitimate criteria utilized in patient selection? In the United Kingdom, the prevailing answer is clearly "yes." As a Cabinet health care spokesman commented, "The assessment of whether individual renal patients would benefit from treatment is a matter for the clinical judgment of the doctors involved" (Whitney, in *Parlimentary Debates,* 1985b; see also Wing, 1979, p. 163). Though the nature and application of these medical criteria may be disputed, almost no one dissents from the proposition that medical criteria are the best (if not the only) guide to patient selection. The sole criticism emanating from the medical community would seem to be that implementation of the ideal has been, like all human endeavors, imperfect.

It is not difficult to speculate as to why such a view should have become so universal. After all, physicians make the actual choices, and their authority and expertise extend only to medical matters. Moreover, to speak exclusively of medical criteria is to suggest to the lay public an objective, rather mechanical reasoning procedure, the very impersonality of which may seem a reassuring protection against favoritism and abuse. Of course, this view may be quite naive and misleading, but it is no less widespread for that.

Yet the judgment that only medical criteria should be applied is also a normative judgment. It is true, of course, that treating only patients with the best prognoses is the most effective use of scarce resources; more patients per unit of resources can be treated in this way than by any alternative approach. Some observers might retort, however, that efficiency is not the highest value. Ought dialyzing ten Charles Mansons be preferred to dialyzing five Mozarts (or five of my saintly uncles) merely because the Mansons have better prognoses? Upon such questions the consensus supporting exclusive reliance on medical criteria must founder. Even physicians appear, on occasion, to share this kind of reservation. When one consultant wrote that "one would have to rank on the positive side – ability to help the community by working" (Challah et al., 1984, p. 1122), he was clearly uttering an ethical and not a clinical judgment.

If medical criteria should not function as the sole selection test, however, it may well be reasonable to insist that patient candidates at least meet certain minimum medical standards. In this way, medical criteria could be used to establish a candidate pool and avoid a grossly irresponsible waste of resources on patients with very poor prognoses (Childress, 1981, p. 91).

The root problem, however, is that to the extent that microallocative decisions reflect macroallocations, they are true tragic choices (Calabresi and Bobbitt, 1978). Society spares only some ESRD patients from suffering and death, finds it awkward to face its abandonment of many helpless and blameless citizens, and prefers that physicians make the selections according to their own impenetrable divinations – and do so privately. Medical criteria, if they were widely discussed, doubtlessly would be revealed as inadequate, but it is the nature of tragic choices that no criteria can achieve nearly universal acceptance. However much a detached analyst may deplore it, therefore, there may be an irresistible tendency to transmute certain kinds of normative decisions about resources into technical decisions about treatment. "Human kind," Eliot (1958) wrote, "cannot bear very much reality" (p. 118).

SECONDARY CONSEQUENCES OF MICROALLOCATIVE PRESSURES

Microallocative pressures, it is important to realize, influence not only such fundamental questions as whether to treat and what therapy to utilize, but also a large number of more mundane matters. Some of these appear to have only moderate medical significance. For example, the United Kingdom pioneered the reuse of disposable dialyzers, "asking patients to accept a marginally second-class style of therapy so that the total number treated may be increased" ([Wing, 1985a, pp. 263–4] though one wonders how many patients were truly asked or even informed about the practice). In any case, the practice remains more widespread and the actual reuse of individual dialyzers more frequent than in almost any other nation. It

Table 17. *Hepatitis B cases per thousand patients on hospital dialysis, 1986*

Country	Patients	Staff
UK	2.8	0
FRG	3.3	0.3
France	8.0	0.3
Italy	7.9	1.6
Spain	7.8	1.1

Source: European Dialysis and Transplant Association.

is generally conceded that reuse is associated with somewhat higher morbidity, but inasmuch as mortality is unaffected, the practice has been taken up by many other countries, including the United States (Bok and Levin, 1982; National Center for Health Services Research and Health Care Technology, 1986; Wineman, 1986; but cf. Heinz, 1986). Economic pressures have made the savings appear more important than the morbidity costs (Wauters et al., 1978, p. 373; Knapp, 1982, p. 848; but cf. Caplan, 1984).

It must also be said that the pervasive stress on saving money has not prevented UK renal units from compiling an unsurpassed record regarding the incidence of viral hepatitis,[6] though the exceptionally low incidence of the disease in the United Kingdom unquestionably has contributed to this achievement (Table 17). The average for all European Dialysis and Transplant Association member nations is 18.1 patient and 3.2 staff cases per thousand patients in dialysis.

Other consequences of microallocative pressures, however, have not been quite so benign. "Until recently," one Liverpool nephrologist reported, "we had no hospital facilities for sustaining patients awaiting a transplant, and we had to take patients on the waiting list for transplantation without prior dialysis. This was not

[6] A cynic would add that part of the enthusiasm for the effort against hepatitis may have stemmed from its presenting a risk to staff, as well as to patients. Indeed, in the six years preceding the issuance of a major advisory group report on hepatitis and ESRD, no less than 120 staff members developed hepatitis, of whom 6 died (DHSS, 1972, p. 12).

very successful. The transplant operation carried a 25 percent mortality, and the waiting list itself carried a 60 percent mortality because patients used to die before kidneys became available" (Bone, in Anderson et al., 1978, p. 19).[7] Similarly, a London nephrologist contended that what "probably happened in the past is that because of a shortage of dialysis places, people were not put back on dialysis after graft failure and therefore died." Moreover, he charged, "the transplanters and their physician colleagues pushed too hard on treatment to save grafts and patients died of all the horrible complications with which we are only too familiar, whereas adequate dialysis provision would allow these patients to be treated, and would allow them to return to dialysis" (Cameron, in Anderson et al., 1978, p. 67). And a nephrologist who was interviewed volunteered that he and his colleagues prescribed lower dosages of some drugs in order to save money.

THE IMPACT ON OLDER PATIENTS

The prime victims of these microallocative pressures, of course, have been the ESRD patients, chiefly patients aged sixty-five and over. Intake rates in the United Kingdom decline rather drastically past this point, particularly when contrasted with those of comparable Western European nations.

Part of the problem derives simply from the fact that although ESRD occasionally afflicts even very young children, it is principally a condition of old age. Not only is there a greater incidence of primary renal disease (like glomerulonephritis) among the elderly; more important, ESRD frequently presents as a secondary disease to such age-related diseases as congestive heart failure, hypertension, atherosclerosis, and diabetes mellitus. Furthermore, whereas the typical young adult with impaired renal function can probably point to only one cause of the problem, the older patient is usually faced with multiple causes (e.g., cumulative pathophysiological effects of

---

7 This practice seems to have become rare. A 1983 survey of twenty-six renal units, for example, disclosed that less than 3.2% of the patients on waiting lists for transplants were not receiving dialysis (Sells et al., 1985, p. 195).

age-induced renal dysfunction, prerenal disturbances, primary renal diseases, postrenal obstructive uropathy, drug-induced uropathy resulting from poorly managed multiple drug therapies [Samiy, 1983, p. 469]). About 85 percent of the deaths ascribed to ESRD in the United Kingdom occur in patients over the age of sixty-four, and another 10 percent in patients from age fifty-five to sixty-four.

A second reason is that older patients tend to be more expensive to treat than younger patients. Over the age of seventy, they are not considered suitable for transplantation, even in Scandinavia (Brynger et al., 1986, p. 13), for graft and survival rates tend to be lower and the incidence of cardiovascular complications higher. Nor are older patients always good candidates for home dialysis either, because of a decreased ability to cope or the likely presence of extrarenal diseases or a multiply caused ESRD. A disproportionate number, therefore, can be treated only by hospital dialysis, the most costly of the alternative therapies.

A third reason is that the prognosis for older patients tends to be somewhat poorer than that for younger patients, though good results are generally obtained. A large American study of five-year patient survivals, for example, concluded that the relative risk of dialysis patients aged sixty through sixty-nine was 167 percent of the risk of the reference group, that of patients seventy through seventy-nine was 244 percent, and that of patients aged eighty and above was 310 percent (Held et al., 1987, p. 646).

The prevalence of older patients among the ESRD population has meant that from the beginning age has played a prominent role in guiding physicians' decisions as to whether to treat. At first, resources were so scarce that not a ripple was created when a prominent nephrologist reported in the *British Medical Journal* that "most [renal] units" rejected patients over the age of fifty (Ogg, 1970, p. 412). Indeed, it seemed to have been taken for granted within the medical community that some rather low age limit was indispensable to the patient selection process (Shaldon, 1968a, p. 522), though whether it should be forty-five, fifty, or fifty-five was subject to minor dispute. Toward the end of the 1970s, however, greater funding together with certain medical developments permitted a gradual increase in age limits, so that by 1982 a fairly typical set of regions could announce that the "elderly up to seventy years of age are all now considered suitable for therapy for renal failure" (Joint Renal Services Planning Group, 1982, p. 21). That today most patients aged sixty-five and over continue to be denied treatment, therefore, is far more likely to reflect decisions taken by general practitioners or general medicine consultants than by nephrologists. As one nephrologist put it, "Relatives of these patients are usually told by their family doctors that he or she is medically unsuitable for the treatment, but this is just a white lie" (Cameron, in Massam, 1982). In any case, there is no doubt that, in the words of another nephrologist, "age is one of the most important factors taken into consideration, if not the most important factor."

None of these factual circumstances, however, satisfactorily explains why older patients have fared so poorly in the United Kingdom. It is true that the UK population has a slightly larger proportion of elderly than many others; in 1983, 21.34 percent of the population was aged sixty or over, as compared with 19.71 percent in the FRG, 20.04 percent in France, and 18.90 percent in Italy (*Eurostat Demographic Statistics,* 1984). But these differences are small. And, after all, it is not only in the United Kingdom that ESRD afflicts mainly older patients or that older patients are more costly to treat or that older patients present somewhat poorer prognoses. These generalizations also apply to the FRG, France, Italy, the United States, and more than a dozen other nations, which nonetheless find it possible to treat the overwhelming majority of their older ESRD patients. When Canadian and American physicians were asked, for example, how they would respond to a series of hypothetical cases, only 1 percent chose to withhold treatment from patients over the age of sixty (Deber et al., 1985, p. 101). No, it is impossible to deduce a policy – an "ought" – from a string of facts – an "is" – for this quite neglects the element of official choice. The facts no more preclude a liberal treatment policy in the United Kingdom than they guarantee one in the United States; it is all a matter of what influential decision makers – in the DHSS, the RHAs, the renal units, and so on – decide ought to be done.

IS AGE A MEDICAL CRITERION?

Much of this discretionary element is obscured in the United Kingdom by the widely shared beliefs that the decision as to whom to treat is wholly a medical decision and that age constitutes a legitimate medical criterion. Certainly, there is no doubt that advancing age has important implications for the kidneys. Even among healthy persons, the mass of the kidney shrinks by a third to a quarter by age seventy, by which time the number of functioning nephron units has subsequently declined, resulting in a steady falling off in the glomerular filtration rate (Rowe et al., 1976, p. 155). As a consequence, as two geriatricians observed, "the aged kidney is much less able to respond to changes in hydration, solute load, and cardiac output" (Frocht and Fillet, 1984, p. 30).

As far as ESRD is concerned, the condition is somewhat more difficult to identify in older patients, in whom standard serum creatinine tests tend to understate the extent of renal failure and extrarenal diseases may complicate diagnosis. Management may also pose special problems and require extra care, mainly because of the likelihood of coexisting diseases. As for dialysis itself, though success rates plainly decline with age, they remain quite good even among the elderly. Indeed, even though older patients tend to be more difficult to manage medically than younger patients, they tend to be easier to manage psychologically; they adhere to the required diet, practice self-limitation more readily, and exhibit less frustration due to their sedentary habits and lower expectations (Rathus and Bernheim, 1978; Westlie et al., 1984).

Is age, then, a legitimate medical criterion? The answer, it appears, must be: It depends. It depends, that is, on whether age is used in a "soft" fashion (i.e., to alert physicians to a congeries of problems) or in a "hard" fashion (i.e., as a more or less rigid boundary that settles questions of treatment itself). If the former, age would seem invaluable to sound decision making; if the latter, age would appear to substitute for decision making.[8]

---

[8] That age might be used in a "hard" and "soft" fashion – and only in the latter way as a medical criterion – has been ignored not only by numerous physicians, but

One problem is that age cohorts – particularly those consisting of patients under the age of seventy – are far too heterogeneous to permit extrapolations to be made about individuals with the confidence that life-or-death choices demand. Patients of age sixty-five, for example, may *in general* have poorer prognoses than patients of age fifty, but *some* patients of age sixty-five will have better prognoses than *some* patients of age fifty. Sound clinical judgment, therefore, would seem to require not the mechanical rejection of patients over sixty-five, but rather the assessment of patients on an individual basis. Anything else would be tantamount to renouncing the role of the physician in favor of that of a clerk, assigning patients to "accept" or "reject" files after reading their birthdays.

A second problem is that the decision to treat is, as one nephrologist termed it, "open-ended." That is, it entails an indefinite obligation (or what one neurosurgeon called a "cycle of commitment" [Jennett, 1985]); for dialysis is in no sense a curative therapy and even transplants are problematical. Thus, the physician must not simply consider whether treating the patient in his current condition is indicated, but also predict whether continuing to treat him a few years later will be indicated, inherently a very speculative exercise. In this regard, one nephrologist related a moving story of a middle-aged diabetic ESRD patient, who had worked as a painter at a large department store at the time his treatment commenced but after a year had deteriorated to the point where a leg had to be amputated. Immobile, unemployed, and passive, he had become a far different man from the one he had been a short time earlier. In his present condition, he might well have been rejected for treatment. But the decision to withdraw treatment, almost universally viewed as far harsher than the decision to deny treatment initially, is taken

also by some otherwise highly sophisticated analysts. Calabresi, for example, though faulting the UK patient selection system for an unsubstantiated class bias, takes at face value assurances that only medical criteria are applied. Indeed, maintaining that clinical judgment is "mechanistic," he claims that the aged "seem to have been excluded from the pool of possible recipients because they are less good medical risks," as if clinical judgment did not contain large elements of the subjective and the discretionary and as if all patients over the age of fifty-five were essentially alike (Calabresi and Bobbitt, 1978, pp. 184–5).

only with the greatest reluctance, and so the patient was continued on dialysis. With older patients, for whom the prospect of deterioration looms larger, physicians naturally must worry about the future as much as the present.

In the United Kingdom, this preoccupation with future developments is apt to be especially intense, for as one London nephrologist noted, "the UK prides itself on knowing when to stop."[9] In practical terms, this appears to translate into an unwillingness to start older patients on dialysis for fear of having later to confront the problem of deciding whether to take them off.

As a matter of actual practice, then, how is the age factor used? The observer, unfortunately, must rely principally upon anecdote, impression, and rather raw treatment pattern data. Despite these serious limitations, though, the answer would seem pretty clear: The "hard" use of age as a rigid line demarcating those to be treated from those to be denied treatment predominates. This appears to be the case far more among general practitioners and general medicine consultants than among nephrologists, but so crucial is the matter of referral that this consideration in no way mitigates the force of the practice.

That age so commonly continues to masquerade as a medical criterion in patient selection suggests that it is not without some utility, at least in the eyes of those who make use of it. The most obvious advantage of relying on age (or on any firm rule of thumb) is that it obviates the need to agonize over specific decisions. Instead of having to confront their own imperfect knowledge and impartiality on a patient-by-patient basis, physicians simply categorize patients on the basis of a general rule. In place of uncertainty and subjectivity are certainty and objectivity, and the expenditure of time and effort is minimized as well. Moreover, the blame for selection error and

---

[9] Although UK physicians seem to pride themselves on their tough-mindedness, this quality may also be found abroad. A Minneapolis study, for example, revealed that long-term dialysis was halted in 9% of all cases and in 17% of patients over the age of sixty (Neu and Kjellstrand, 1986), and a smaller Canadian study found that 28% of all long-term dialysis deaths resulted from discontinuance (Rodin et al., 1981). In half of the Minneapolis cases and a third of the Canadian cases, the patients made the decisions.

the pain of rejecting some patients for treatment can be laid on the general rule, not the physician. However flawed a medical criterion age may be, in short, it is plainly of immense value to decision makers seeking to avoid stress, guilt, and discomfort and to save time and effort by trading their discretion for the automatic implementation of a principle.

But age is not used simply as a medical proxy variable, a convenient shorthand term for a set of afflictions that are assumed to appear at certain points in the life cycle. Age may also be used as a normative proxy variable. Age cutoff points for treatment, that is, may reflect a judgment not that the patient cannot be successfully treated, but that the patient is really not worthy of treatment. Other things being equal, the older the patient is past his midfifties, the more expensive he is likely to be to treat and the briefer the success of that treatment is likely to be. As a matter of elemental justice, therefore, some physicians may conclude that a proper concern for the greatest good for the greatest number would dictate a preference for younger ESRD patients over older ones (e.g., Kjellstrand, in *Dialysis and Transplantation,* 1986, p. 348). "Inevitably, " as one distinguished and compassionate nephrologist sadly acknowledged, "a patient who would consume more than his 'fair share' of resources may be denied treatment" (Wing, 1979, p. 162). Indeed, from a societal perspective – and although nephrologists may tend to compare renal patients with one another, general practitioners and general medicine consultants may tend to think in terms of far broader patient populations – some physicians may conclude that dialyzing older patients ranks rather low as a health care priority.

In this, the UK experience with ESRD is hardly unusual. In the United States, for example, where ageism has been a fashionable and prominent concern for many years, recent studies indicate that older patients are more likely than younger patients to receive inadequate treatment for breast cancer (Greenfield et al., 1987) and may be denied care on the basis of perceived but nonexistent dementia (Wetle and Levkoff, 1984). Similarly, widely utilized cost–benefit and cost–effectiveness analyses are said to be biased against the elderly, whose economic prospects tend to be weaker than those of younger claimants (Avorn, 1984). In the United Kingdom, where sensitivity to ageism appears to be less developed, the bias may well be greater.

Are there, then, any ethical problems with the United Kingdom's age-based renal policy? Oddly, it is an American philosopher, Norman Daniels, who has confronted this question most extensively, and his answer is yes. Daniels argues that health systems should transfer wealth from younger age groups to older ones, for since each cohort ages, this transfer amounts to one generation's saving for its own future needs. This converts "an *interpersonal* distribution problem, with all its attendant worries about age-bias, into an *intrapersonal* problem of rational or prudential savings." From this perspective, "the age criterion operates within a life and not between lives" and "each moment of life is equally valuable" (Daniels, 1985, pp. 96, 98, 104–5).[10]

Of course, as Daniels concedes, one difficulty with this is the inherent uncertainty with which we must view the future. Persons who "saved" for the future a half-century ago could hardly have known that dialysis would emerge as a treatment for ESRD in time for their old age, nor can we predict what treatments will emerge in the decades to come. Nor can we know what diseases we will need treated or even whether we will be alive. Nor, platitudes about "equally valuable" moments of life to the contrary notwithstanding, can we know if we will even wish to stay alive.

Two facts give this uncertainty additional power. The first is that if history is any guide, the elderly receive in benefits vastly more than they pay into the system. That is, if the system were a true insurance system, as Daniels maintains, today's aged would receive a far smaller array of benefits than they do. In other words, what exists is exactly the generational transfer system that Daniels would deny. (The NHS does not even pretend to be an insurance system as America's Social Security does, but Daniels [1985, p. 93] considers it one anyway.)

---

[10] Although it is not altogether clear, Daniels seems to disapprove of the British practice of age rationing, though he concedes that it is "plausible" to reserve certain life-extending technologies for one's younger years in order to maximize the chance of having a normal life span (Daniels, 1985, p. 93).

The second fact is that whether viewed as intertemporal or intergenerational, the system is not voluntary but coercive. Thus, although Daniels speaks repeatedly of persons *choosing* to save, in truth the choice is not theirs at all, except in the indirect sense that the public chose representatives who voted for the system and continue to support it. Government makes the effective choice for individuals by way of compulsory schemes, which may be funded out of general revenues (as in the United Kingdom) or an identifiable pool (as in America); if individuals were truly free to choose, the laws would be permissive and not coercive.

In this regard, what Daniels does not consider is the value of the rather conventional American conservative idea that individuals should be encouraged to look out for themselves – by purchasing insurance or annuities, for example – and that only if they are too poor to do this should their fellow taxpayers be compelled to help them. According to this view, it is moral and financial folly to discourage people from providing for their own old age, to reward them for their lack of foresight, or to aid those who do not require it. In addition, it reinforces the stereotype of the elderly as weak and dependent and of old age as a period of unrelieved suffering (see Halper, 1980). Viewed from this perspective, the great defect of the British approach is less the refusal to treat the elderly than the failure to inform society of that fact, so that people could avail themselves of the opportunity to look out for themselves.

THE IMPACT ON MEDICAL PERSONNEL

If the prime victims of these microallocative pressures are ESRD patients, hyperscarcity takes a heavy toll from nephrologists and other medical personnel as well; for the process of selection, according to some observers, forces physicians to act as judges, sometimes in the face of fears about their own imperfect knowledge and objectivity. Rejecting patients desiring treatment may be particularly difficult because it may seem contrary to physicians' medical training and to the ethic of the welfare state into which they have been socialized. That the nephrologist ordinarily makes the decision alone (though typically after consultation with other members of the renal unit) also generates a certain stressful ambivalence; an unconscious wish for omnipotence may produce some enjoyment from the exercise of power, while the decision to say no may generate guilt that is often accompanied by an emotional withdrawal from the patients under care (Kaplan De-Nour and Czaczkes, 1968; Shaldon, 1968b). Such feelings may reflect medical training that deliberately "bypasses existing moralizing" in favor of "grappling with a grotesque pragmatic reality that cannot be ignored" (Konner, 1987); the experiential barriers are such that outsiders simply cannot, merely by observation and imagination, place themselves in doctors' shoes. Such feelings are probably not uncommon among all kinds of physicians responsible for the long-term care of patients with potentially fatal diseases.

However, an observer who for many years has been committed to viewing patient selection from the patient's viewpoint claimed that an ominous development was more typical. At the beginning, she said, young physicians are "appalled" at letting treatable patients die; after a while, "they learn to stomach it"; and within a couple of years, it "becomes a part of their lives," an accepted element of the routine. In this sense, she argued, most participating physicians can be compared to the "good Germans" who gradually accommodated themselves to the "final solution" and whose active cooperation in the annihilation of much of European Jewry was essential to the success of the enterprise. Far from being burdened with guilt, the physician, in order to cope with the necessity of rejecting treatable patients, instead hardens his heart, she maintains. Meanwhile, easing the doctor's rejection decision somewhat is the "clinical myth" that renal failure "is a pleasant way to die" (Knapp, 1982, p. 847; Challah et al., 1984, p. 1122; but cf. Roher, 1959).

Yet even this view must find a place for the terrible anguish repeatedly and publicly expressed by many of the United Kingdom's leading nephrologists (see, e.g., Bewick, in London *Times,* 1984). Unwilling simply to exit and make a bad situation worse, a number have given voice to their frustration over macroallocations in a way that outsiders can only find moving and heroic (cf. Hirschman, 1970).

"In the final showdown," however, one physician administrator maintained, "nephrologists are not willing to fight for resources." Mrs. Ward, he pointed out, has been unable to find a nephrologist who will help her bring a lawsuit to establish a right to treatment and instead is regarded with considerable unease as "a dangerous woman." Whether this reluctance to fight is merely another instance of British "up-puttingness" or instead reflects peer pressure to "act responsibly" or simply fear of seeming "too flashy," he found hard to say. But gestures such as one nephrologist's well-publicized assertions of a refusal to sign death certificates for untreated ESRD patients he dismissed as merely "peeing in the ocean."

THE DECISION ETHIC

The picture that emerges is very different from the sentimental portrait of the physician as the patient's agent, singlemindedly pursuing the patient's interests as he would have his own interests pursued. For in addition, the physician must play two other distinct roles: One involves his obligations to larger social ends (equity, efficiency, etc.) and the other to his personal goals (professional reputation, public prestige, etc.).

The physician's concern with larger social ends is entirely natural, for he functions not in atomized isolation but within a huge structure that provides him with credentials, patients, income, and much else that helps to define him as a doctor and as a person. But the same structure that is so vital in shaping, rewarding, and protecting him exerts innumerable reciprocal pressures to conform to the structure's values. As an American legal scholar observed in another context, "The goal of individual freedom is at the same time dependent on and incompatible with the communal coercive action that is necessary to achieve it" (Kennedy, 1979, p. 211).

Thus, unlike the idealized physician, whose theoretical autonomy is constrained only by sound medical considerations and legal and contractual obligations, the real-life physician is seriously limited by practical considerations. He routinely selects non-hospital-based therapies not because they are necessarily superior – for some patients they may be superior, for others they may be suboptimal, and for still others they may not be suitable – but because their lower cost renders them the only ones available. As a consequence, some patients will receive optimal treatment, some suboptimal, and some none at all. Though ESRD patients may reveal these pressures in their starkest form, they are certainly not unique to this context. Indeed, one UK physician has proclaimed the "end of clinical freedom," maintaining that it died "accidentally," crushed between rising costs of new forms of investigation and treatment and the financial limits inevitable in an economy that cannot expand indefinitely (Hampton, 1983, p. 1238; but cf. Rendall, 1985).

In resigning himself to this, the clinician is not submitting to cynicism. On the contrary, he is likely to be acting in what he himself perceives as a highly ethical manner. But it is not the popular ethic of an absolute right to treatment, but instead a more hardheaded utilitarian ethic of choosing to treat many low-cost patients rather than few high-cost ones.

Consider what this means in concrete terms. One physician, who himself underwent a kidney transplant, discussed the issue candidly some years ago:

> I have made a point of asking a number of nephrologists a telling question, "Would you, if you were established on dialysis, choose to have a renal transplant?" The invariable answer is "I would stay on dialysis." These same doctors recommend renal transplantation to their patients. I can perfectly understand their attitude: by offering transplantation they are able to do more good to more patients with the available resources. (Henry, 1978, p. 217)

With similar frankness, a leading nephrologist wrote:

> I must create propaganda in my unit which puts pressure on patients not to get stuck on the limited hospital dialysis facilities but to submit themselves and their families to the incessant demands of home dialysis or to volunteer for transplantation. (Wing, 1981, p. 162; but cf. Clunie et al., 1970, p. 29; Crosby and Jones, 1970, p. 574; Luke, 1983, p. 1594; Wilson, 1983, p. 332)

To an observer, this tactic may seem entirely understandable, even laudable. But it can hardly be described as the mere mechanical exercise of clinical judgment.

As to the physician's concern with his own personal goals, the issue is complicated by the long-standing convention that it is somehow dishonorable for doctors to consider their own interests. Indeed, physicians frequently speak of an obligation to pursue "entirely disinterestedly" the goals of other people. With respect to ESRD patients, this attitude translates into a pride in working brutally long hours, taking on time-consuming and emotionally draining tasks (like arranging kidney donations) without a thought to compensation, and in general, as one eminent nephrologist expressed it, "doing more than one's duty." The system, indeed, presumes such civic-spiritedness, which must be counted as one of the main themes of the British medical culture (see Hirschman, 1985).

Coexisting with what one physician termed "this martyr complex" is often a profound sense of loyalty to the system, flaws and all. If one works for the NHS, the physicians seemed to say, one must abide by its rules, including its financial constraints. "Doctors have to be fairly responsible about resources," as one nephrologist put it. "You could sink the lifeboat by adding too many people." Whereas Americans might protest that additional lifeboats are required, British physicians seem more prone to accept the situation as given and to try to make the best of it.

THE PHYSICIAN AS POLITICAL ACTOR

By this point it has become clear that the physician is not merely a medical actor, though as a medical doctor that is his title and that is his training. In addition, the physician is a political actor – which is to say he not only must make "clinical judgments" and practice "good medicine," but also must authoritatively allocate resources (Easton, 1953, p. 130). Faced with a situation of rather oppressive scarcity, he must decide who gets what, when, and how – classic political questions (Lasswell, 1936). And though relatively few people will be affected by his decisions, the impact on these few will be difficult to exaggerate, for nothing less than life or death is involved.

As agents of the state, that is, physicians in their clinical roles exercise discretion in the allocation of scarce resources and thereby perform the central distributive political task. "Political" in this context, therefore, is not at all confined to the well-known pressure-group activities of such organizations as the BMA or to partisan or other electoral behavior. The point is not that doctors can also act politically, but that doctoring itself can be a political act. As one Newcastle nephrologist put it, "The people who make the decisions here are only too aware that every time a problem patient goes on dialysis it means that five or ten geriatric sick, and even those simply in need of loving care, are left to gay abandon" (Wardle, 1983). Or as another physician noted, "One man's provision is another man's deprivation" (Hampton, 1983, p. 1237).

Of course, this political role is nowhere explicitly acknowledged. This is not a trivial matter, for it helps to ensure that the vast majority of patients and their families – and even a few physicians themselves – will be blind to the true nature of the situation. Thus blind, they will mistake political judgments for medical ones and be far more likely to acquiesce. The fiction that the selection process is purely medical, in other words, clearly functions as a powerful legitimator of rejection. It is important for its acceptance by patients and their families, that is, that the selection process not only be just but appear to be just, and this requires that it appear intelligible and patently reasonable to ordinary people (Rescher, 1969, pp. 1976–86; cf. Powell, 1976, p. 38). The ritualistic pronouncement of "clinical judgment" evidently fulfills that need, though sometimes at the cost of honesty and candor.

The unacknowledged political character of the physician's role also forces upon him an agonizing conflict of interest. In his manifest fuction as healer, he sees his patient's welfare as his primary obligation; in his latent function as resource allocator, he is primarily beholder to the DHSS (cf. Merton, 1949, pp. 21–81). Though it implicitly recognizes the problem, DHSS policy is more platitude than solution:

Hospital consultants have clinical autonomy and are fully responsible for the treatment they prescribe for their patients.

They are required to act within the broad limits of acceptable medical practice and within policy for the use of resources, but they are not held accountable to DHSS authorities for their clinical judgments. (Committee of Inquiry into Normansfield Hospital, 1978, pp. 424–5)

But what if the physician's clinical judgment – for which he cannot be "held accountable" – conflicts with "policy for the use of resources" – within which he is "required to act"? What, in other words, if his manifest and latent functions are incompatible? In cases of severe scarcity (as in ESRD), both functions can be made to appear to be honored only through serious misrepresentation. Of course, it is much easier to deceive patients than bureaucrats. As one nephrologist told the *Times,* "Some of us have to tell lies to older patients, partly to make the patients more comfortable and partly to make ourselves more comfortable. We have to say to them that their hearts are too dodgy to stand the strain of dialysis" (Wing, in Ferriman, 1980). To the other burdens of the physician, then, must sometimes be added the demeaning "necessity" of lying (Calabresi and Bobbitt, 1978, pp. 24–6; cf. Ward, 1985).[11]

Not only the individual patient and his physician, however, suffer from this conflict of interests. A consensus has long existed that there is a larger societal interest in protecting the integrity of the doctor–patient relationship, an interest enshrined, for example, in the physician's freedom from coercion to testify about his patient's medical affairs in a court of law. That relationship depends on trust, and trust, in turn, depends on the physician's not being seen as serving any master before the patient, an appearance evidently maintained only through occasional resort to subterfuge and manipulation.[12] The physician, in other words, is widely viewed as the

---

[11] A MORI poll disclosed that among thirteen groups of professionals, doctors trailed only the clergy – and here by a very slight margin – in their capacity to command public trust (London *Times,* 1984).

[12] Irrespective of physician's good intentions, falsehoods intended to deceive patients into believing that they are untreatable breach doctors' duty to care for their patients and may raise the possibility of civil or even criminal proceedings (Douglas, 1985).

patient's agent. That is, the pattern is seen as delegating authority to the physician, who, by dint of his experience and expertise, is obliged to act in the patient's interest.

The refusal to acknowledge the physician's political role openly has also meant that the decision-making process has escaped serious outside scrutiny, for allocative decisions have been treated as if they were conventional medical decisions. Thus, the kinds of questions regarding dialysis and transplantation that were raised in the United States in the 1960s have simply never been explicitly addressed by responsible UK political and bureaucratic leaders, but instead merely left to physicians.

Consider some of the questions that have been ignored: Who selects the selectors? Shall they operate singly, in ad hoc groups, or in a more institutionalized structure? What should their qualifications be? (Medical competence, of course, but what of societal representativeness or philosophical expertise?) Should the social worth of competing patients be weighed and, if so, how? (Past performance? future potential? personal decency? responsibility for dependents?) Is the selection process so strewn with imponderables that the only sensible course is to throw up one's hands and call for a lottery, which at least would respect the value of equality (Gorovitz, 1966, p. 7; Siemsen, 1978, p. 88; Childress, 1979, p. 138)?[13] So completely have UK physicians monopolized the microallocative decision-making process that virtually everyone concerned has taken the monopoly for granted, accepted it as a "given," and never seriously considered the merits of alternative systems.

---

[13] The original committee in Seattle rejected such an approach as an irresponsible abdication of its duty to choose, and an American commentator assailed randomization as a "refusal to be rational" and "a deliberate dehumanization, reducing us to the level of things and blind chance" (Fletcher, n.d.); clearly, nearly all UK physicians today would agree. One London nephrologist, however, stood the "lottery" argument on its head: Since it cannot be demonstrated that one life is more valuable than another, he reasoned, no one could term his choices of whom to treat ethically mistaken. And a survey of 453 medical directors of dialysis and transplantation facilities in the United States revealed that were rationing to become necessary, 31% favored considering random selection (Kilner, 1988, p. 145).

SOME IMPLICATIONS OF THE PHYSICIAN'S
POLITICAL ROLE

This is not to argue that the United Kingdom adopt an earlier American practice in which hospitals often relied on selection committees composed of lay people and physicians, who were given no guidelines and developed no fixed criteria themselves (Murray et al., 1962, p. 315; Fox and Swazey, 1974).[14] The result, it is generally conceded, was not really satisfactory (see, e.g., Sanders and Duke-minier, 1968, pp. 377–8), despite the unquestionably good intentions of those who took part. In London, where one nephrologist reported that "many of us [were] horrified" by the committees (Wing, 1985a, p. 55), reactions to these efforts appear to have been especially hostile.

Nor is it to argue for the institutionalized presence of other interests. Their representatives, lacking the authority bases of physicians, would likely be dominated by them and rendered ineffective. And if not ineffective, they might be naive or wrongheaded and greatly complicate an already immensely complex situation. Almost certainly, in any case, these interests would tend to press for treatment, for who else but representatives of patient, nurse, social worker, or other caring groups would feel intensely enough about the matter to become involved and seek a position of influence?[15]

Even the hospital ethics committees that have become ubiquitous in the United States may not be the answer. Partly, this is because

[14] A contemporary popular account that generated a storm of controversy was that of Alexander (1962).

[15] In any case, as a former chief medical officer rather delicately put it, "suggestions for joint medical–nonmedical hemodialysis selection procedures in this country . . . have not been welcomed" by the medical community (Godber, 1975, p. 8). A pioneering nephrologist put the matter more bluntly: "Who is to implement the selection? In my opinion it must ultimately be the responsibility of the consultants in charge of the renal units. . . . I can see no reason for delegating this responsibility to lay persons. Surely the latter would be better employed if they could be persuaded to devote their time and energy to raise more and more money for us to spend on our patients" (Shackman, 1967, p. 624). Although today such attitudes are less frequently expressed so nakedly, they are very far from extinct.

the committees have other missions that may conflict with their ethical obligation, because they lack the procedural safeguards of fairness that are taken for granted in the courts, and because group dynamics within committees may have an unwarranted effect on the results (Lo, 1987). Principally, though, the problem with the ethics committee is that unless ethical criteria are laid down beforehand, the committee will proceed in an improvisational, inconsistent fashion that may well be no more satisfactory than the informal practices it is designed to supersede. Labeling a body an "ethics committee" may be a bureaucratically effective means of disposing of the problem, but unless the committee's standards and procedures are clearly spelled out and widely accepted, it is really not in a position to deliver on its promises.

Still, one may argue that the United Kingdom's decision-making process often seems to exhibit a formless, almost casual character that is hardly in keeping with its life-or-death significance. Greater structure, it is true, might prove a little less convenient and a little more costly than current practices. Yet it is hard to see why a refusal to treat should not require at least one nephrologist's opinion. Indeed, given the stakes involved it may not be excessive to require that even two consider the case, in order to maximize the likelihood that all options be explored in the most up to date context. In the United States, it is generally accepted (and for some purposes required) that a patient will obtain a second medical opinion before undergoing some surgical procedures; it may not be presumptuous to suggest the need of a second opinion to the United Kingdom before an ESRD patient is denied treatment (but cf. Bayliss, 1988).[16]

Should the patient himself participate in the discussions? Cer-

---

[16] When this suggestion was made earlier (Halper, 1985), one nephrologist countered that with "four out of five district general hospitals [having] no member of staff trained in modern renal medicine, [the patients] may have to travel fifty to 100 miles to a major tertiary referral center. Because chronic renal disease often presents as an acute uremic emergency, patients are frequently *in extremis* before the need for such consultation is perceived." The real need, therefore, he contended, is for more and more widely distributed nephrologists (Wing, 1985a, p. 54).

tainly, it is difficult to imagine any discussion a patient would find more stressful. Desperate, arguing for his life, not knowing exactly what information may be of help and therefore compelled to bare his soul or plead for pity, the patient may find himself denuded of privacy and self-respect. Even if his efforts succeed, he may retain scars from the confrontation; if he fails, his bitterness may blight much of his remaining time.

Nor is it clear that the decision itself would necessarily be improved by his presence, for in place of medical or ethical expertise his main contribution might well be an issue-clouding emotionalism. The discomfort this might generate for physicians and their staffs, moreover, might be hard to exaggerate. Indeed, in order to avoid such agonizing confrontations, some physicians might even decide to treat patients when medical indications would clearly seem to suggest the reverse (see Schwartz and Aaron, 1984, p. 56). It is not surprising, then, that a 1982 survey of American hospital ethics committees revealed that only 19 percent permitted patients to attend meetings (Younger et al., 1983).[17]

At the same time, however, it *is* the patient's life that is on the line, and though many patients may prefer to distance themselves passively from the decision making, others might want an opportunity to defend their interests actively. Accused criminals have such a right, of course, and though it may be objected that the doctor–patient relationship ought not to be made into an adversarial proceeding, the fact remains that a physician's decision may so profoundly conflict with a patient's wishes that it would be disingenuous to speak as if doctor and patient must perforce be on the same side. There is a place for paternalism in medicine, of course, but in a democracy premised upon the individual's pursuit of his own interests, a heavy burden must fall to those claiming to represent another's interests so fully that he himself can be banished from the proceedings that may determine whether he lives or dies.

And it is to argue, too, that there is a fundamental lack of con-

[17] In perhaps the best known brief treatment of the issues raised when patients request specific interventions, no mention whatever is made of resource constraints or of the physician's role as gatekeeper (Brett and McCullough, 1986).

gruence between the physician's medical role, which is built on clinical autonomy, and his political role as an allocator, which implies effective accountability. As a medical actor, in the words of a former DHSS chief medical officer, "each consultant is the monitor of his own work and that of his 'junior' " and, indeed, he need not even "submit it to collective review, which is therefore poorly developed" (Godber, 1982, p. 371). As a result, the "final arbiter of a doctor's conduct is his conscience, influenced in turn by his personal code" (Warren, 1979, p. 25).

Such heavy reliance on self-restraint may suffice for medical actors. Indeed, all the physicians interviewed stressed that individual variations among patients made the individual clinical judgment by the doctor in charge indispensable. The alternative, they all pointed out, was a clinical judgment made by some physician-bureaucrat who never examined the patient and whose rules would inescapably be so rigid as to be unworkable (Wing, 1985a, p. 55).

Yet physicians are political actors, too, and in democracies we normally expect the presence of institutionalized external restraints when political actors are involved. No mechanisms – no formal statements on treating young children, persons aged sixty-five or older, diabetics, those unable to speak English or of low intelligence, or other controversial patient populations – in fact, virtually no explicit policy statements whatever have been forthcoming from either the DHSS or the RHAs. But as these difficult, often personally wrenching decisions are remanded to physicians on the line, effective accountability is sacrificed. As the *Lancet* editorialized, "In the face of fixed resources going into the Health Service, priorities have to be settled. It has to be decided and acknowledged openly who can be dialyzed and who cannot be dialyzed. A limit has to be composed" (*Lancet*, 1981, p. 596).

How atypical, though, it might be asked, is the nephrologist's unacknowledged political role in ESRD treatment? "We do this every day," a geriatrician who was interviewed pointed out, referring to resource allocation. Surely other specialists would agree. The nephrologist, therefore, is hardly alone, though the fact that his therapies are both very costly and effective in prolonging useful life might magnify the importance and controversial nature of his role.

If intellectually his decision is made easier by the certainty that refusal to treat means death, that very knowledge may fire the emotions and impede rationality. The differences between the nephrologist and other consultants, in short, may often be more differences of degree than of kind.

What this suggests is that the problems attaching to the nephrologist's position – conflicts of interest, absence of accountability machinery, and so on – are not peculiar to him or to ESRD, but to a considerable extent are generalizable to hospital consultants as a class. To the degree that this is true, the continuing refusal by political authorities to compel the DHSS to address the situation may contribute to patient and physician hardships throughout the Health Service. It remains to ask, however, how realistic such calls actually are for the development of workable, explicit rationing schemes.

RATIONING

"What we have here," declared one renal physician, "is rationing." For more than a decade (Cooper, 1977; Mechanic, 1977; Aaron and Schwartz, 1984), nearly every discussion of health care resource allocation has featured this term. So confused has usage become, however, that it is well to recall that "rationing" refers simply to means of resource allocation at below market price. Clearly, though, the physician was correct: The United Kingdom rations ESRD treatment.[18]

The question is, however, what kind of rationing does the NHS impose? For though rationing schemes tend to share certain

---

[18] Of course, it is possible to imagine a system in which government did not ration ESRD treatment, but instead merely left the matter to the private marketplace. Those with sufficient money could either purchase dialysis services or donor kidneys, or purchase insurance to guard against the risk of ESRD; the nonpoor could be taxed to provide insurance for the poor. Advocates might contend that this approach would maximize individual autonomy and responsibility; opponents might reply that it would be punitively harsh and blind to societal obligations. Wherever merit lies, however, it is plain that proposals of this nature are so far out of harmony with the times that they are rarely granted even a polite hearing (see Perry, 1980).

qualities, they also differ widely in many important respects. All rationing schemes are alike, for example, in that they represent efforts to cope with scarcity; we ration, say, health care services, but not air. And nearly all rationing is connected with a sense of justice or, perhaps more commonly, injustice. That is, it is felt that market allocations are unjust – for example, that they put the poor at an unfair disadvantage – and so an artificial system is created that is believed to be morally more defensible.

Yet rationing may follow any number of principles. Goods and services may be allocated on the basis of need, merit, or virtue, for instance – or by bribery, political influence, threat of physical violence, or any number of other unsavory means.[19]

More significantly, there are different kinds of rationing processes. Rationing processes, for one thing, may differ in the consistency with which they operate. Given a single rationer applying the same logic to a stable supply-and-demand pattern, a high level of consistency would seem to be assured. Change one or more of the "givens," however, and consistency is to that degree imperiled. In the United Kingdom, of course, there is no central rationer, with a list of available treatment slots to be filled in one hand and a rank-ordered list of patients in the other. In place of a central rationer, as a Glasgow medical sociologist observed in a different context, is "a

---

[19] In the United States, some disgruntled patients and physicians have charged that kidney transplants are sometimes rationed according to the recipient's willingness to give money to the transplanting hospital. Specifically, they have maintained that Saudi royalty and their associates have been moved to the head of the queue at Presbyterian University Hospital in Pittsburgh, a leading transplant center, and have in return endowed a chair at the University of Pittsburgh, which owns the hospital. Instead of proposing that such financial considerations be eliminated, however, the complainants argued that the number of foreigners receiving transplants in the United States be severly limited, if not actually reduced to zero; in this rationing scheme, nationality would operate as a key principle (Gruson, 1985a,b). A 1986 DHHS report claimed that about 300 foreigners received cadaver transplants in the United States and that an additional 200 to 250 kidneys were shipped overseas for foreign transplants. Had Americans received the transplants, the report noted, Medicare would have received tens of millions of dollars from forgone dialysis. The report urged that a strong preference be given to Americans for transplantation.

number of people [making] dispersed contributions to an overall logic which may be only dimly perceived" (Williams, 1984, p. 244). Clinical autonomy and the devolution of authority to districts and regions, in short, guarantee a rationing pattern, in which chance – which general practitioner does the patient see? to which consultant is he sent? – is frequently the governing factor.

In this regard, it is important to highlight the distinction between implicit and explicit rationing. Under implicit rationing, the criteria are not announced nor is the decision-making process or its results exposed. Indeed, typically, it is not even acknowledged that rationing has occurred. Rather, allocations simply "happen."

We tend to think of implicit rationing in two contexts. In the first, there is a strong sense of trust and community, as members share values and goals and are bound by ties of habit and affection, as in a family. In the second, an autocrat simply enforces his will and would tolerate limits on his capacity to ration no more than he would tolerate restrictions on other important areas of his authority.

With explicit rationing, the criteria are announced and the results of the process (if not the process itself) are made public. It would seem to fit relationships among strangers rather better than among members of a community and those committed to the rule of law rather better than autocrats determined to govern by unchecked command.

How, then, is one to explain the implicit system prevailing in the Health Service's rationing of ESRD treatment? The answer lies in the kinds of decisions that are called for; if rationing requires merely the spur of injustice to get it going, its structure requires a shared sense of justice for its operation. It is not enough to agree that the market cannot be left to its own devices; in addition, there must be agreement on a substitute. Here, of course, is where the problems really begin, for there is no real consensus as to what justice consists of, apart from a vacuous agreement on platitudes and pieties that hardly apply themselves.

Under certain circumstances, of course, nearly everyone concedes that officials can sit as philosopher-kings and set down a rationing scheme, but normally these are temporary periods, justified by an obvious emergency (like a war or the pollution of a water supply), and do not involve tragic choices but only mere inconvenience. Indeed, it is difficult to name even a handful of instances in which tragic choices are made by explicit rationing. Even the much discussed Seattle selection committee exercised explicit rationing only in the sense that it became widely known for its allocative role. Certainly, the criteria it applied were never made explicit – in fact, there seem to have been no clearly spelled out, consistently applied criteria – and the results of its work were not presented to the public for evaluation. Nor was the committee, whose members' names were kept secret, accountable to the public or to anyone else.

With tragic choices, an explicit rationing scheme must carry a particularly heavy burden in order to establish its legitimacy, for such choices literally and symbolically raise the supreme issue of life or death. In his classic work on the theory of social and economic organization, Weber (1947) identified three bases of legitimacy: the legal, the traditional, and the charismatic. People may feel that they ought to obey because the command is the law, because it follows long-standing custom, or because it emanates from an extraordinarily gifted leader. The rule of law, with its rational justifications and distinctions, is most characteristic of modern society. Normally, however, it does not exist in pure form but rather in combination with one or both of the other bases of legitimacy. The other bases, though, are so weak regarding tragic choices that they are unable to provide the requisite support for the legal argumentation: There is no set of traditional values and procedures for making explicit tragic-choice rationing, nor has any charismatic figure come to dominate the process. Legal rules, therefore, would appear naked to their enemies, and this obvious vulnerability has doubtless deterred interested persons from venturing rationing schemes.

That ESRD selection decisions are tragic choices, of course, would inhibit the development of explicit rationing in any system. In addition, though, a number of other factors present in the United Kingdom reinforce the tendency toward the implicit approach: the famous British tradition of pragmatic improvisation; a lack of consensus as to health priorities among physicians and among health officials; the paternalistic self-image of the physician and the patient's still potent traditional deference to authority; the structure and procedures of the NHS that increase patient vulnerability as they impede effective accountability; indeed, the central assumption of the NHS itself, namely, that it should respond to professionally determined need rather than to consumer-determined demand (Klein, 1984b). Technology, too, may greatly complicate explicit rationing by continually changing the nature of the goods and services to be divided up, by repeatedly altering supply-and-demand patterns and thus upsetting vested interests, and by requiring a freedom of control for further innovation that cannot easily coexist with the restraints rationing itself ordinarily entails.

Even if an agreement on the desirability of explicit rationing could be reached, moreover, a question would remain as to how well defined the selection criteria ought to be. Narrow, rigid rules, of course, would carry with them a herd of problems: Among physicians, such rules would generate resentment, lower morale, and dampen the spirit of cooperation, altruism, and institutional loyalty; among the public, they would, when applied in an unpopular way, encourage the corrosive belief in the prevalence of government-imposed injustice; enforcement would consume substantial resources and accentuate bureaucratic tendencies to emphasize adherence to rules at the expense of efficiency and mercy; time lags in adapting rules to technological developments would cause serious hardships and dissatisfaction; and so on.

Broad and flexible rules might sidestep these difficulties, but only because they would provide enough official discretion effectively to continue the old practice of implicit rationing.

In this light, consider, for example, the explicit rationing system advanced by the renowned American renal surgeon Thomas E. Starzl and his associates for the equitable selection of cadaveric kidney recipients. The system gives recipients points for time on a waiting list, quality of the antigen match, extent of reactive antibodies, medical emergency, and logistical factors. During 1986, fully 98 percent of the 270 transplantations performed at the University of Pittsburgh followed Starzl's scheme (Starzl et al., 1987), and the United Network for Organ Sharing, which maintains national waiting lists, adopted this system for the entire United States.

The Starzl system represents an effort to replace ad hoc or rule-of-thumb practices with a consistent or objective approach and clearly reflects considerable thought and years of hands-on experience.

At the same time, however, the weaknesses of the scheme are obvious. It is not simply that other physicians may quibble about specific point scales (Matas and Tellis, 1987) or the problem of storing kidneys (Hunsicker, 1987). More basically, both the weights assigned and the factors included are fundamentally arbitrary. Why should waiting time be worth a maximum of ten points, antigens twelve, antibodies ten, urgency ten, and logistics six? Why should the ordinal rankings be added, when the intervals are clearly unequal? Why restrict nonmedical criteria solely to waiting time? To none of these questions is the answer self-evident, though to none of these questions did the authors respond in their leading article on the subject. Despite repeated references to objectivity and computerization, therefore, the validity of the Starzl selection system appears open to serious and numerous challenges.

In addition to the problem of rationing resources to ESRD patients, there is the matter of rationing resources to ESRD itself in preference to other health care categories. This is true not only because it is impossible to be confident about cost estimates of ESRD therapies, but also because it is exceedingly difficult to balance the claims of ESRD against the claims of the other good causes demanding Health Service funding. Indeed, the common metaphor of balancing is itself profoundly misleading, for it suggests that the "heavier" of the competing claims can be determined as objectively as the heavier weight on a scale. In fact, though, there is no constant, impersonal force like gravity pulling equally on the claims, and so the determination of which is heavier is very largely subjective.

Efforts have been made, of course, to quantify the various claims in order to determine which offer the most efficient use of resources. The results, however, have not clarified matters much. Thus, one set of analysts applying reasonable cost–premium assumptions to a variety of conditions concluded that the NHS could afford to treat ESRD (Roberts, 1985, p. 90), whereas in the preceding year a health economist calculated the quality-adjusted life years gained by ESRD treatments to be far costlier than those of some of their most common competitors (Williams, 1984; but cf. Jennett, 1985). Different analysts using different techniques obtain different results with different policy implications. And it would be naive to expect that a consensus will emerge in support of one technique, thereby turning off disagreements like water from a tap.

Moreover, all the problems involved in dividing up the NHS pie exist – in even more complex and intractable forms – in dividing up the whole public-sector pie, and are even stickier with the whole gross domestic product pie.

None of this is to say that the overall merits of explicit rationing do not argue for its adoption, either generally or in the case of ESRD specifically. The problems, after all, may merely be a regrettable, inescapable cost of doing business and be vastly exceeded by the advantages. But it is to say that the reasons that explicit rationing does not strike policy makers as either feasible or in their own best interests are powerful and almost beyond counting. Whatever the abstract arguments in support of particular selection criteria, therefore, it might be necessary to contract a kind of terminal hopefulness in order to believe that explicit rationing constitutes a practical technique for reforming UK ESRD policy in the near future.

Despite all the inconsistencies and vagaries of implicit rationing, however, it has failed to generate any real public outcry. Nor has it tarnished the symbolism that represents the NHS as the incarnation of "socialist equity and collectivist compassion" (Klein, 1985, p. 42). How is this to be explained? The simplest answer is that rationing is not tied to money – better-off patients are not moved to the front of the queue – and this lends it a sheen of fairness. Of course, this need not mean that money is of no importance whatever: Higher-income patients and their families may be more likely to push for referral and treatment and may even be able to seek treatment in the private sector. But these advantages appear to be seen as peripheral exceptions to the rule, and the principle that patient income does not determine patient selection is fairly widely accepted.[20] Although

[20] What is not widely noted is the contention that queuing, like randomization, is "literally irresponsible, a rejection of the burden" of choosing (Fletcher, n.d.).

philosophers may dismiss this view as irredeemably simplistic, much of the public seems to respond to it as down to earth and easy to grasp.

RATIONING – OUT OF THE CLOSET?

If rationing was not the NHS's "dirty little secret," still it probably never was spoken of so openly and so bitterly as in late 1987 and 1988. Almost on a daily basis, critics of the government denounced bed closures, staff shortages, cancellations of clinical sessions, and restrictions on clinical activity – almost invariably with reference to rationing.

For their part, Tories tended to reply, as did Andrew Rowe, a Mid-Kent MP, "Health care provision creates demand in excess of supply, and it always will. So there will always be rationing. . . . It is therefore sentimental and muddle-headed hypocrisy for the opposition to pretend otherwise."

What was new, however, were signs that physicians were not so willing to acquiesce silently to the system. One reason that rationing had proved so effective was that not only medical care was rationed; so was knowledge of the rationing itself. Thus, unlike a person who requires a ration ticket (say) to purchase meat, a patient does not himself literally take the purchasing action and learn of the system firsthand. Indeed, since physicians have normally obscured medical rationing behind a fog of medical rationalizations, the patient is likely to be aware of it only in a hazy, impersonal way and may not fully appreciate its impact on his own life. By late 1987, there were clear indications that some physicians were no longer willing to play the game.

The reason for the change in many physicians' attitudes does not appear to be that, in fact, rationing had become more stringent than ever. Plainly, that was not the case. Instead, a number of physicians seemed to perceive an unraveling of a long-standing if quite unofficial understanding. With this arrangement, physicians had agreed to live within budget constraints and in return were granted an autonomy that essentially freed them from effective scrutiny. Some physicians appeared to believe that the Thatcher government had unilaterally abrogated the understanding by refusing to pour large sums into the NHS and by instead talking of increasing productivity. And the government, these doctors believed, was actuated not by expediency, which would soon blow away, but by principle, which could be expected to endure; for with a balanced budget and relative prosperity, the government could have made many more funds available to the Health Service. It was not financial exigencies, as in the early 1980s, but instead a determination to restrain public expenditures and pursue greater efficiences that lay behind the refusal to continue to honor fully the long-standing physician–government arrangement. The tough-minded prime minister, seeking value for money and seeing the medical profession's traditional practices as an impediment to the achievement of this goal, was willing to sacrifice some physician autonomy in order to get it.

In response, physicians became increasingly eager to decry rationing to the media, especially the London media. In one move that generated considerable attention, for example, Nigel Harris, a prominent physician who had campaigned on television for Mrs. Thatcher a few months earlier, appeared at 10 Downing Street with a petition signed by 1,169 doctors denouncing her new initiatives for hospitals and clinics. The Labour party and others opposed to the government quickly joined in, Neil Kinnock, for instance, charging that "blood is flowing through the bandages the Tories are trying to wrap around" the NHS (in Raines, 1987). Public perception that the government was at war with the Health Service began to take hold and to spread. Even Mrs. Thatcher, who does not give ground easily or often, felt compelled to offer an additional 100 million pounds to the NHS as an emergency appropriation.

It is hard to predict how widespread the rationing revelation phenomenon will become or how long it will last. But by threatening to bring into the open a rationing whose chief advantage is its implicit character, recent events may be striking at one of the main props of the NHS itself.[21]

---

[21] The NHS's practice of implicit rationing runs counter to the general rule that we favor secrecy in private matters (privacy) and openness in public matters (accountability) (Bok, 1984). To the extent that the practice misleads patients, it also raises the issue of the relationship of illusion to fairness (Baumol, 1986, pp. 220–2).

A QUESTION OF BENEFICENCE

In all of this practical talk, it is easy to lose sight of a major ethical question: To what extent is the physician actively obliged to benefit his patients? Or to apply it to the ESRD context: To what extent is the physician actively obliged to seek treatment for a treatable patient?

The physician, of course, is by no means the sole actor in the drama, and if the patient fails to receive treatment, one may also perhaps blame the NHS central office, the RHA, or even the patient and his family; if any of these were more committed to the cause or more aggressive in temperament, the treatment that was denied might instead have been forthcoming. Yet having acknowledged this, one must also acknowledge that it is the physician who is fundamentally in charge of patient care, and so it is at his door that the question must principally be addressed.

It is not necessary to pause long to consider whether physicians have special moral obligations distinct from those we all owe each other. Some have argued that we all share the same moral duties, though tradition, the necessity for technical expertise, and other factors mislead us into assuming that the obligations of doctors are different; the contexts in which the obligations are applied may be different, but the obligations themselves, it is said, are the same (Downie, 1986).

Certainly the medical community, however, takes it for granted that its beneficent obligation sets it apart. It is frequently contended, for example, that inasmuch as society has provided the physician with his education, income, and so forth, he is reciprocally obliged to treat those patients who appear before him (cf. May, 1975; Camenisch, 1979). Underscoring this, the Hippocratic oath requires physicians to "come for the benefit of the sick," when it is possible to do so. It is therefore said to be an error to view physicians as self-interested actors, with only perfunctory duties owed to the larger world around them (Sieghart, 1985).

This is not to say that the physician's obligation is open-ended to the extent that he may routinely be required to assume major risks to his own life or to cast off all but his professional role in a single-minded pursuit of patient welfare (Slote, 1977, pp. 125–7). The physician can hardly be held to the standard of a saint or a hero. These reservations, however, do not apply to ESRD, where treatment imposes risks and hardships only on patients, whose lives are forever altered, if not dominated, by the condition; from the physician's perspective, nothing supererogatory is involved.

Beauchamp and Childress (1982) have more broadly expressed the conditions under which beneficence can be ethically required:

> X has a duty of beneficence toward Y only if . . . (1) Y is at risk of significant loss or change, (2) X's action is needed to prevent this loss, (3) X's action would probably prevent it, (4) X's action would not present significant risk to X, and (5) the benefit that Y will probably gain outweighs any harm that X is likely to suffer. (p. 153)

All these conditions would clearly apply to a physician–patient ESRD situation.

Such a rigidly obligatory beneficence, however, is not without its problems. Does it require, for instance, that in close cases the physician opt for treatment, even if his best judgment is to withhold it? And how is the close-case category to be kept from inexorably expanding? Does the physician's duty violate the norm of proportionality; in exchange for society's very modest investment in him, can the physician legitimately be asked to devote a large part of his resources to society? Would such a broad view of the physician's beneficence aid in recruiting and retaining doctors or would it instead prove counterproductive? Does beneficence require physicians to behave better than their fellows and, in that sense, to be better persons; and is this realistic and desirable? The question of beneficence, in short, itself poses many questions. Still, it is hard to see how harsh and too often uninformed gatekeeper naysaying can conform with the obligations of physicians' beneficence, however it may be defined.

CONCLUSIONS

In the making of a microallocative decision about whether to treat a given patient, the patient himself normally plays a passive role.

More important are the general practitioner and general medicine hospital consultant, who decide on referral, but it is the nephrologist who usually makes the most careful decision as to whether to treat. Although ostensibly guided by clinical judgment, however, he probably soon learns that the decision-making process is subjective and variable. More than this, he is confined by the scarcity of resources, which necessitates a certain amount of "corner cutting" and dictates treatment patterns that direct some patients toward suboptimal therapies and exclude others from treatment altogether.

It is not hard to speculate about how medical criteria have come to monopolize legitimacy in ESRD patient selection. Nor, on reflection, is it difficult to see that the exclusive rhetorical reliance on medical criteria – whatever the criteria actually employed – reflects a normative judgment as to how the microallocative political decision ought to be made. It is possible, of course, to debate the wisdom of all this ad infinitum.

The real point, however, is not whether the normative decision enthroning medical criteria is sound. Such decisions by their nature cannot be proved valid, as if they were theorems in geometry, nor are they likely ever to please all interested parties. Instead, the point would seem to be whether a democratic society ought to continue to tolerate the current decision-making process; for the process encourages normative decisions to be made by persons with no special qualifications or training in normative matters and who neither represent community views nor are effectively accountable to any outside authority. And because the normative character of the decision is typically mistaken by patients and their families for a medical rationale, the process has by and large escaped serious scrutiny. It is, of course, convenient for political leaders to pass the task onto bureaucrats and for bureaucrats to pass it on to physicians. As one nephrologist observed, it is a commonplace for renal physicians to declare that they are "doing the dirty work for the politician" (Wing, 1985a, p. 53). More than that, there are obvious good (and politically expedient) reasons for defending the tradition of clinical autonomy. Who, after all, is in a better position to reach decisions pertaining to a patient's welfare than his physician? Can anyone really argue that regulations promulgated by officials or politicians who have never even seen the patient – and who may be quite lacking in pertinent medical expertise – ought to take precedence over the judgment of the physician in charge? Would the doctor–patient relationship benefit from being further bureaucratized? Would competent and strong-minded physicians even put up with such a scheme? Is the discomfort with current practices merely a function of the low treatment rates that reflect macro- and not microallocative pressures and that would be present in any case? The familiar questions arrive in crowds and are not easily dispersed.

Yet the current system – or nonsystem – raises questions as well. Should even physicians retain such unrestrained authority in matters of life and death? Is the sense of justice offended by the knowledge that patients who would be accepted for treatment by specialists are often rejected by doctors whose relevant experience and expertise may be modest, if not obsolete? Is the physician left with an unresolvable conflict of interest, ostensibly pursuing the patient's best interest but often feeling compelled to place a societal interest in efficient resource allocation first? Should decisions and decision guidelines of this magnitude be hidden from public view? Should ethical issues be ignored on the pretense that the exclusive rhetorical reliance on medical criteria does not itself represent an unexamined ethical judgment? Is faith in physicians really a substitute for faith in procedures? And if the rigidities of bureaucratic regulation make for too blunt a decision-making tool, why should physicians who use age and other criteria like a club be permitted to continue in this fashion? In response to all this, it hardly seems sufficient for bureaucrats to observe that patient selection is left to the physicians and for physicians to reply that resource allocation is left to the bureaucrats. In any case, recent events that have focused attention on rationing may be changing the tempo at which the old buck-passing dance used to be carried on.

4. Some premature conclusions

Perhaps because it confirms humanity's general hope for progress, the impact of medicine upon society has for decades been a popular theme both in official rhetoric and in private speech. Of course, not all health gains have been due to medicine – indeed, improved sanitation, nutrition, housing, education, and so forth have clearly had far greater impact – but the public has tended to confuse the two and to credit increased life expectancy and improved vigor chiefly to medicine (McKeown, 1976; McKinlay and McKinlay, 1977; Levine et al., 1983). Further, medicine, unlike science in general, is usually thought of as an almost unalloyed good. Where science's name is mottled by nuclear weapons and environmental depradations, medicine's is barely blemished at all.

Medicine, moreover, not only has helped to shape individuals' outlooks on themselves and their futures, but has also consumed such vast quantities of resources, financial, intellectual, and technological, that its very appetite has had major effects on social life. Indeed, so essential is contemporary medicine to the notion of modernity that it is quite impossible even to imagine a society advanced in all areas save that. Few developments have seemed better able to confirm the possibility of progress than twentieth-century medicine.

But in the tangle of upbeat clichés, it is easy to lose sight of the fact that society has had an enormous impact upon medicine, too. The great advances in medical knowledge and practice, for one thing, have not simply arrived, like so many unordered desserts brought by a confused waiter, nor can medicine credit only itself for these developments. Instead, one must point to what Titmuss (1968) tellingly called "the invasion of medicine by the natural sciences" (p. 183), which has helped to transform medical training, care, and organization and left physicians increasingly dependent on chemists, biologists, engineers, and a host of other specialists.

More than this, society's influence is manifested through its political and bureaucratic agents, who have determined that medicine merits the immense allocations to which it has grown accustomed. In the case of ESRD, more specifically, it is society that has determined that it will fund treatment, at least under some circumstances. The determination of these circumstances illustrates how society can shape medicine, and inescapably it is a painful process. This is because it entails letting some persons die, not because they are unworthy to live but simply because under some implicit or explicit schema to be applied in a context of scarcity, they are felt to be less worthy than some others.

Yet if the process is painful, it is instructive, too, for if it inquires into whom it will save, society cannot help also inquiring into what kind of health service it has and wants and what kind of society it is and ought to be. All of this, however, requires that the question of who will be saved be openly raised. Thus far, the United Kingdom has evidently found this an easier question to answer than to ask.

Paralleling the interaction of society and medicine is the interaction of the macro- and microallocative processes within medicine itself. For purposes of analysis and convenience, this study has treated them separately. In this sense, it is possible to view the ESRD microallocative process as a natural consequence of the tradition of clinical autonomy interacting with the multitudinous variations among physicians. That is, physicians are granted vast discretionary authority to determine which patients to treat, and different physicians produce different treatment patterns, depending on training, biases, interests, and a number of other medical and nonmedical factors (cf. Glover, 1938; Royal College of Radiologists, 1979; Wennberg et al., 1982). Underlying this is the recognition that many key physicians' decisions are not compelled by an indisputable logic, but instead are choices presented by analogical reasoning on which experts may differ. Viewed from this perspective, disparities in treatment patterns are likely to persist so long as physicians retain their autonomy and distinctive individuality – in short, certainly for the near future.

THE UNITED KINGDOM LIVING WITHIN ITS MEANS

In another sense, the ESRD microallocative process reflects larger macroallocative pressures. For the scarcity of resources allocated to ESRD patients is not irremediable (like, say, the scarcity of Rembrandt portraits), but rather is a function of an implicit policy decision against reallocating resources in sufficient quantities to relieve it. Put differently, the scarcity is not so much imposed on society as imposed by society, or at least by its agents. Clearly, if enough resources were made available (perhaps less than 10 pounds per taxpayer per year), virtually all ESRD patients could be treated. With the necessity of denying treatment effectively eliminated, the significance of clinical autonomy and physician variation as determinants of patient selection would effectively be eliminated, too.[1]

Seen from this vantage, the United Kingdom's experience with ESRD is simply that of a welfare state endeavoring to live within its means. In the larger view and measured in terms of direct costs, the United Kingdom has been remarkably successful; it devotes a smaller part of its gross national product to health care, and operates under a lower rate of health care cost inflation, than does almost any other industrialized nation. At the same time, though, its ESRD treatment patterns remind all other Western democracies caught up in the quest for cost containment and cutbacks in entitlements that this involves sacrifices not only from stereotypically prosperous physicians and inefficient hospitals, but also from vulnerable and blameless patients who arouse pity, not indignation. In this light, the UK experience teaches again that there is no free lunch and, indeed, that the innocent and helpless may be left with the highest price to pay.

Yet to acknowledge that the United Kingdom must live within its means is not to concede the justice of every decision made in this

---

[1] Thus, in the United States, physicians applauded Medicare's coverage of ESRD patients, mainly because it spared them the burden of making tragic choices (Eisenberg, 1979).

name. Like a sore that will not heal, the question just will not go away: In order for the United Kingdom to live within its means, must so many ESRD patients be abandoned to die? The obvious answer is no. In the absence of a consensus on measuring moral or economic importance, it is simply disingenuous to point to a public expenditure of which one disapproves and announce that the nation simply cannot afford it, particularly in the late 1980s, when Britain has returned to relative prosperity. So trifling a burden as 10 pounds per taxpayer, in any case, could hardly be written off as excessive, given the vastly incommensurate benefits of prolonging useful life for thousands of persons. Death upstages everything, including money.

A less obvious answer, however, must also intrude; for setting aside a modest allocation for ESRD may, in principle and in practice, entail setting aside like amounts for a plethora of other worthy causes. And as the late Senator Everett McKinley Dirksen used to lament, "A billion here, a billion there, and the first thing you know, you're talking about real money." If ESRD is seen as an exemplar of a larger problem – must living within its means compel a society to consign treatable patients to death? – the response may not be quite so plain.

How, then, can one judge the United Kingdom's ESRD policy?

A RIGHT TO HEALTH CARE?

One answer is that the United Kingdom's policy can be evaluated in terms of a more fundamental right to health care (or, in the more extreme form, to "optimal health" itself [Faculty of Community Medicine, 1986, p. 4]). "Right" here is an ethical and not a legal term, and refers to a societal obligation to provide patients with appropriate treatment when they demand it (cf. Fried, 1975a). As such, right is connected with the notion of obligation in three senses. First, a right is seen simply as an obligation perceived from the beneficiary's perspective; second, a right reflects an *in rem* claim against the whole community, rather than an *in personam* claim that one person may raise against another; and, third, the enjoyment of a right is generally seen as creating or reinforcing a duty to meet one's own obligations. My assertion of a right to a kidney transplant, therefore, would be just another way of saying that society through its agents is obligated to obtain the organ, perform the surgery, and so on, and that I, as a member of society, am reciprocally obligated to support another person's assertion of a right to a transplant.

Sometimes, the right to health care is stated in a more or less unqualified way, without mention of conditions or limitations (cf. Williams, 1962; Outka, 1974; Veatch, 1976; McCullough, 1979). With perhaps a few peripheral exclusionary criteria, such as residency (but cf. Dagger, 1985), an unqualified right operates quite irrespective of the personal qualities of the claimant. Age, race, ability to pay, moral worth, contribution to society – these characteristics and dozens more are simply irrelevant. The only decisive variable is medical need, which is often conceived as an objective, almost self-applying criterion.

In broad terms, there are three commonly voiced arguments for this position. The first is that in order to utilize such generally accepted rights as the right to speak or to vote, the individual must receive adequate health care. Thus, for an untreated ESRD patient, these other rights would progressively lose their meaning until with his death they would disappear like a light switched off. The existence of these other rights, in other words, is said to imply a correlative right to health care as a necessary precondition.

Some would reply, however, that in the name of strengthening political rights, this argument would effectively remove the essence of a great political issue from the democratic agenda – namely, to what extent should taxpayers fund health care? Critics would also observe that the argument for health care could be extended to cover virtually all important social concerns – housing, education, and so on – thereby removing them from the agenda, too. Thus denuded of significance, the agenda would be left brief and trivial. And so in the process of building the correlative rights, the rationale for the underlying primary rights would be so severely cut back that it would be rendered quite incapable of supporting the grand new structures resting upon it. It is hardly credible, therefore, that the original formulators and defenders of political rights intended that they be read to entail such immense social welfare obligations. On the contrary, political rights were initially seen as imposing obligations upon the individual to make full and responsible use of them, and not upon his fellows to help him do so.

A second argument rests on the Aristotelian notion of justice that requires that like be treated as like. As Williams (1962) put it: "Leaving aside preventive medicine, the proper ground of distribution [of health care] is ill health. . . . [T]he situation of those whose needs are the same not receiving the same treatment, though the needs are the ground of the treatment . . . is an irrational state of affairs" (see also Marmor, 1985, pp. 105–6). Similarly, an egalitarian theologian maintains that the essential moral equality of humanity entails the obligation of health care systems to offer "the amount of health care needed to provide a level of health equal, insofar as possible, to other persons' health" (Veatch, 1976).

However, the contention that like be treated as like, so unassailable in theory, can easily prove naive and mechanical in practice, for it quite ignores resource scarcity and problems of ranking claimants. In any system that is not highly centralized, that is, different subunits will make different priority rankings, so that one might favor ESRD patients and another, say, arthroplasty. In such cases, where each side can make a plausible defense, reasonable observers will also differ, and only the most arrogant will dare to declare that the question of how to allocate resources admits of only one legitimate solution.

By the same token, some will fail to see how an alleged moral equality of humanity has unambiguous implications for health care systems. Instead, one might as well argue that the obligations fall either on the individual or the family to look out for themselves or as an uncoercible moral but not legal duty to look after one's fellows. It is a long leap from asserting that you and I are morally equal to taxing you to treat the ESRD with which I am afflicted.

Nor, because each case is necessarily unique, is it always obvious when a pair of cases are sufficiently similar to be treated as if they were alike. Ought we to focus exclusively on present symptoms, for example, or also take into account pertinent past behavior or prognoses for the future? To what extent (if any), for example, do a patient's desires or conduct shape his right to health care? Does intensity of demand reinforce his claim? Suppose he eschews medical orthodoxy for rolfing? Christian Science? diagnosis by divination from chicken entrails? (Alternative medicine, such as homeopathy or acupuncture, is normally unavailable through the NHS.) Does a patient waive his right to health care by improvident health practices (like a dialysis patient's ignoring his dietary restrictions)? If he is unwilling to forswear the pleasures of neglect, ought society, like some indulgent Daddy Warbucks, simply to pick up the tab? Is our obligation to the individual so powerful that it is unaffected by his own failure to look out for himself? And when, short of death, does the obligation end – if it ends at all? Thus, far from settling the issue, proclaiming that like should be treated as like merely restates it, for it leaves us asking which attributes we should select for comparison, and how numerous, significant, and close the similarities should be.

A third argument is the communitarian position that needs create rights. It is probably fair to say that the modern welfare state, indeed, the modern popular understanding of social justice itself, rests on the concept of need. It is not only Marx who favors distribution "to each according to his needs"; President Reagan, too, professed a commitment to the "truly needy." When people who disagree about nearly everything else agree on aiding the needy, however, it most likely means that they are simply using the word in different senses (when they are not cynically dissembling [cf. Halper, 1973]). And "need," of course, has proved notoriously resistant to efforts at definitional precision: In ordinary speech "need" is often merely a synonym for "want," and prominent social critics, perhaps in imitation of Marx's "false consciousness," have often distinguished true from false (i.e., manipulated) needs (e.g., Galbraith, 1958; Marcuse, 1964, p. 21). Others have spoken of "need" as what is "detrimental . . . to our natures as men and specific persons" (McCloskey, 1976; cf. Braybooke, 1968, p. 90), as if the meaning of this phrase were not nearly as opaque as the term it purports to clarify.

Whatever definitional problems that attach to the term "need" in most circumstances, however, would seem to be quite absent in the case of ESRD, for the stark simplicity of the situation deters all word play: ESRD patients *need* treatment in order to stay alive.

Yet the determination of needs, even in such a circumscribed medical setting, may be harder to explicate than might at first appear. An ESRD patient, it is true, needs treatment to stay alive. In other words, once alive, he may decide that he needs other things, but the very existence of these secondary needs presupposes the primacy of life. As sensible as this seems, however, individuals (and not only ESRD patients) do not always rank staying alive as their first goal. Many have always felt that staying alive is less desirable than escaping physical pain or mental suffering, as in the myth of Sybylla, who having been granted her wish for eternal life spent most of that life pleading for death; and in nonmedical settings history is replete with examples of those who have willingly given their lives for family and friends, for secular or religious ideals, or for many other purposes. In fact, it is obvious that most people would not be willing to do *anything* to stay alive; some taboos, whether against eating pork or human flesh, are so potent that many people would literally die rather than violate them. Social conditioning, in other words, may create needs against which even the requirements of biology may prove unavailing.[2] What is interesting, then, is "how the objective necessities of human existence are filtered through the symbolic processes of culture and of individual perception . . . in that nebulous zone where the so-called objective and subjective dimensions meet" (Leiss, 1976, p. 62). ESRD patients do not invariably choose to continue the treatment that alone can offer them life.

Do needs create rights? In a discursive, impressionistic work, Michael Ignatieff finds the answer in a fortuitously interactive structure of needs themselves. That is, some people require aid to "live to their full potential," and the rest of us, he claims, require feelings of social solidarity that lead us to "have needs on behalf of others" (Ignatieff, 1984, pp. 10, 17). For the most part, it is true, this aid is not passed from one person to another in a gift relationship, but rather is transferred via a welfare bureaucracy, which permits us to "remain a society of strangers. . . . We are reponsible for each other but we

---

[2] A sailor who had been adrift on a tiny raft recalled of his failed effort to eat a gull: "It's easy to say that after five days of hunger you can eat anything. But though you may be starving, you still feel nauseated by a mess of warm bloody feathers with a strong odor of raw fish and mange" (Márquez, 1986).

are not responsible to each other" (Ignatieff, 1984, pp. 10, 17, 18). Still, if we do not need help, Ignatieff believes, we at least need to be helpful. Though the issue of rights does not arise, the practical result would seem to be the same: My need for ESRD treatment would oblige society to provide it.

"From each according to his needs to each according to his needs" may have a pleasingly symmetrical ring, however, but suppose the two needs are not congruent? Might some needs be over-supplied and others undersupplied? Suppose our communitarian needs are satisfied at a level of giving that cannot provide for ESRD patients? Ought government to enforce its definition of need upon unwilling recipients or donors? And why, in any case, ought its definition to be preferred over theirs? The answers are not clear.

Similarly, for Richard Zaner, "human affliction is an appeal for help." The individual, sensing his own "vulnerability and diminishment of selfhood," requires trust and caring. And that he is not responsible for his condition transforms his demand into a call for justice. Thus transformed, his need morally obligates the community in general and the physician in particular to respond with aid (Zaner, 1982). Gene Outka (1972) also finds the "peculiarly random and uncontrollable" character of health needs compelling; the innocence of the patient renders his need for the treatment a right.[3]

[3] The English philosopher Robert Goodin, in a deontological argument with obvious implications for ESRD treatment, carries this stress on vulnerability still farther. Conceding that traditionally it has been taken for granted that we owe a special duty to family and friends (Ross, 1930, p. 21; Parfit, 1984, p. 95), Goodin contends that it is vulnerability that imposes a responsibility on us. Of course, he writes, "those relatively near to us in space and time will be rather more vulnerable to us," but it is the vulnerability and not the proximity that is morally relevant.

From this, Goodin draws two quite stunning implications. The first is that exploiting vulnerability becomes per se immoral. Since no distinctions as to degree or means are suggested, one is left wondering what is to become of the self-interest that drives the world's economic and political life. Vulnerability, after all, is found not only among subjects of tyrannies; all dealings among unequals – in other words, virtually all human relationships – would seem to entail some exploitation of vulnerability. Is all this to be condemned, and, if so, what ought its replacement to be? Under such a system would it ever be permissible to refuse a request from one who believes himself to be vulnerable – and if not, would this

Yet sad though the plight of the blameless victim is, it is not clear why society – which is also blameless – is duty bound to care for him. Such compassionate behavior may certainly be praiseworthy, but why must it be obligatory? Why, in particular, this focus on the victim's lack of responsibility for his plight? If a fireman were burned rescuing a child, would he have a lesser call on society's resources because he assumed a risk by freely choosing to enter the burning building? Should his heroism strip him of his rights?

AN UNQUALIFIED RIGHT?

The problems attaching to the assertion of an unqualified right to health care, however, go far beyond specific flaws in rationales. First, such an assertion mistakes means for ends. It is not good health care that people desire, after all, but rather good health, and health

place the strong at the mercy of the weak and render the strong vulnerable, too? What kind of social relations would be possible in this bizarre world of pervasive, mutually reinforcing vulnerabilities?

Goodin's second implication is that vulnerability entails an officially coercible responsibility, irrespective of how the vulnerability was brought about. That this might "tend to encourage improvident behavior" is dismissed as "a practical rather than a moral matter" (Goodin, 1985, pp. 777, 779, 780). To illustrate this, Goodin offers the example of two victims of a traffic accident, who, brought to a hospital emergency room with similar injuries, "should be treated with equal care and attention, even though one caused the accident and the other one was its innocent victim." The example, however, begs the critical issue of resource limitation by assuming that it is possible to treat both patients. Yet in the making of real-world policy decisions, resource constraints must nearly always be considered, and so a more apposite illustration might be one in which the hospital is capable of treating only one of the two injured in the accident. In this case, other things being equal, it is hard to see why the victim should not be preferred over the perpetrator. Does an ESRD patient really have no greater call on resources than one who negligently or deliberately injured himself?

More generally, Goodin may be read as urging that if I act with the intent of helping the vulnerable but also with the knowledge that my action will in addition encourage the evil, foolish, or destructive behavior that brought about the kind of vulnerability that I now seek to remedy, neither this knowledge nor any of the predictable negative results is of any moral relevance. Though deontologists judge the morality of actions without consideration of their consequences, Goodin's view will clearly seem far too narrow to gain many adherents.

care is only one of several means to that end. Indeed, societally, it is so far from the most important means that a health practices index that omits health care entirely can still predict individual health status and mortality with impressive accuracy (Berkman and Breslow, 1983). No wonder a prominent medical sociologist conceded, "If one wishes to equalize health, equalizing medical care is probably not the most effective strategy" (Starr, 1976; Sagan, 1988).

An exaggerated concern with health care, however, obscures the contributions of other factors to good health, attracts resources away from health-promoting but non-health-care activities (e.g., education, traffic safety, pollution reduction), and thus may actually impede progress toward better health. An unqualified right to health care, therefore, ensures that health care providers will receive more money and may even increase the quality and quantity of health care available, but it need not significantly promote better health.[4]

Second, the assertion of an unqualified right to health care implies mutually conflicting positions on the issue of medical paternalism. Those emphasizing the individual's negative right to pursue his own health care without interference from government may be troubled by the enormous, multitiered complex of regulations and institutions covering professional licensure, drug availability, and so on, all of which assume that health care is such a technical enterprise that the lay person requires officially credentialed experts for his protection – even if he himself may not always recognize it. Those stressing society's obligation to provide health care, on the other hand, will naturally seek to direct money and authority to exactly those forces whose paternalistic qualities may strike their neighbors as offensive. Moreover, by stressing the medical establishment's

[4] Of course, it is possible to argue for the superiority of principles based on rights to policies based on goals, and to insist that "particular programs must be carried out or abandoned because of their impact on particular people, even if the community as a whole is in some ways worse off in consequence" (Dworkin, 1985). In this way, an argument might be framed that would defend the unqualified right to health care, even in the face of incontrovertible evidence that it interfered with the end of raising general standards of health. If lawyers and judges may think in terms of principles, however, executives, legislators, bureaucrats, and other political actors overwhelmingly stress policies – rhetorical declamations to the contrary notwithstanding.

obligation to offer solutions, these advocates may eviscerate the patient's own role, seeing him as essentially passive and unable to contribute to his own health except by swallowing his pills at the appointed times (see Brett and McCullough, 1986).[5]

Third, the assertion of an unqualified right to health care suggests that excellence and equality can be achieved simultaneously, when as the provision of renal services illustrates, this is rarely the case. This is because excellence normally requires the concentration of resources (e.g., at a major teaching hospital), whereas equality entails their dispersion. But if equalizing "up" is typically too expensive to be realistic, equalizing "down" instantly meets stiff resistance from those advantaged elements who are asked to sacrifice merely for the greater good of the greater number.

Fourth, the assertion of an unqualified right to health care raises an endless stream of correlative questions. What health care, for example, is one entitled to? It is one thing to speak of dialysis for an ESRD patient. But what of a hair transplant, or an abortion? The World Health Organization (1958) has defined health as "a state of complete physical, mental, and social well being and not merely the absence of disease or infirmity" (p. 459). Does this imply that anyone not in a state of "complete well being" (i.e., virtually all humankind) has a right to care that will elevate him to this condition, without regard to limitations on resources or the evident absence of means to ensure this complete well-being? Is this perilously close to declaring that we have not only the Jeffersonian right to the pursuit of happiness, but the right to happiness itself? Is it wise or prudent even to ask that society bear such an unbearable burden? Are we entitled to eudaemonia?

What of the impact of implementing an unqualified right to health care upon healthy people? Most of them, of course, would not freely choose to insure themselves and their families against all possible medical eventualities because they implicitly calculate that

[5] Moreover, even those who dismiss the practical consequences of the collision between positive and negative rights may be forced to concede that the two are logically quite unrelated. Libertarians who stress the right of noninterference, therefore, find no right to well-being at the expense of other citizens (Nozick, 1974).

the marginal utility of some of the coverage is not worth the price.[6] With an unqualified-right system, however, healthy people – indeed, virtually everyone – would in effect be coerced into purchasing this full and expensive coverage in the form of higher taxes.

And what of the consequences of encouraging consumption at the expense of production? Compassion, of course, has a fine, noble ring. It does not, however, create wealth, but merely urges its redistribution. Does this suggest that if compassion (and other consumption-oriented drives) is given too many rights at the expense of production, at some point there will be insufficient resources to support that compassion? Relatedly, it may be easy to agree that the only inequalities that should be allowed are those that improve the condition of the worst off (cf. Rawls, 1971, who, however, does not view health as a good capable of being allocated). But if this requires an open-ended commitment to the seriously, frequently incurably ill, we will be forced to rearrange our priorities in ways that may seem neither prudent nor just.[7]

If the right to health care is truly a basic human right, does it necessarily apply equally to everyone? To a demented ninety-year-old in need of dialysis as much as a nine-year-old? To those in one's own country only or to all of humanity? Or does the sheer difficulty of ranking classes of people as to their medical worthiness argue for a lottery system of selection (see Gorovitz, 1966, p. 7; Siemsen, 1978, p. 88; Childress, 1979, p. 138)?

And what of the health care providers? Society may be obligated to allocate sufficient resources for health care – whatever that means and however that is determined – but it is physicians and other health personnel who actually perform the work. Do they have rights – such as determining what tests and treatments to prescribe – that deserve protection, too (Sade, 1971)?

---

[6] This is not mere speculation; a 1982 poll found that fully 56% of Americans with "hardly any" health worries preferred "cheaper and limited" coverage, whereas only 37% preferred "full and expensive" coverage (Reinhold, 1982, p. D23).

[7] In line with this, Sen (1973, p. 16) maintains that utilitarianism would dictate that fewer resources be directed toward the disabled than the normal, who would gain greater utility from each additional increment (but cf. Brandt, 1979, pp. 319–29).

Fifth, the assertion of an unqualified right to health care represents a profoundly apolitical solution to a profoundly political problem. Politics, as the authoritative allocation of values in a society (Easton, 1953), entails a continual scramble among claimants for scarce resources. Denoting health care an unqualified right, however, places it outside the political process, assigning it sufficient – perhaps, in principle at least, unlimited – resources without compelling its advocates to battle with competing claimants. Secure from the ever fluctuating desires of others, dependent neither on their goodwill nor their self-interest, the individual can hunker down behind his acknowledged right and know peace. As a kind of ultimate political victory, in short, winning acceptance of health care as an unqualified right raises it above politics, where life is safe and the rewards better.[8]

But what, it might be objected, is wrong with this? Can any person of voting age have failed to notice that politics is disreputable, if not selfish, dishonest, and demeaning? Who now doubts that

> a politician is an arse upon
> which everyone has sat except a man.
>   (Cummings, 1955, p. 87)

To which the political scientist can retort only that stereotypes aside, politics cannot simply be banished like a party crasher by an upright butler; for politics derives not from the conduct of fools and knaves – though, of course, they can certainly make matters worse – but rather from the scarcity of resources and the incompatibility of

---

[8] Thus, politically, it is essential that the benefit be distributed as of right, rather than as an act of charity. The nature of the alleged obligation, however, is apt to strike many people as so indirect, abstract, or insubstantial, that it may not in fact appear to be a right. It would be clear to all, for example, that I have a right to expect you to keep your promise to me; the obligation is explicit and the connection is personal. Yet if I have ESRD, it may seem harder to assert exactly what I have a right to – to some kind to therapy (what kind, chosen by whom, according to what criteria)? to an income supplement to compensate me for the loss of my job? to life insurance to protect my family? – and exactly who has an obligation to provide it. The obligation, despite election oratory, seems far more implicit and the connection far more impersonal.

human purposes, and more durable bases for a social phenomenon would be hard to discover (Halper, 1981, ch. 1). To exempt any policy, even health policy, from this competition would be to exempt it from effective accountability as well.

Viewed from this angle, it may simply be naive to assert an unqualified right to health care. Given such a right, of course, demand for health care would increase rapidly and indefinitely, and soon call for massive reallocations from other goods and services. How much of this reallocation, though, would the public, the bureaucracy, the elected officials, and the representatives of non-health-care interests tolerate? After all, most of us view good health not as the goal of life but merely as a precondition of its full enjoyment. Indeed, when we are not ill or injured – and most of us are not – we may hardly think of it at all. Rather than giving health care a blank check, then, we may find ourselves assigning equal or even higher priority to other things, some of them foolish or maybe unhealthy things. To acknowledge this is not to denigrate the importance of health care or the intelligence of society, but merely to face facts.

In short, invoking a right to health care, calling for equality of treatment, or declaring a communitarian commitment are not much help in evaluating the United Kingdom's ESRD policy.

A QUALIFIED RIGHT TO HEALTH CARE?

For all these reasons, most persons who speak of an unqualified right to health care do so only as a rhetorical device with which they hope to increase health care's share of available resources. Rights talk, in other words, tends to be more advocacy than philosophy. This is not to deny the practical impact of such declarations. Clearly, they sound a deep communitarian chord to which many citizens reflexively respond. Further, the very act of asserting an unqualified right to health care congratulates its supporters on their compassion and social commitment, and thus may be indispensable for sustaining and energizing many of the foot soldiers in the battle for money.

When we turn from sloganeering to thought, however, we are more likely to encounter advocates of a second kind of right to health care: a qualified right. Usually, this is construed to refer to an

obligation on the part of society not to interfere *unreasonably* with the
individual's pursuit of health care and to provide a *reasonable* level
of that care when the individual demands it. Although it is often
accomplished only implicitly, the insertion of the "reasonable–
unreasonable" qualifier, of course, is the key.

The most ambitious advocates of the qualified-rights approach
probably are two American philosophers, Norman Daniels and
Allan Gibbard. Writing, broadly speaking, in the Rawlsian tradition,
Daniels develops a general theory of justice in health care allocation,
which is grounded in a still more general theory of distributive justice in society.

Health care, Daniels contends, is special because it can relieve
pain and discomfort, ward off premature death, and restore normal
functioning, so that the individual may have the opportunity to carry
out his life plan and achieve happiness. Ordinary inequalities in the
access to goods and services that are routinely tolerated in other contexts, therefore, ought not to be permitted in health care services
(Daniels, 1985, pp. 10–11, 27–8). Specifically, a person can be said
to have a right to health care if "impairment of normal functioning
through disease and disability restricts an individual's opportunity
relative to that portion of the normal range his skills and talents
would have made available to him were he healthy" (Daniels, 1985,
p. 34; cf. Miller, 1976, pp. 133–6; Rawls, 1982, p. 168). Under
health care needs, Daniels includes "adequate nutrition and shelter;
sanitary, safe, unpolluted living and working conditions; energy,
rest, and some other features of life style; preventive, curative, and
rehabilitative personal medical services; and non-medical personal
and social support services" (Daniels, 1985, p. 32).

Daniels's approach has the advantage of allowing for passage
through the life cycle and represents an effort to distinguish essential
from nonessential care. Also, in contrast to many writers who remain vague as to whether or to what extent the right to health care
should be limited, Daniels targets his arguments at exactly these
critical areas. Further, Daniels avoids the familiar trap of assuming
that health care is the chief determinant of health.

Yet it would seem that Daniels also provokes a number of questions. The first thing to note is that when he asserts that health care is

special, he is making an assertion not simply about conventional medical care, broadly or narrowly construed, but about a vast panoply of social welfare goods and services as well. Indeed, although rejecting the World Health Organization's definition of health as "an idealized level of well being" (Daniels, 1985, p. 29), his own list of societal obligations is so comprehensive that, as a practical matter, the official burden might be about the same under either rationale. And this is an extraordinarily heavy burden, so heavy that few if any societies would be fully able to meet it. In fact, the very weight of the burden raises many of the same questions raised by unqualified-rights plans – for example, what of the loss of freedom implicit in such a massive transfer of resources and duties to government? Can consumption take precedence over production, which must be logically and temporally prior? Ought virtually the entire domestic agenda to be removed from the political process?

There is also a question as to how special health care really is. Of course, every kind of activity is unique and, in that sense, special; it is only from a distance that the uninformed, as if gazing at a crowded stadium, fail to notice the uniqueness of individuals and see only an undifferentiated mass. The real question is whether health care, even as construed by Daniels to cover virtually the entire array of social welfare services, is sufficiently different from other activities to merit different treatment.

In a classic article, Arrow (1963) argued that health care is special by dint of the risk and uncertainty attaching to it; individuals do not know what health care they will need, when they will need it, what is available, and so forth – though they do know that the consequences of making a mistake may be disastrous. Whatever the merits of this view, however, it plainly does not apply to Daniels's presentation; for he does not confine himself to traditional health care needs, but includes items like nutrition and shelter, which are required on a continuing, predictable basis and do not raise the same issues of risk and uncertainty at all. In either case, however, it may well be that "what makes health care special . . . is that so many people, consumers and producers, believe that it *is* special" (Halper, 1987, p. 161).

Daniels's contention that health care is special is predicated on the connection of health care to the individual's maintaining his normal functioning as a member of the human species, species functioning to the individual's normal opportunity range, that range to implementing his life plan, and that plan to his sense of well-being. Health care institutions help protect individuals against serious infringements on their opportunities, and society, Daniels concludes, is obligated to guarantee individuals fair equality of opportunity to receive health care.

The texture of Daniels's discussion here is too rich and subtle to be conveyed by a synopsis. It does not denigrate his work, therefore, to note that it is simply not intended to settle, by itself, the host of specific trade-offs required in the implementation of any general allocative plan, even one meeting the broad requirements of justice as set forth in his theory. Its practical utility, to ESRD policy evaluation, therefore, is necessarily rather limited.

Gibbard, like Daniels, also rejects the unqualified-rights position, noting that "resources may be too scarce" and that "equity cannot require the impossible" or the "economically infeasible." Moreover, even leaving aside the element of scarcity, he notes, "there are ways of allocating economic burdens that are so onerous that it would be better, ethically speaking, for no one to receive certain kinds of life-saving treatment, than for the burdens to be imposed and for everyone to be assured of getting those treatments if in need of them." Further, he argues that the unqualified-rights position would in effect require everyone to insure himself against all health risks, even though this would strike some individuals as irrationally depriving them of the opportunity to spend their money in other ways (Gibbard, 1982, pp. 413, 414, 416, 418).

Instead, Gibbard believes that equity entails only a "decent minimum" level of health care, which the individual may supplement with insurance, if he so wishes. A decent minimum Gibbard defines as "those kinds of health care which it would be prudent for anyone, even at the decent economic miniumum, to insure himself for, if he could buy any package of health insurance he chose at its inclusive social cost." Although it is impossible to demarcate the boundaries of the concept precisely, Gibbard (1982) indicates that health care is sufficiently important for the individual's life prospects that the minimum coverage would be "extensive" and, unless obviously futile or "extraordinarily expensive," would include "all treatment that was advisable on purely medical grounds" (pp. 421, 422, 423).

Why, however, ought one to be *entitled* to this level of services? For one thing, Gibbard maintains, it follows from the presumption that everyone is entitled to a decent minimum of economic welfare in general, a presumption that would apply in the best economically feasible state. Second, it would be advantageous from a utilitarian point of view to transfer funds from high-income persons, who would spend their marginal income on less urgent needs, to low-income persons' health care, which is more urgent (Gibbard, 1982, pp. 421–2).

Gibbard acknowledges that this approach has certain practical problems. Requiring a decent minimum level of care lacks the robust simplicity of preserving life at all costs, which, however inadequate as an ethical rule, may well inspire health professionals to deliver better care (see Appelbaum and Klein, 1986). He also fears that the public would come to resent health professionals as playing God, for they would apply principles of vast importance without the benefit of clear standards that would permit accountability. Nor, Gibbard concedes, does he take into account the loss in the quality of interpersonal relationships that might ensue from the realization that society does not compel all desirable health care to be provided to those in need. Here, however, Gibbard observes commonsensically that "we should not feel that we owe each other efforts that it is irrational for anyone to secure for himself" (Gibbard, 1982, pp. 425–7).

Throughout, Gibbard writes with immense sensitivity, to both economic and noneconomic factors. Dismissive of conventional wisdom, he does not at all denigrate individuals who have not thought deeply about the problems he discusses; on the contrary, he is sympathetic to their limitations and anxieties, and strives to take their shortcomings into account. Gibbard, moreover, is also very realistic and well aware of the difficulties of formulating and applying specific ethical criteria.

Yet, perhaps unavoidably, Gibbard's analysis, like a strip of bacon white with fat, is streaked with questions. Is it really self-evident, as redistributionists have often claimed (e.g., Pigou, 1932, p. 89; Lerner, 1947, p. 29), that suppressing the evil of luxury can subsidize suppressing the evil of want? The assets of the wealthy by and large are not stored in mattresses or expended on caviar, but rather consist of productive capital that can be diverted to consumption only at a cost in productivity that may lower living standards generally. The utilitarian argument that the poor benefit more from marginal income, therefore, can be reversed to read that society may benefit more from the investments of the rich than the consumption of the poor. The chief winners in redistribution, therefore, are sometimes merely candidates who profit electorally or government officials, who devise, implement, and monitor the policies and keep a share of the resources for their trouble.

And what of "expensiveness"? In Gibbard's analysis, does it refer only to marginal costs, or are average costs included, too? The answer may help determine the size and nature of research and development commitments, an issue with great implications for health care. Can the phrase "purely medical grounds" be uttered as if it were an objective formula that applies itself and is therefore free of all human uncertainties, errors, and value judgments? And "prudent" may have an obvious meaning to one crossing a city street, but how useful is it to a healthy person addressing the remote and indeterminate risks that disease and injury might pose? In such a circumstance, it is hard to construct a prudent person analogous to the legal fiction of the tort law's reasonable man, for the requisite specifics are by definition absent. Thus, one finds oneself thinking in terms of risk-averse Rawlsians, fearing every harmful possibility, or adventuresome Nozickians, viewing uncertainty mostly in terms of opportunities. Obviously, these two personality types will be associated with radically different decisions as to how much current consumption or investment ought to be forgone in the name of insurance.

Nor does the question of what constitutes a decent minimum have a definitive answer; for as Gibbard admits, evaluations can be presumed to change as a consequence of relative economic prosperity, public opinion, and any number of factors. And not only are societal expectations as to decent minimums constantly undergoing transformation; in addition, the medical technology that helps maintain the flux is always leading policy makers into uncharted areas.

More basically, it is difficult to see how a vaguely qualified right would differ in practice from an ordinary claim; for viewed from a perspective that both Daniels and Gibbard would reject, all a qualified right asserts is that an individual is entitled to as much health care as the society by way of its policy makers decides it can afford.

A LIBERTARIAN DENIAL?

At the other pole may be found libertarians, like the eminent philosopher and physician H. Tristram Engelhardt, Jr., who view health care less as a social than as a personal concern. It is true, Engelhardt concedes, that ESRD patients have lost what he calls the natural lottery, in that their lives are in jeopardy through no fault of their own. And almost all such persons have also lost the social lottery, in that they lack the resources required to secure treatment. But though this is surely unfortunate, he acknowledges, it is not unfair, because society is not the cause of the difficulty. A society, therefore, may go far beyond its duty, as the United States does, but it should not be criticized if, like the United Kingdom, it takes a constricted view, for society is not obligated to pay to rectify a condition for which it was in no way responsible.

Underlying this is the belief that it is not only individuals like ESRD patients who may advance ethical claims for resources; for ethics is concerned not only with beneficence, but also with respecting the liberty of individuals "to determine the use of their private energies and resources." That is, other members of society are seen as having a right to dispose of the property they have legitimately acquired, a right that a free and pluralistic society is bound to respect, except for coercively obtaining the few resources needed to carry on a small class of so-called nightwatchman functions.[9]

---

[9] In this, Engelhardt recalls Nozick's (1974) by now famous argument that individuals can acquire property rights by their own efforts or by trading with those

From Engelhardt's viewpoint, therefore, two things are plain. First, if an ESRD patient goes untreated for want of money, money is not merely a bookkeeping abstraction in a government budget or a mass of paper and coins. Rather, money represents the wealth of a society, produced by generations of human effort and constituting a principal means by which the individual exercises liberty and creates his own destiny. Second, need may argue for charity but, impotent in the face of the individual's suzerainty over his own property, cannot argue for coerced, goverment-directed redistribution – not even in matters of life and death. Unlike Daniels's for example, Englehardt's approach admits of clear and specific applications to policy areas such as ESRD.

Of course, some people may believe that by thus enthroning private preferences, societal priorities become indefensibly disordered. Still, libertarians emphasize, individual choices must be respected and coercion minimized; "free societies are characterized by the commitment to live with the tragedies that result from the decision of free individuals not to participate in the beneficent endeavors of others" (Engelhardt, 1984). And so what Ignatieff, Daniels, Zaner, and others would surely take to be errors in priorities, according to Engelhardt must be accepted as an inescapable cost of maintaining a free society. The lesson would seem to be that individuals should insure themselves against such calamities, and if they are unable (or perhaps unwilling) to do so, private charity must be looked to for the resources; and if these prove insufficient, then, unhappily, some patients must die. The alternative would be coercively to take the property of innocent bystanders, to discourage individual responsibility, and to reduce the role of private giving.

Not surprisingly, many find this scenario unbearably harsh. An atomized world that maximizes individual freedom might prove wonderfully vigorous, productive, and creative. But losers in the struggle may suffer terribly, and even nonlosers may feel uncomfortably anxious, insecure, and guilty.

who have already acquired these rights, and that these rights are so extensive that they preclude the existence of redistributive "rights"; for it is the resources that these "rights" would coercively redistribute that the property rights guarantee against redistribution.

That the unfortunate would be able to rely on private, uncoerced charity, moreover, will strike many as the sheerest folly. One reason is that among many large donors, charity represents merely a selfish desire to reduce the donor's tax bill; in a "nightwatchman society," however, taxes would presumably be so low that this incentive for giving would be effectively eliminated. A second reason is that potential small donors must be persuaded that their gift will make a difference. On an individual basis, though, this is a patently false claim, and so organizations frequently deal with potential donors as a class. "If *everyone* were to give 10 pounds per year, ESRD treatments for all those in need would be guaranteed," I may be told; but because I know that in reality only a tiny fraction will give and I am unwilling to donate more than 10 pounds, I write off the whole effort as a lost cause. If, however, the 10 pounds were coercively taken from me and from all other taxpayers, I would know that sufficient funds would be collected to achieve the goal, and so I would readily submit. Paradoxically, then, it may be the very element of coercion that renders one a willing donor.

Finally, one cannot avoid feeling that Engelhardt's rigorously individualistic world view is inhospitable to the pervasive interdependence of individuals that communitarians would stress. One does not on one's own even become an ESRD patient; others must first have become physicians. Given this vast web of functional and ethical interdependence, most individuals have not been content with a state whose coercive powers run only to protection against force and fraud.

CAVEATS FOR THE DIFFERING APPROACHES

In evaluating debates on the right to health care, the prudent observer may wish to keep a few caveats in mind. First, it is not always clear to outsiders whether a system features an unqualified or a qualified right to health care. Americans, for example, having learned that the NHS provides health care to all Britons at little or no charge at the point of service, usually conclude that the United Kingdom guarantees an unqualified right to health care. As many ESRD patients know to their sorrow, this impression is quite false.

Second, inasmuch as no system, actual or reasonably proposed, offers a totally unqualified right to health care, it may not be particularly useful to conceive of unqualified and qualified rights as a dichotomy. Instead, they might better be thought of as poles on a continuum. Arguments against a purely unqualified right, therefore, are apt to seem like shots directed at a straw man.

Conceiving of the rights issue in continuum terms also clarifies part of the policy maker's problem by placing it in a directional context. After World War II, for example, when there was a broad consensus that Britons were receiving far too little health care, policy makers could talk loosely about the right to health care and simply provide more of it. After proceeding in this direction for forty years, however, the policy makers' situation has become much more difficult. By now, the question of where on the continuum the line ought to be drawn – that is, how much and what kinds of care a right to health care entails – has already become rather contentious.

Third, though it seems obvious *a priori* that an unqualified right to health care will seem more attractive to providers and consumers and a qualified right to those paying the bills, this, indeed, may not always be the case. This is true not simply because individuals may be activated by feelings other than material self-interest. Complicating the picture is the fact that many taxpayers view themselves or members of their families as potential providers or, more likely, consumers, and this potential role may sometimes seem more salient to them than their role as taxpayers.

Fourth, though we may be repelled by Wildean characters who know the price of everything and the value of nothing, talk of rights and reforms compels us to try to price values. How much, to re-ask a familiar question, is a life worth? Normally, what we really mean when we ask this question is, how much compensation should be due for wrongful loss of life or how much should be spent to safeguard it from a particular risk? The answers, of course, vary widely, there being no generally accepted formula for determining such matters.[10]

---

[10] Arguably, there is something useful about the prevailing confusion as to the dollar value of life, injury, or disease; for this very element of uncertainty makes it harder for government and business to look on individual calamities as a predictable cost of doing business and may induce a certain sense of caution.

Nor is it clear how much the individual values his own life. Some would observe that, in the last analysis, life is all we have, and so each of us normally can be expected to view our own irreplaceable life as priceless. As one economist put it, "Death is an awesome and indivisible event that goes but once to a customer in a single large size" (Schelling, 1984, p. 158). Others would reply that as individuals we take avoidable risks every day (consider the smoker, the jaywalker, the driver without a seatbelt), and as societies we routinely select policies that cost lives (whether deciding to build bridges, set highway speed limits, or fight wars). Indeed, insurance companies, airlines, courts, and government agencies assign financial values to life all the time. Nor is this only a recent practice. The ancient Babylonians in the Code of Hammurabi featured a complex compensation system for death, as did the Aztecs, the medieval English, and a number of other societies. And many nations and religions honor martyrs, who gave their lives in pursuit of what they – and often we – take to be a higher good. All this, however, may be obscured by "society's humanitarian self-image" (Blumstein, 1976, p. 233), which requires that life be described as sacred and that some victims of catastrophes be transformed by the media from unknown individuals to stereotypical symbols and be rescued at immense cost and great risk. (This is why a few "identifiable" lives invariably have a vastly more disproportionate call on public resources than a much larger number of "statistical" lives.)

The same kinds of pricing questions arise with injury and disease, and with far greater frequency.

In health care, these issues emerge most forcefully over expensive medical technology, such as that involved in dialysis and transplantation. When Massachusetts General Hospital declined to establish a heart transplantation program on the ground that it would not further "the greatest good for the greatest number" (Knox, 1980; Leaf, 1980), it was voicing a concern that some observers would apply to ESRD as well.

Fifth, it is probably naive to imagine that any set of rules can be devised that can mechanically be applied to almost everyone's satisfaction. The chief rationale for such rules is their simplicity and hence the ease of their administration. Such rules, that is, would have to be straightforward and be triggered by a very few quickly discoverable facts. Yet, as when age cutoffs were applied to ESRD patients, the procedure's very simplicity ensures a coarseness of decision making that leads to counterproductive results (i.e., screening out otherwise qualified candidates, who happen to be overage). Although rules reduce administrative discretion and encourage the perception of impersonal uniformity and predictability of treatment, they also fail to capture the true and complete purpose their authors intended. Rules have other shortcomings – they give those with a talent for rule manipulation an advantage, for instance – but it is their inescapable incapacity to operationalize their purpose fully that generates much of the dissatisfaction.

Broader rules, however – like the standard, "Select patients fairly" – suffer from a lethal vagueness and a lack of consensus as to the meaning of key terms. Subjectivity, arbitrariness, abuse – all that we associate with the old cliché about the rule of men and not law – are guaranteed.

In legal systems, the problems associated with simple and broad rules are amenable to substantial amelioration. Exceptions and qualifications to the simple rule become established; the details of the broader rule are filled in as it is applied in specific contexts. All this depends, however, upon formal adjudicative bodies, written justifications for decisions, the rule of precedent, a willingness to change slowly as if by the accretion of geological sediments, and so much more. No one suggests that such a system would be appropriate for medical decision making. And yet in the absence of *some* substitute structures and procedures, the problems of applying rules might receive little explicit, systematic attention, let alone relief.

Sixth, arguably, any discussion that confines itself to questions of rights and individual choices, whether of general public policy or individual patient selection, is too narrow to suffice. According to this view, the proper ethical unit for analysis is not the specific action but rather the entire life. Each person is capable of choosing to become any of a number of possible selves, it is said; these choices follow from specific decisions as to how to deal with the tasks, needs, and desires that arise in his life. As an authentic being, he understands his circumstances and the ethical consequences of his behavior; or as an inauthentic being, he merely follows the standard operating procedures set down by others. Language, whether medical jargon, bureaucratic circumlocutions, or moral platitudes, can mislead, desensitize, make the inauthentic appear more authoritative, and deflect the individual from self-mastery. Authentic personal existence, therefore, entails an unending struggle and thus can never take the form of mere submission to rules, even to rules widely supported by an ethical consensus. Hence, it is an error to conceive of morality as so many discrete decisions, whether made with a utilitarian view to the consequences or a deontological obediance to ethical laws. Compartmentalized discussions, like those on ESRD, are as doomed to failure as efforts to bail out only one end of a sinking boat.

SOME COMMENTS ON THE UNITED KINGDOM

If it is difficult to evaluate the United Kingdom's ESRD policy by relying on first principles (like a right to health care) or on general theories of justice in health care (like Daniels's or Gibbard's), at least it might be possible to examine the policy from a less rarified plane. Which is to ask: Are the United Kingdom's ESRD policies consistent with the general principles governing the NHS?

This, of course, is not an easy question to answer either. It is hard enough under the best circumstances to develop an explicit rationing system to deal with tragic choices, but when the bureaucracy, reflecting a long national tradition of reticence in public and even private life, raises secrecy and obfuscation to the level of *haut art,* the pursuit of general principles is apt to seem like a fool's errand.

Despite occasional brave talk about "generalizing the best health advice and treatment [with] no limitation on the kind of assistance given" (Bevan, in *Parliamentary Debates,* 1946, col. 45), few in Britain see this as anything other than a remote, perhaps even utopian end point or a politician's rhetorical flourish. Instead, there is a broad, practical consensus that the system should concentrate on providing the "services that most people use most of the time" (Abel-Smith, 1978, p. 19). Behind this lies a pair of uneasily coexisting convictions. One is the profound belief that the provision of health care is a social and not merely a personal problem. Society, it is felt, not only has an interest in combating infectious diseases, educating the public as to its own health needs, and safeguarding those unable to care for themselves; in addition, there is a social interest in restoring the ill to normal functioning so that they can help bear society's burdens and a social interest in maintaining a sense of fellow feeling and solidarity. "People want rights," Tawney (1972 [1913]) declared three-quarters of a century ago, "in order that they may perform duties" (p. 56). The other conviction is that Britain is a nation of limited resources and limited economic prospects. Hard choices must be made; value for money must be sought; frills must be forgone.

Although perhaps loosely tied to the rule-of-thumb utilitarianism that has dominated much of British policy thinking for generations, the health care consensus is far more a state of mind than a philosophy. What it offers is a sense of practical goals and constraints, and to problem solvers this is no small advantage. Even its most obvious weaknesses are useful to those charged with making the system work. Whereas critics might complain that the outlook commits the system to the perpetuation of existing treatment patterns, for example, bureaucrats are likely to find security and comfort in the status quo. By embracing the familiar, the "services for most people" approach justifies and fortifies long-standing incrementalism, and to officials who are overwhelmingly incrementalists, this can only seem a good thing.

Furthermore, the inescapable task of line drawing, which to qualified-rights philosophers poses such insuperable problems, is to the NHS policy maker operating within a broad consensus quite another matter. For him, to call for definitive answers to allocative problems is to ignore the positive values of ambiguity and tension in a society of interests competing for advantage. Put differently, to the policy maker the essential problem of line drawing may represent not so much an absence of intellectual clarity as a simple invitation to negotiate, compromise, and bargain. The political solutions that result will inevitably be filled with inconsistencies – such as the radical differences in ESRD treatment rates from one region in the

United Kingdom to another – but to a practical individual this is only an inescapable cost of doing business.

It is the political character of the "services for most people" position, then, that is its chief attraction, for it offers something both to rights and to marketplace advocates. To rights advocates, it is construed as a commitment that certain worst cases will not be permitted and reinforces a hope that in the future the minimum level will rise. To marketplace advocates, however, the "services for most people" position both allows those with the resources and the inclination to purchase greater than minimum care and guards against what they take to be an excessive public commitment. Thus, in the United Kingdom, health care rights emerge as less extensive than such political rights as the right to speak or vote or even such resource-consuming rights as the right to a grade-school education or to fire protection. At the same time – and this depends entirely upon where the line is drawn – the "services for most people" position can provide substantial protection for those incapable of meeting their own needs.

How well, then, does the United Kingdom's ESRD policy meet its own basic operating principle? Given the prevailing budgetary and bureaucratic constraints, the answer would seem to be: not all that badly. Of course, ESRD raises life-or-death issues, and this gives its claims special power and poignancy. And yet the NHS is less intimidated by death than are a number of other systems. That is, it does not shrink from the truth that death cannot be avoided nor from the corollary that it ought not to be delayed at all costs; for in British eyes, an American type of preoccupation with death necessarily slights other concerns and produces an indefensibly skewed allocation of resources. Thus, even more than its life-and-death character, ESRD's comparative rarity and the comparative costliness of its treatments are apt to strike British policy makers as decisive attributes. In a system committed to treating most people's needs, dialysis and transplantation can never fit comfortably. Thus, whereas some ESRD advocates may view a radical extension of services as a policy required by the NHS's humanitarian mission, many will grant ESRD treatment only a rather low priority: Not only are these therapies not services that most people use most of the time; they also are so costly that they can be provided only if some of the more common services go unprovided.

A NOTE ON PROCEDURAL RIGHTS

In the real world of the United Kingdom, neither rights talk nor libertarianism has carried the day. In their place is a pattern of patient selection that varies enormously from place to place and from physician to physician. What this suggests is that more central than the question of a substantive right to treatment may be the question of a procedural right to be fairly considered for treatment.

In other words, quite irrespective of questions as to the justice of actual ESRD treatment decisions, questions arise as to the justice of the prevailing UK decision-making process, which employs vague and shifting criteria, makes no effort to enforce consistency, and gives little opportunity for influence to those whose very lives are at stake. Compounding all this, the system hides itself from public view, so that its workings remain almost totally unknown to all outsiders, who are thus denied even the chance to know what has transpired, let alone the opportunity to try to change things.

If the queries come easily, however, the answers do not. For it is much easier to specify what a decision-making process should not be than what it should be and to neglect intractable problems of implementation as if they were too vulgar to merit serious discussion. Thus, theoretical arguments for explicit rationing that ignore the so far insuperable problems of applying it to tragic choices run the risk of being dismissed as irrelevant. No thoughtful observer, in short, can proceed with certitude.

It is a hopeful sign, therefore, that UK physicians and others have finally begun to examine the selection process (e.g., Challah et al., 1984). It would be reckless to predict what further examination might reveal or what operational changes might be advanced, though the final resolution will presumably reflect the unique British values, traditions, and practices. Given the widespread dissatisfaction with the selection process among those with the greatest expertise and experience, however, it would be more reckless still to pretend that no further examination is necessary. Indeed, given the stakes, a refusal to examine current options is really no option at all.

Meanwhile, working in an environment of scarcity, eager to retain their position, and nourished intellectually by a long utilitarian tradition of balancing interests, UK policy makers recoil from theoretical rhetoric as a child would from a dead mouse in a dustpan. Partially, this can be accounted for by a natural aversion to a way of thought that would reduce their own flexibility and discretion – in a word, power – on entirely abstract grounds. More important, rights talk is disabled by its fundamental indifference to resource constraints, and libertarianism by its disdain for bureaucracy per se.

Instead, policy makers tend to think in terms of interests. There are never enough resources to treat or to seek aggressively the cure for every malady, they know; there are always more potentially beneficial claims (and claimants) than can be met at any realistic level of health care funding; thus, some interests will be allocated more resources, others less or none, and nearly all will be dissatisfied with what they receive.

Again, must some ESRD patients die so that the United Kingdom can live within its means? Clearly, other advanced industrialized nations have offered different answers, and it is tempting to conclude that they cannot all be wrong and the United Kingdom right – particularly when the United Kingdom is proclaiming by word and deed its determination to move in their direction.

One answer, of course, is that it is, indeed, quite possible that the consensus supporting broad ESRD treatment patterns is mistaken. The pertinent policy decisions, after all, need not have followed serious ethical thought and analysis, but rather have been expedient responses to short-term political pressures that now carry consequences that were unforeseen at the time. Certainly, for example, Congress's perfunctory approval of including ESRD under Medicare revealed no hint that advocates saw the annual cost climbing to 2 billion dollars in fifteen years.

More fundamentally, however, barring the imposition of a rigid priority ranking that would place health care first, policy makers would be forced to admit: Perhaps ESRD patients need not be left to perish, but some sizable number of treatable patients afflicted with other diseases probably would have to be ignored. Even in America, it has become commonplace to read that "we are rapidly approaching an economic threshold that will inherently limit the development and diffusion of new methods of treatment" (Evans et al., 1986, p. 1896); the United Kingdom presumably passed this threshold years earlier. It is easy to deplore this conclusion and to argue for a health-care-dominated priority system, of course, but a free people, mostly healthy and given to focusing on the near term, has never supported such a system. Nor does it seem likely to change its mind.

LAST WORDS

And so the familiar debate between rights and interests grinds on. But the words cannot erase the image of a treatable ESRD patient drifting inevitably toward death or cancel the indelible realization that there, but for the grace of God, go us all. The easiest misfortunes to bear are surely the misfortunes of others.

References

Aaron, H. J., and Schwartz, W. B. 1984. *The Painful Prescription.* Washington, D.C.: Brookings Institution.

Abel-Smith, B. 1978. Minimum adequate levels of personal health care: History and justification. *Milbank Memorial Fund Quarterly* 56: 7–21.

Abram, H. S. 1972. The psychiatrist: The treatment of chronic renal failure and the prolongation of life, III. *American Journal of Psychiatry* 128: 1534–9.

Abram, H. S., and Wadlington, W. 1968. Selection of patients for artificial and transplanted organs. *Annals of Internal Medicine* 69: 615–20.

Acchiardo, S. R., Moore, L. W., and Cockrell, S. 1986. Does low protein diet halt the progression of renal insufficiency? *Clinical Nephrology* 25: 289–94.

Alexander, S. 1962. They decide who lives, who dies: Medical miracle puts a moral burden on a small community. *Life,* Nov. 6, pp. 102–25.

Alford, R. R. 1975. *Health Care Politics: Ideology and Interest Group Barriers to Reform.* University of Chicago Press.

Allen, D., Hartley, M., and Makinson, G. T. 1987. Performance indicators in in the National Health Service. *Social Policy and Administration* 21: 70–84.

Almeder, R. F. 1979. The role of moral considerations in reallocation of exotic medical life saving therapy. In J. M. Humer and R. F. Almeder, eds., *Biomedical Ethics and the Law,* 543–55. New York: Plenum Press.

Anderson, D. 1985. Life and death: An inescapable choice. London *Times,* July 30, p. 10, col. 6.

Anderson, J. L., Parson, F. M., and Jones, I. E., eds., 1978. *Living with Renal Failure.* Lancaster: MTP Press.

Annas, G. J. 1988. The paradoxes of organ procurement. *American Journal of Public Health* 78: 621–2.

Appelbaum, P. S., and Klein, J. 1986. Therefore choose death? *Commentary* 81 (April): 23–29.

Arrow, K. 1963. Uncertainty and the welfare economics of medical care. *American Economic Review* 53: 41–73.

Avorn, J. 1984. Benefit and cost analysis in geriatric care: Turning age discrimination into health policy. *New England Journal of Medicine* 310: 1294–1301.

Bachrach, P., and Baratz, M. 1963. Decisions and nondecisions: An analytical framework. *American Political Science Review* 57: 634–42.

Baillod, R. A., Comty, C., Ilahi, M., Konotey-Ahulu, F. I. D., Sevitt, L., and Shaldon, S. 1965. Overnight haemodialysis in the home. In D. N. S. Kerr, ed., *Proceedings of the European Dialysis and Transplant Association, II,* 99–103. Amsterdam: Excerpta Medica.

Baldamus, C. A. 1983. Clinical value and technical feasibility of long-term hemofiltration. *Asaio Journal* 6: 192–6.

Banting, K. 1979. *Poverty, Politics and Policy.* London: Macmillan Press.

Barker, E. 1938. *The Citizen's Choice.* Cambridge University Press.

Basson, M. D. 1979. Choosing among candidates for scarce medical resources. *Journal of Medicine and Philosophy* 4: 313–33.

Baumol, W. I. 1986. *Superfairness: Applications and Theory.* Cambridge, Mass.: MIT Press.

Bayliss, R. 1988. Second opinions. *Lancet* 1: 808–9.

Beauchamp, T. L. 1979. Can we stop or withhold dialysis? *Controversies in Nephrology* 1: 163–70.

   1978. The allocation of scarce medical resources. In T. L. Beauchamp and L. Walters, eds., *Contemporary Issues in Bioethics,*   – . Belmont, Calif.: Dickenson.

Beauchamp, T. L., and Childress, J. F. 1983. *Principles of Biomedical Ethics,* 2d ed. New York: Oxford University Press.

Beer, S. H. 1982a. *Britain against Itself: The Political Contradictions of Collectivism.* London: Faber & Faber.

   1982b. *British Politics in the Collectivist Age.* New York: Knopf.

   1956. Pressure groups and parties in Britain. *American Political Science Review* 50: 1–23.

Beesley, M. E. 1985. Management and the health district. *Social Policy and Administration* 19: 145–53.

Bendixen, H. H. 1977. The cost of intensive care. In J. P. Bunker, R. A. Barnes, and F. Mosteller, eds., *Costs, Risks and Benefits of Surgery,* 372–84. New York: Oxford University Press.

Bennett, G. 1979. *Patients and Their Doctors.* London: Ballière Tyndall.

Bennett, S. E., Russell, G. I., and Walls, J. 1983. Low protein diets in uraemia. *British Medical Journal* 287: 1344–5.

Berger, P. S., Albert, B. E., and Longnecker, R. E. 1983. Dialysis therapy for diabetics. *Diabetic Nephropathy* 2 (Feb.): 22–5.

Berkman, L. F., and Breslow, D. 1983. *Health and Ways of Living.* New York: Oxford University Press.

Berlyne, G. M. 1982. Over 50 and uremic equals death. *Nephron* 31: 189–90.

Best, G., Dennis, J., and Draper, P. 1977. *Health, the Mass Media and the National Health Service.* London: Guy's Hospital, Unit for the Study of Health Policy, Department of Community Medicine.

Bevan, G., et al. 1980. *Health Care Priorities and Management.* London: Croom Helm.

Blagg, C. R., and Scribner, B. H. 1976. Dialysis: Medical, psychosocial, and economic problems universal to the dialysis patient. In B. M. Brenner and F. C. Rector, eds., *The Kidney,* 2 vols., 1: 1705–44. Philadelphia: Saunders.

Blumstein, J. F. 1976. Constitutional perspectives on governmental decisions affecting human life and health. *Law and Contemporary Problems* 40:231–305.

Bok, D., and Levin, N. W. 1982. Can we do without dialysis re-use? *International Journal of Artificial Organs* 5: 4–5.

Bok, S. 1984. *Secrets: On the Ethics of Concealment and Revelation.* New York: Oxford University Press.

Borel, J. F. 1976. Comparative study of in vitro and in vivo drug effects on cell-mediated cytotoxicity. *Immunology* 31: 631–41.

Borel, J. F., Feurer, C., Gubler, H. U., and Stähelin, H. 1976. Biological effects of cyclosporine A: A new anti-lymphocytic agent. *Agents Actions* 6: 468–75.

Borel, J. F., Feurer, C., Magnée, C., and Stähelin, H. 1977. Effects of the new anti-lymphocytic peptide cyclosporine A in animals. *Immunology* 32: 1017–25.

Brahams, D. 1987. An attempt to remedy through the courts a lack of NHS funding. *Lancet* 2: 1342–3.

1984. Enforcing a duty to care for patients in the NHS. *Lancet* 2: 1224–5.

Branch, R. A., Clark, G. W., Cochrane, A. L., Jones, J. H., and Scarborough, H. 1971. Incidence of uraemia and requirements for maintenance dialysis. *British Medical Journal* 1: 249–54.

Brandt, R. 1979. *A Theory of the Right and the Good.* Oxford: Clarendon Press.

Braybrooke, D. 1968. Let needs diminish that preferences may prosper. In *Studies in Moral Philosophy,* American Philosophical Quarterly Monograph Series, No. 1. Oxford: Blackwell Publisher.

Brescia, N. J., Cimino, J. E., Appel, M. D., and Hurwich, B. J. 1966. Chronic hemodialysis using venopuncture and a surgically created arteriovenous fistula. *New England Journal of Medicine* 275: 1089–92.

Brett, A. S., and McCullough, L. B. 1986. When patients request specific interventions. *New England Journal of Medicine* 315: 134–51.

British Medical Journal. 1981. 283: 261–2.

    1978. 2: 1449–59.

Bryan, F. A., Jr. 1981. The patient and the family in home dialysis. *Controversies in Nephrology* 3: 406–25.

Brynger, H., Persson, H., and Blohmé, I. 1986. Renal transplantation in elderly patients. *Transplantation Proceedings* 18: 12–13 (suppl. 3).

Bulpitt, J. 1983. *Territory and Power in the United Kingdom.* Manchester University Press.

Butcher, A. 1982. Doctors slam life-or-death cash squeeze. Birmingham *Post,* Nov. 6, p. 3, col. 2.

Butts, M., Irving, D., and Whitt, C. 1981. *From Principles to Practice.* London: Nuffield Provincial Hospitals Trust.

Calabresi, G., and Bobbitt, P. 1978. *Tragic Choices.* New York: Norton.

Calne, R. Y., et al. 1978. Cyclosporine A in patients receiving renal allografts from cadaver donors. *Lancet* 2: 1323–7.

Calne, R. Y., et al. 1981. Cyclosporine A in cadaveric organ transplantation. *British Medical Journal* 282: 934–6.

Calne, R. Y., et al. 1979. Cyclosporine A initially as the only immunosuppressant in 34 recipients of cadaveric organs. *Lancet* 2: 1033–6.

Camenisch, P. F. 1979. The right to health care: A contractual approach. *Soundings* 62: 293–310.

Cameron, J. S. 1983a. The management of diabetic renal failure in the United Kingdom. *Diabetic Nephropathy* 2 (May): 1–2.

    1983b. Cost no object in NHS budget. London *Times,* Oct. 24, p. 15, col. 5.

Cameron, J. S., and Challah, S. 1986. Treatment of end stage renal failure due to diabetes in the United Kingdom, 1975–84. *Lancet* 2: 962–6.

Cameron, J. S., Chantler, C., Haycock, G., Ogg, C. S., and Williams, D. G. 1981. Audit in renal failure. *British Medical Journal* 283: 555.

Campbell, J. D., and Campbell, A. R. 1978. The social and economic costs of end-stage renal disease. *New England Journal of Medicine* 289: 386–92.

Canadian Multicentre Transplant Study Group. 1986. A randomized clinical trial of cyclosporine in cadaveric renal transplantation: Analysis of three years. *New England Journal of Medicine* 314: 1219–25.

1983. A randomized clinical trial of cyclosporine in cadaveric renal transplantation. *New England Journal of Medicine* 309: 809–15.

Capelli, J. P., Camiscioli, T. C., Vallorani, D. O., and Bobeck, J. D. 1985. Comparative analysis of survival on home hemodialysis, in-center hemodialysis and chronic peritoneal dialysis (CAPD–IPD) therapies. *Dialysis and Transplantation* 14: 38–52.

Caplan, A. L. 1984. Dialyzers: To reuse or not to reuse, ethics is the question. *American Journal of Nephrology* 4: 128–31.

Carpenter, C. B., and Strom, T. B. 1982. Transplantation: Immunogenetic and clinical aspects – part I. *Hospital Practice* 17: 125–34.

Cartwright, A., and Anderson, R. 1981. *General Practice Revisited: A Second Study of Patients and Their Doctors.* London: Tavistock.

Castle, B. 1980. *The Castle Diaries.* London: Weidenfeld.

Cattell, W. R. 1979. Men, money or machine. *Journal of Medical Engineering and Technology* 3: 1–3.

1978. The status of haemodialysis. In J. L. Anderson, F. M. Parson, and E. D. Jones, eds., *Living with Renal Failure,* 21–32. Lancaster: MTP Press.

Challah, S., Wing, A. J., Bauer, R., Morris, R. W., and Schroeder, S. A. 1984. Negative selection of patients for dialysis and transplantation in the United Kingdom. *British Medical Journal* 288: 1119–22.

Challenger-Gumbs, E. 1985. Overcoming ethnic barriers. *Nursing Mirror,* July 31, pp. 42–3.

Chaplin, N. W. 1982. *Health Care in the United Kingdom.* London: Kluwer Medical.

Chapman, L. 1978. *Your Disobedient Servent.* London: Chatto & Windus.

Chester, A. C., Rakowski, T. A., Argy, W. P., Giacalone, A., and Schreiner, G. E. 1979. Hemodialysis in the eighth and ninth decades of life. *Archives of Internal Medicine* 139: 1001–5.

Childress, J. F. 1981. *Priorities in Medical Ethics.* Philadelphia: Westminster Press.

1979. A right to health care? *Journal of Medicine and Philosophy* 4: 132–47.

Clunie, G. J. A., Hartley, L. C. J., and Morgan, T. O. 1970. Ethics and experimentation. *Lancet* 2: 39.

Committee of Inquiry into Normansfield Hospital. 1978. *Report,* Cmnd. 7537. London: HMSO.

Controversies in Nephrology. 1979. 1: 123–35.

Cook, R. 1983. Owing to pressure of space . . . London *Times,* Dec. 5, p. 12, col. 6.

Cooper, M. H. 1977. *Rationing Health Care.* London: Croom Helm.

Council for Science and Society. 1982. *Expensive Medical Techniques: Report for a Working Party.* London: Council for Science and Society.

Crosby, D. L., and Jones, J. H. 1970. Regular haemodialysis and renal transplantation. *Lancet* 2: 574–5.

Crossman, R. 1975. *Diaries of a Cabinet Minister.* London: Hamilton.
    1972. *A Politician's View of Health Service Planning.* University of Glasgow Press.

Cummings, E. E. 1955. *100 Selected Poems.* New York: Grove Press.

Czaczkes, J. W., and Kaplan De-Nour, A. 1978. *Chronic Hemodialysis as a Way of Life.* New York: Brunner/Mazel.

Dagger, R. 1985. Rights, boundaries, and the bonds of community: A qualified defense of moral parochialism. *American Political Science Review* 79: 436–47.

Dahl, R. A., and Lindblom, C. A. 1953. *Politics, Economics, and Welfare.* New York: Harper & Row.

Daniels, N. 1985. *Just Health Care.* Cambridge University Press.

Davenport, S. 1986. Fearless champion of a dying cause. *Yorkshire Post,* May 21, p. 3, col. 3.

Davies, P. 1985. London's hospitals: No more fat to trim? *Health and Social Services Journal* 94: 608–9.

Davison, A. M., Read, D. J., and Lewins, A. M. 1984. Underutilized hospital haemodialysis resources. *Lancet* 1: 723–5.

Deber, R. B., Blidner, I. N., Carr, L. M., and Barnsley, J. M. 1985. The impact of selected patient characteristics on practitioners' treatment recommendations for end-stage renal disease. *Medical Care* 23: 95–109.

Delano, B. G., Lundin, A. P., and Friedman, E. A. 1982. Success of home hemodialysis in purportedly unacceptable patients. *Nephron* 31: 191–3.

Dempster, M. A. H., and Wildavsky, A. 1979. On change: Or, there is no magic size for an increment. *Political Studies* 27: 371–89.

Dennis, C. W. 1971. Regular hemodialysis and renal transplantation. In G. McLachlan, ed., *Portfolio for Health: The Role and Program of the DHSS in Health Services Research,* 143–7. London: Oxford University Press for the Nuffield Provinicial Hospitals Trust.

Department of Health and Social Security. 1976a. *National Health Service Planning System.* London: HMSO.

1976b. *Prevention and Health: Everybody's Business.* London: HMSO.

1976c. *Priorities for the Health and Personal Social Services in England.* London: DHSS.

1975. *First Interim Report of the Resources Allocation Working Party.* London: HMSO.

1972. *Hepatitis and the Treatment of Chronic Renal Failure: Report of the Advisory Group, 1970–1972.* London: DHSS.

Department of Health and Social Security, NHS Management Inquiry Team. 1983. *Recommendations on the Effective Use of Manpower and Related Resources.* London: DHSS.

de Wardener, H. E. 1966. Some ethical and economic problems associated with intermittent haemodialysis. In G. E. W. Wolstenholme and M. O' Connor, eds., *Ethics and Medical Progress: With Special Reference to Transplantation,* 104–18. London: Churchill.

Dialysis and Transplantation. 1986. 15: 300–5, 348–56.

Dick, D. 1983. How long can NHS ignore quality control? *Health and Social Services Journal,* July 28, pp. 898–9.

Donadio, J. V., et al. 1984. Membranoproliferative glomerulonephritis: A prospective clinical trial of platelet-inhibitor therapy. *New England Journal of Medicine* 310: 1421–6.

Douglas, J. F. 1985. Renal failure and the law. *Lancet* 1: 1318–21.

Downie, R. S. 1986. Professional ethics. *Journal of Medical Ethics* 12: 64–5.

Downs, A. 1967. *Inside Bureaucracy.* Boston: Little, Brown.

Drewry, G., ed. 1985. *The New Select Committees: A Study of the 1979 Reforms.* Oxford University Press.

Dror, Y. 1968. *Public Policy Reexamined.* San Francisco: Chandler.

Durenberger, D. 1985. Remarks. *Congressional Record,* Nov. 14, p. S15455 (daily ed.).

Dworkin, R. 1985. *A Matter of Principle.* Cambridge, Mass.: Harvard University Press.

Easton, D. 1953. *The Political System: An Inquiry into the State of Political Science.* New York: Knopf.

Eckstein, H. 1960. *Pressure Group Politics: The Case of the British Medical Association.* London: Allen & Unwin.

1958. *The English Health Service: Its Origins, Structure, and Achievements.* Cambridge, Mass.: Harvard University Press.

Eddy, D. M. 1982. Clinical policies and the quality of clinical practice. *New England Journal of Medicine* 307: 343–7.

Edwards, B. 1984. A picture of health. London *Times,* May 7, p. 12, col. 2.

Eggers, P. W., Connerton, R., and McMullan, M. 1984. The Medicare experience with end-stage renal disease: Trends in incidence, prevalance, and survival. *Health Care Financing Review* 5: 69–88.

——— 1979. Sociological influences on decision-making by clinicians. *Annals of Internal Medicine* 90: 957–64.

Eisenberg, J. M. 1979. Sociological influences on decision-making by clinicians. *Annals of Internal Medicine* 90: 957–64.

Elcock, H. 1979. *Strategic Planning Process in Regional and Local Government.* Hull Papers in Politics, University of Hull, February.

——— 1978. Regional government in action: The members of two regional health authorities. *Public Administration* 56: 379–97.

Elcock, H., and Haywood, S. 1980. *The Buck Stops Where? Accountability and Control in the National Health Service.* Hull, England: University of Hull, Institute for Health Services.

Elder v. *Beal.* 1979. 609 F.2d 695 (3d cir.).

Elian, M., and Dean, G. 1985. To tell or not to tell the diagnosis of multiple sclerosis. *Lancet* 2: 27–8.

Eliot, T. S. 1958. Burnt Norton. In *The Complete Poems and Plays, 1901–1950.* New York: Harcourt, Brace.

Engelhardt, H. T., Jr. 1984. Shattuck Lecture: Allocating scarce medical resources and the availability of organ transplantation. *New England Journal of Medicine* 311: 66–71.

*Eurostat Demographic Statistics.*1984. Luxembourg: Statistical Office of the European Communities.

Evans, R. W., et al. 1985. The quality of life of patients with end-stage renal disease. *New England Journal of Medicine* 312: 553–9.

Evans, R. W., Manninen, D. L., Garrison, L. P., and Maier, A. M. 1986. Donor availability as the primal determinant of the future of heart transplantation. *Journal of the American Medical Association* 255: 1892–8.

Faculty of Community Medicine of the Royal College of Physicians. 1986. *Health for All by the Year 2000: Charter for Action.* London: Faculty of Community Medicine.

Farmer, C. V., Snowden, A., and Parsons, V. 1979. The prevalence of psychiatric illness among patients on home dialysis. *Psychological Medicine* 9: 509–14.

Ferraro, K. F., Dixon, R. D., and Kinlaw, B. J. R. 1986. Measuring compliance among in-center hemodialysis patients. *Dialysis and Transplantation* 15: 226–36, 266.

Ferriman, A. 1982a. Child kidney victims "go untreated and die." London *Times,* Jan. 15, p. 3, col. 7.

1982b. Step back in kidney treatment. London *Times,* Jan. 29, p. 3, col. 1.

1980. 1000 kidney patients die "because treatment unavailable." London *Times,* Mar. 20, p. 4, col. 1.

Festenstein, H., Doyle, P., and Holmes, J. 1986. Long-term follow-up in London transplant group recipients of cadaver renal allografts. *New England Journal of Medicine* 314: 7–14.

Fischbach, M., Attal, Y., and Geisart, J. 1984. Hemodiafiltration versus hemofiltration in children. *International Journal of Pediatric Nephrology* 5: 151–4.

Fitzgerald, R. 1988. Must every Britain suffer the "British disease"? A note on the inevitability of instituational sclerosis. Unpublished manuscript, Department of Political Science, State University of New York at Buffalo.

Fletcher, J. N. D. n.d. *The Greatest Good of the Greatest Number: A New Frontier in the Morality of Medical Care,* Sanger Lecture No. 7. Richmond: Medical College of Virginia, Virginia Commonwealth University.

Fox, R. C. 1975. Long-term dialysis. *American Journal of Medicine* 59: 702–12.

Fox, R. C., and Swazey, J. P. 1974. *The Courage to Fail.* University of Chicago Press.

Fried, C. 1975a. Rights and health care: Beyond equity and efficiency. *New England Journal of Medicine* 293: 241–5.

1975b. Equality and rights in medical care. *Hastings Center Report* 5 (Feb.): 29–34.

Friend, R., Singleterry, Y., Mendell, N. R., Nurse, H. 1986. Group participation and survival among patients with end-stage renal disease. *American Journal of Public Health* 76: 670–2.

Frocht, A., and Fillet, H. 1984. Renal Disease in the geriatric patient. *Journal of the American Geriatric Society* 32: 28–43.

Gabriel, R. 1983. Chronic renal failure in the UK: Referral, funding and staffing. In F. M. Parson and C. S. Ogg, eds., *Renal Failure: Who Cares?* 35–40. Lancaster: MTP Press.

Galbraith, J. K. 1958. *The Affluent Society.* Boston: Houghton Mifflin.

Gallup. 1985. *Political Index No. 293.* London: Gallup Poll, Jan.

Garcia-Garcia, G., et al. 1985. Results of treatment in patients with end-stage renal disease: A multivariate analysis of risk factors and survival in 341 successive patients. *American Journal of Kidney Diseases* 5: 10–18.

Gathorne-Hardy, J. 1984. *Doctors: The Lives and Work of GPs.* London: Weidenfeld & Nicolson.

Gaze, H. 1985. The unequal equation. *Nursing Times,* Feb. 13, pp. 16–17.

General Accounting Office. 1986. *Comments on HHS Proposal to Revise End Stage Renal Disease Facility Payment Rates.* GAO/HRD-86-126BR, July.

1985. *Changes Needed in Medicare Payments to Physicians under the End-Stage Renal Disease Program,* GAO/HRD-85-14, Feb. 1.

General Medical Council, 1987. *Professional Conduct and Discipline: Fitness to Practise.* London: General Medical Council.

Gentry, W. D., and Davis, G. C. 1972. Cross sectional analysis of psychological adaptation to chronic hemodialysis. *Journal of Chronic Diseases* 25: 545–50.

George, C. R. P. 1983. Feasibility of home haemodialysis with simplified techniques. *Lancet* 2: 285–97.

Gibbard, A. 1982. The prospective Pareto principle and its application to questions of equity of access to health care: A philosophical examination. *Milbank Memorial Fund Quarterly* 60: 399–428.

Giles, G., and Davison, A. 1985. Are renal services efficient? *Health and Social Services Journal* 94: 546–8.

Gillie, O. 1983. Call to doctors to boycott kidney cuts. London *Sunday Times,* Oct. 16, p. 2, col. 4.

Giordano, C. 1982. Protein restriction in chronic renal failure. *Kidney International* 1982: 401–8.

Giovanetti, S. 1986. Answers to ten questions on the dietary treatment of chronic renal failure. *Lancet* 2: 1140–2.

Glassman, B. M., and Siegal, A. 1970. Personality correlates of survival in a long term hemodialysis program. *Archives of General Psychiatry* 22: 566–74.

Glover, J. A. 1938. The incidence of tonsillectomy in school children. *Proceedings of the Royal Society of Medicine* 31: 1219–36.

Godber, G. 1982. The British health system: Achievements and limitations. *Israeli Journal of Medical Science* 18: 365–73.

1975. *Change in Medicine.* London: Nuffield Provincial Hospitals Trust.

1968. Intermittent haemodialysis in the home. Letter of Chief Medical Officer to General Practitioners, April.

Goodin, R. E. 1985. Vulnerabilities and responsibilities: An ethical defense of the welfare state. *American Political Science Review* 79: 774–87.

Gorovitz, S. 1966. Ethics and the allocation of medical resources. *Medical Research in Engineering* 5: 5–7.

Graham, N. G., Dombal, F. T., and Goligher, J. C. 1971. Reliability of physical signs in patients with severe attacks of ulcerative colitis. *British Medical Journal* 2: 746–8.

Gray, A. 1984. NHS: Less real growth. *Public Money* 3 (June): 39.

Greenberg, D. S. 1978. Washington report: Renal politics. *New England Journal of Medicine* 298: 1427–8.

Greenfield, S., Blanco, D. M., Elashoff, R. M., and Ganz, P. A. 1987. Patterns of care related to age of breast cancer patients. *Journal of the American Medical Association* 257: 2766–70.

Grimes, D. S., and Allen, D. 1985. Griffiths and professionalism. *British Medical Journal* 290: 1367–8.

Grist, L. 1981. Are some doctors pulling the plug? *General Practitioner,* Oct. 16, p. 73.

Gruson, L. 1985a. Some doctors move to bar transplants to foreign patients. *New York Times,* Aug. 10, p. 1, col. 4.

1985b. Center for transplants aids Pittsburgh ascent. *New York Times,* Sept. 16, p. A10, col. 2.

Guillebaud, C. W. 1956. *Report of the Committee of Enquiry into the Cost of the National Health Service* Cmnd. 9663. London: HMSO.

Haas, T., Dongradi, G., Villeboeuf, F., deVeil, E., Verrier, J., and Hillion, D. 1985. Technical and clinical data on high-performance hemofiltration: Twelve patients during one year. *Artificial Organs* 9: 164–8.

Halper, T. 1987. DRGs and the idea of a just price. *Journal of Medicine and Philosophy* 12: 155–64.

1985. End-stage renal failure and the aged in the United Kingdom. *International Journal of Technology Assessment in Health Care* 1: 41–52.

1981. *Power, Politics, and American Democracy.* Glencoe: Scott, Foresman.

1980. The double-edged sword: Paternalism as a policy in the problems of aging. *Milbank Memorial Fund Quarterly* 58: 472–99.

1973. The new "deserving poor" and the old. *Polity* 6: 71–86.

Ham, C. 1982. *Health Policy in Britain: The Politics and Organization of the National Health Service.* London: Macmillan Press.

Hamilton, A. 1985. Extra funds for liver transplants. London *Times,* Jan. 30, p. 2, col. 4.

Hamilton, D. N. H., and Briggs, J. D. 1978. Current status of renal transplantation. In J. L. Anderson, F. M. Parson, and D. E. Jones, eds., *Living With Renal Failure,* 33–45, Lancaster: MTP Press.

Hampers, C. L., Schupak, E., Lowrie, E. G., and Lazarus, J. M. 1973. *Long-Term Hemodialysis: The Management of the Patient with Chronic Renal Failure,* 2d ed. New York: Grune & Stratton.

Hampton, J. R. 1983. The end of clinical freedom. *British Medical Journal* 287: 1237–8.

Harding, J. 1982. *New kidney patients are turned away.* Bristol Evening Post, Nov. 5, p. 3, col. 7.

Harris v. McRae. 1980. 448 U.S. 297.

Hart, V. 1978. *Distrust and Democracy: Political Distrust in Britain and America.* Cambridge University Press.

Hartwig, R. E. 1987. The paradox of malevolent/benevolent bureaucracy. Paper presented at the annual convention of the Georgia Political Science Association, Savannah, Ga.

Haywood, S., and Hunter, D. J. 1982. Consultative processes in health policy in the United Kingdom: A view from the centre. *Public Administration* 60: 145–62.

Health Care Financing Administration. 1987. *Medical Coverage of Kidney Dialysis and Kidney Transplant Services.* Washington, D. C.: Department of Health and Health Services.

Heclo, H. 1972. Review article: Policy analysis. *British Journal of Political Science* 2: 83–108.

Heinz, J. 1986. Disposable dialysis devices: Is reuse abuse? *Dialysis and Transplantation* 15: 447.

Held, P. J., Pauly, M. V., and Diamond, L. 1987. Survival analysis of patients undergoing dialysis. *Journal of the American Medical Association* 257: 645–50.

Henderson, L. V. 1935. Physician and patient as social system. *New England Journal of Medicine* 212: 819–23.

Henderson, L. W., Ford, C., Colton, C. K., Bluemlé, L. W., and Bixler, H. J. 1970. Uremic blood cleansing by dialfiltration using a hollow fiber ultrafilter. *Transactions of the American Society for Artificial Internal Organs* 16: 107–14.

Henry, J. A. 1978. Haemodialysis and transplantation: A personal view. In J. L. Anderson, F. M. Parson, and D. E. Jones, eds., *Living With Renal Failure,* 215–22. Lancaster: MTP Press.

Hiatt, H. H. 1987. *America's Health in the Balance: Choice or Change?* New York: Harper & Row.

  1975. Protecting the medical commons: Who is responsible? *New England Journal of Medicine* 302: 235–41.

Hiatt, R. A., and Friedman, G. D. 1982. The frequency of kidney and urinary diseases in a defined population. *Kidney International* 22: 63–8.

Hirschman, A. O. 1985. Against parsimony: Three easy ways of complicat-

Klein, R. 1985. Why Britain's Conservatives support a socialist health care system. *Health Affairs* 4: 41–58.

1984a. The politics of ideology vs. the reality of politics: The case of Britain's National Health Service in the 1980's. *Milbank Memorial Fund Quarterly* 62: 82–109.

1984b. Rationing health care. *British Medical Journal* 289: 143–4.

1983a. The NHS and the theatre of inadequacy. *Universities Quarterly* 37: 201–15.

1983b. *The Politics of the National Health Service.* London: Longman Group.

1981. Health services. In P. M. Jackson, ed., *Government Policy Initiatives 1979–80: Some Case Studies in Public Administration,* 161–80. London: RIPA.

1978. Parliamentary accountability and the NHS: Need for separate committee. *British Medical Journal* 1: 1498–99, 1501.

Knapp, M. S. 1982. Renal failure: Dilemmas and developments. *British Medical Journal* 284: 847–50.

Knox, R. A. 1980. Heart transplants: To pay or not to pay. *Science* 209: 570–5.

Kolff, W. J. 1986. Retrospective on artificial organs and the role of the Transactions – American Society for Artificial Organs. *Artificial Organs* 10: 263–5.

1965. First clinical experience with the artificial kidney. *Annals of Internal Medicine* 62: 608–19.

1947. *New ways of treating Uraemia: The Artificial Kidney, Peritoneal Lavage, Intestinal Lavage.* London, Churchill.

Kolff, W. J., Berk, H. T. H. J., Welle, M., van der Ley, A. J. W., van Dijk, E. C., and van Noordwijk, J. 1944. The artificial kidney: A dialyser with a great area. *Acta Medica Scandinavica* 117: 121–34.

Konner, M. 1987. *Becoming a Doctor: A Journey of Initiation in Medical School.* New York: Viking.

Koopman, C., Eisenthal, S., and Stoeckle, J. D. 1984. Ethnicity in reporting pain, emotional distress and requests of medical outpatients. *Social Science and Medicine* 18: 487–90.

Laing, W. 1980. End-stage renal failure. *OHE Briefing,* no. 11.

1979. Cost effectiveness. *Journal of Medical Engineering and Technology* 3: 113.

1978. *Renal Failure: A Priority in Health?* London: Office of Health Economics.

Laing, W., and Taylor, D. 1982. *Hip Replacement and the NHS.* London: Office of Health Economics.

Lancet. 1984. 1: 717.

   1981. 1: 594–96.

   1961. 2: 821–22.

Large, B., and Ahmed, R. 1981. Audit in renal failure. *British Medical Journal* 293: 556.

Lasswell, H. D. 1936. *Politics: Who Gets What, When, How.* New York: McGraw-Hill.

Lasswell, H. D., and Kaplan, A. 1950. *Power and Society: A Framework for Political Inquiry.* New Haven, Conn.: Yale University Press.

Leaf, A. 1980. The MGH trustees say no to heart transplants. *New England Journal of Medicine* 302: 87–8.

Lee, K., and Mills, A. 1982. *Policy Making in the Health Sector.* London: Croom Helm.

Legrain, M. C. 1983. Diabetics with end-stage renal disease: "The best buy." *Diabetic Nephropathy* 2 (Aug.): 1–3.

LeGrande, J. 1978. The distribution of public expenditures in the case of health care. *Economics* 45: 125–42.

Leiss, W. 1976. *The Limits to Satisfaction: An Essay on the Problem of Needs and Commodities.* University of Toronto Press.

Lerner, A. P. 1947. *The Economics of Control,* 3d ed. New York: Macmillan.

Levine, S., Feldman, J. J., and Elinson, J. 1983. Does medical care do any good? In D. Mechanic, ed., *Handbook of Health, Health Care, and the Health Professions,* 394–404. New York: Free Press.

Levy, N. B. 1983. Sexual dysfunction of haemodialysis patients. *Clinical and Experimental Dialysis and Apheresis* 7: 275–88.

   1979. Psychological problems of the patient on hemodialysis and their treatment. *Psychotherapy and Psychosomatics* 31: 260–6.

Lewis, B. R. 1979. *Kidney Donorship Transplantation: A Social Marketing Problem.* Occasional paper no. 7902, University of Manchester Institute of Science and Technology, Department of Management Sciences.

Lindblom, C. E. 1965. *The Intelligence of Democracy: Decision Making through Mutual Adjustment.* New York: Free Press.

   1959. Incrementalism: The science of "muddling through." *Public Administration Review* 19: 79–88.

Lipsey, D. 1983. Health before defense. London *Sunday Times,* Nov. 6, p. 2, col. 6.

Lively, W. J. 1982. Symptoms of anxiety and depression in patients undergoing chronic hemodialysis. *Journal of Psychosomatic Research* 26: 581–4.

Lo, B. 1987. Behind closed doors. *New England Journal of Medicine* 317: 46–50.

London *Hampstead and Highgate Express*. 1983. Oct. 21, p. 3, col. 2.

London *Times*. 1987. Nov. 26, p. 44, col. 1.

    1985. Jan. 9, p. 11, col. 1.

    1984. Sept. 27, p. 3, col. 3.

    1983a. Nov. 21, p. 4, col. 3.

    1983b. Nov. 18, p. 13, col. 7.

    1983c. Nov. 10, p. 4, col. 6.

    1983d. Oct. 19, p. 13, col. 1.

    1981a. Feb. 5, p. 3, col. 5.

    1981b. July 24, p. 15, col. 1.

    1978. Apr. 21, p. 4, col. 4.

    1975. Jan. 31, p. 15, col. 1.

    1972. Dec. 4, p. 17, col. 6.

Loury, M. R. 1979. Frequency of depressive disorders in patients entering home hemodialysis. *Journal of Nervous and Mental Diseases* 167: 199–204.

Luke, R. G. 1983. Renal replacement therapy. *New England Journal of Medicine* 308: 1593–5.

Lupton, R., ed., 1979. *Caring for Children in Renal Failure: Report of the Conference Held at the King's Fund Centre, October 9, 1979.* London: King's Fund Centre.

Lynn, K., Buttimore, A. L., Bailey, R. R., and Swainson, C. P. 1984. Universal home haemodialysis. *Lancet* 1: 105.

Lysaght, M. J. 1985. Contemporary ESRD therapy: Quagmire or eschaton. *Contributions to Nephrology* 44: 275–84.

MacGreggor, F. C. 1979. *After Plastic Surgery: Adaptation and Adjustment.* New York: Praeger.

Mackenzie, W. J. M. 1976. Models of English politics. In R. Rose, ed., *Studies in British Politics,* 3d ed., 5–15. New York: St. Martin's Press.

Macpherson, S. 1986. Kidney transplantation in the United Kingdom. *International Journal of Technology Assessment in Health Care* 2: 497–506.

Maher, B. A., Lamping, D. L., Dickinson, C. A., Murawski, B. J., Olivier, D. C., and Santiago, G. C. 1983. Psychosocial aspects of chronic hemodialysis: The National Cooperative Dialysis Study. *Kidney International* (suppl.) 23: S-50-57.

Maher v. *Roe.* 1977. 432 U.S. 464.

Malcolm, A. H. 1986a. Extending life or prolonging death? *New York Times,* Mar. 23, IV, p. 24, col. 3.

—— 1986b. Is there too little order in the transplantation business? *New York Times,* Apr. 13, IV, p. 10, col. 1.

Mallick, N. P., Gokal, R., Johnson, R. W. G. 1983. Effect of cut in NHS budget. London *Times,* Oct. 24, p. 15, col. 5.

Mancini, P. V. 1984. *The Cost of Treating End-Stage Renal Failure.* London: Department of Health and Social Security, Economics Advisers' Office.

Marcuse, H. 1964. *One Dimensional Man.* Boston: Beacon Press.

Marmor, T. 1985. A political scientist's view. *Bulletin of the New York Academy of Medicine* 61: 101–6.

Marplan, Ltd. 1979. *Public Attitudes to Kidney Donations: Report of a Survey Prepared for the Central Office of Information on Behalf of the Department of Health and Social Security,* London: DHSS.

Márquez, G. G. 1986. *The Story of a Shipwrecked Sailor.* Trans. R. Hogan. New York: Knopf.

Martin-Malo, A. 1984. Effects of haemodialysis and haemofiltration on myocardial function. *Contributions to Nephrology* 41: 403–8.

Massam, A. 1982. Doctor attacks "kidney scandal." London *Evening Standard,* Jan. 7, p. 14, col. 6.

Matas, A. J., and Tellis, V. A. 1987. Selection of kidney recipients. *Journal of the American Medical Association* 257: 1328.

Mausner, J. S., Clark, J. K., Coles, B. I, and Menduke, H. 1978. An areawide survey of treated end-stage renal disease. *American Journal of Public Health* 68: 166–9.

Maxwell, M. H., Rockney, R. E., Kleeman, C. R., and Twiss, M. R. 1959. Peritoneal dialysis: Technique and applications. *Journal of the American Medical Association* 170: 917–23.

Maxwell, R. 1984. International health comparisons: What can they tell us? *Public Money* 3 (Mar.): 35–40.

—— 1981. *Health and Wealth: An International Study of Health Care Spending.* Lexington, Mass.: Heath.

May, W. F. 1975. Code and covenant or philanthropy and contract? *Hastings Center Report* 5 (Dec.): 29–38.

Maynard, A. 1986. Financing the UK National Health Service. *Health Policy* 6: 329–40.

McCloskey, J. H. 1976. Human needs, rights, and political values. *American Philosophical Quarterly* 13: 1–11.

McCormick, J. S. 1986. Diagnosis: The need for demystification. *Lancet* 2: 1434–5.

McCullough, L. B. 1979. The right to health care. *Ethics in Science and Medicine* 6: 1–9.

McGeown, M. G. 1978. Selection of patients: Integration between dialysis and transplantation. In W. Drukker, F. M. Parson, and J. P. Maher, eds., *Replacement of Renal Function by Dialysis,* 418–25. The Hague: Nijhoff.

1972. Chronic renal failure in Northern Ireland. *Lancet* 1: 307–10.

McKinlay, J. B., and McKinlay, S. M. 1977. The questionable contribution of medical measures to the decline of mortality in the U.S. in the twentieth century. *Milbank Memorial Fund Quarterly* 55: 405–28.

McKeown, T. 1976. *The Role of Medicine: Dream, Mirage, or Nemesis.* London: Nuffield Provincial Hospitals Trust.

McPherson, K. 1985. The political argument on health costs. *British Medical Journal* 290: 1679–80.

Mechanic, D. 1979. *Future Issues in Health Care.* New York: Free Press.

1977. The growth of medical technology and bureaucracy: Implications for medical care. *Midbank Memorial Fund Quarterly* 55: 61–78.

Medical Services Study Group of the Royal College of Physicians. 1981. Deaths from chronic renal failure under the age of 50. *British Medical Journal* 283: 283–6.

Merion, R. M., White, D. J. G., Thiru, S., Evans, D. B., and Calne, R. Y. 1984. Cyclosporine: Five years' experience in cadaveric renal transplantation. *New England Journal of Medicine* 310: 148–54.

Merrill, J. P., Murray, J. E., Harrison, J. H., and Guild, W. R. 1956. Successful homotransplantation of the human kidney between identical twins. *Journal of the American Medical Association* 160: 277–82.

Merrill, J. P., Schupak, E., Cameron, E., and Hampers, C. L. 1964. Hemodialysis in the home. *Journal of the American Medical Association* 190: 468–70.

Merritt, R., and Toff, G. 1986. State health reports. *Nation's Health,* April, p. 16, col. 1.

Merton, R. K. 1949. *Social Theory and Social Structure: Toward the Codification of Theory and Research.* New York: Free Press.

Michael, J., and Adu, D. 1981. Audit in renal failure. *British Medical Journal* 203: 556.

Miller, D. 1976. *Social Justice.* Oxford: Clarendon Press.

Milne, J. F., Golden, J. S., and Fibus, L. 1978. Sexual dysfunction in renal failure: A survey of chronic hemodialysis patients. *International Journal of Psychiatry in Medicine* 8: 335–45.

Moore, F. D. 1972. *Transplant: The Give and Take of Tissue Transplantation.* New York: Simon & Schuster.

Morgan, G. 1979. All party committees in the House of Commons. *Parliamentary Affairs* 32: 56–65.

Morris, G. P. 1983. Enforcing a duty to care: The kidney patient and the NHS. *Law Society's Gazette* 80: 3156, 3164–5.

Moss, L. 1982. *People and Government in 1978: A Survey of Opinion in England and Wales.* Birkbeck College, University of London.

Mumford, L. 1934. *Technics and Civilization.* New York: Harcourt, Brace.

Murray, J. S., Tu, W. H., Albers, J. B., Burnell, J. M., and Scribner, B. H. 1962. A community hemodialysis center for the treatment of chronic uremia. *Transactions of the American Society for Artificial Internal Organs* 8: 315–20.

Nahas, A. M., and Coles, G. A. 1986. Dietary treatment of chronic renal failure: Ten unanswered questions. *Lancet* 1: 597–600.

Najam, J. M., and Levine, S. 1981. Evaluating the impact of medical care and technologies on the quality of life: A review and critique. *Social Science and Medicine* 15: 107–15.

National Center for Health Services Research and Health Care Technology (NCHSR). 1986. The reuse of hemodialysis devices labeled "for single use only" (Health Technology Assessment, Rep. No. 11), Rockville, Md.

National Kidney Research Fund. 1982. *Some Kidney Disease Is Preventable.* Harrow, Middlesex.

Neu, S., and Kjellstrand, C. M. 1986. Stopping long-term dialysis. *New England Journal of Medicine* 314: 14–20.

Newhouse, J. P. 1977. Medical care expenditures: A cross-national survey. *Journal of Human Resources* 16: 115–25.

NHS Management Board. 1986. *Review of the Resource Allocation Working Party Foundation.* London: Department of Health and Social Security.

Norton, P. 1981. *The Commons in Perspective.* Oxford: Robertson.

Nozick, R. 1974. *Anarchy, State, and Utopia.* New York: Basic Books.

Office of Population Censuses and Surveys. 1984. *Mortality Statistics, Causes.* London: HMSO.

Ogg, C. S. 1970. Maintenance haemodialysis and renal transplantation. *British Medical Journal* 4: 412–15.

O'Higgins, M. 1984. *House of Commons: A Study of the Views of MPs.* University of Bath, Centre for the Analysis of Social Policy.

Olson, M. 1982. *The Rise and Decline of Nations: Economic Growth, Stagflation, and Social Rigidities.* New Haven, Conn.: Yale University Press.

⎯ 1965. *The Logic of Collective Action.* Cambridge, Mass.: Harvard University Press.

Orwell, G. 1968 [1940]. *My Country Right or Left, 1940–1943,* ed. S. Orwell and I. Angus. New York: Harcourt Brace Jovanovich.

Outka, G. 1974. Social justice and the equal access to health care. *Journal of Religious Ethics* 2: 11–32.

Parfit, D. 1984. *Reasons and Persons.* Oxford: Clarendon Press.

Parkhouse, J., Campbell, M. G., Hambleton, B. A., and Philips, P. R. 1983. Career preferences of doctors qualifying in the UK in 1980. *Health Trends* 15 (Feb.): 12–14.

Parliamentary Debates, House of Commons (Hansard). 1986a. 6th ser., vol. 91, col. 698w, Jan. 16.

⎯ 1986b. 6th ser., vol. 91, col. 140w, Feb. 4.

⎯ 1985a. 6th ser., vol. 77, col. 407w, Apr. 23.

⎯ 1985b. 6th ser., vol. 89, col. 311w, Dec. 19.

⎯ 1942. 5th series, vol. 422, col. 45, Apr. 30.

Parson, F. M. 1982. History of Dialysis in the United Kingdom. *Dialysis and Transplantation* 11: 22–4.

⎯ 1967. A true "doctor's dilemma." *British Medical Journal* 1: 623.

Parson, F. M., and Ogg, C. S., eds., 1983. *Renal Failure: Who Cares?* Lancaster: MTP Press.

Parsons, T. 1951. *The Social System.* New York: Free Press.

Parsons, V., and Lock, P. M. 1981. Audit in renal failure. *British Medical Journal* 283: 556.

⎯ 1980. Triage and the patient with renal failure. *Journal of Medical Ethics* 6: 173–6.

Pendreigh, D. M., et al. 1972. Survey of chronic renal failure in Scotland. *Lancet* 1: 304–7.

Perry, C. 1980. Human organs and the open market. *Ethics* 91: 63–71.

Pigou, A. C. 1932. *Economics of Welfare,* 4th ed. London: Macmillan Press.

Plough, A. L., and Salem, S. 1982. Social and contextual factors in the analysis of mortality in end-stage renal disease patients: Implications for health policy. *American Journal of Public Health* 72: 1293–5.

Powell, J. E. 1976. *Medicine and Politics: 1975 and After.* Tunbridge Wells: Pitman Medical.

Poynton, D. 1983. Developments in financial management systems. *Public Finance and Accountancy* 10 (Oct.): 23–5.

Prentice, T. 1985. 850 kidney patients a year at risk. London *Times,* July 26, p. 3, col. 1.

Pressman, J., and Wildavsky, A. 1973. *Implementation.* Berkeley: University of California Press.

Prottas, J., and Batten, H. L. 1988. Health professionals and hospital administrators in organ procurement: Attitudes, reservations, and their resolutions. *American Journal of Public Health* 78: 642–5.

Prottas, J., Segal, M., and Sapolsky, H. M. 1983. Cross-national differences in dialysis rates. *Health Care Financing Review* 4 (Mar.): 91–103.

Quellhorst, E., Scheunemann, B., and Hildebrand, U. 1980. Hemofiltration: Technique and clinical application. *International Journal of Artificial Organs* 3: 209–10.

1983. Long-term results of regular hemofiltration. *Blood Purification* 1: 70–9.

Quinton, W. E., Dillard, D., and Scribner, B. H. 1960. Cannulation of blood vessels for prolonged hemodialysis. *Transactions of the American Society for Artificial Internal Organs* 6: 104–9.

Raines, H. 1987. Bowing to foes: Thatcher backs health fund. *New York Times,* Dec. 17, p. A18, col. 1.

Ranadé, W. 1985. Motives and behavior in district health authorities. *Public Administration* 63: 185–200.

Rantzen, E., and Woodward, S. 1985. *Ben: The Story of Ben Hardwick.* London: BBC.

Rathaus, M., and Bernheim, J. 1978. Are your elderly patients good candidates for dialysis? *Geriatrics* 33: 56–66.

Rawls, J. 1982. Social unity and primary goods. In A. K. Sen, ed., *Utilitarianism and Beyond,* 159–85. Cambridge University Press.

1971. *A Theory of Justice.* Cambridge, Mass.: Harvard University Press.

Regen, A. M., and Stewart, J. 1982. An essay on the government of health: the case for local authority control. *Social Policy and Administration* 16: 19–43.

Regina v. *Secretary of State for Social Services, ex parte Hincks et al.* 1980. 123 SJ 436.

Register, C. 1987. *Living with Chronic Illness: Days of Patience and Passion.* New York: Free Press.

Reichsman, F., and Levy, N. B. 1972. Problems in adaptations to maintenance hemodialysis. *Archives of Internal Medicine* 130: 859–65.

Reinhold, R. 1982. Competition held key to lower medical costs. *New York Times,* Apr. 1, p. A1, col. 2.

Rennie, D., Rettig, R. A., and Wing, A. J. 1985. Limited resources and the treatment of end-stage renal failure in Britain and the United States. *Quarterly Journal of Medicine* (n.s.) 56: 321–36.

Rescher, N. 1969. The allocation of exotic lifesaving therapy. *Ethics* 79: 173–86.

Review Body of Top Salaries. 1983. *Review of Parliamentary Pay and Allowances*, vol. 2: *Surveys and Studies* (Cmnd. 881-II). London: HMSO.

Rhodes, R. A. W. 1979. Research into central–local relations in Britain: A framework for analysis. In *Central–Local Government Relations*, app. I. London: Social Science Research Council.

Richards, V. 1985. The real England. *Encounter* 65 (June): 57–61.

Richardson, J. J., and Jordan, A. G. 1979. *Governing under Pressure.* Oxford: Robertson.

Richmond, J. M., et al. 1982. Psychological and physiological factors predicting the outcome of home dialysis. *Clinical Nephrology* 17: 109–13.

Roberts, C. J. 1985. How much can the NHS afford to spend to save a life or avoid a severe disability? *Lancet* 1: 89–91.

Robinson, H. B. 1978. Selection of patients for dialysis and transplantation. In J. L. Anderson, F. M. Parson, and D. E. Jones, eds., *Living With Renal Failure*, 9–18. Lancaster: MTP Press.

Rodin, G. M., Chmara, J., Ennis, J., Fenton, S., Locking, H., and Steinhouse, K. 1981. Stopping life-sustaining medical treatment: Psychiatric considerations in the termination of renal dialysis. *Canadian Journal of Psychiatry* 26: 540–4.

Roher, M. 1959. *Days of Living.* Toronto: Ryerson Press.

Roper, J. 1978. $50m for NHS seen as derisory. London *Times,* Apr. 12, p. 4, col. 8.

Rosa, A. A., Fryd, D. S., and Kjellstrand, C. M. 1980. Dialysis symptoms and stabilization in long term disease. *Archives of Internal Medicine* 140: 804–7.

Rose, R. 1986. *Politics in England: Persistence and Change*, 4th ed. Boston: Little, Brown.

Rosman, J. B., Donker, A. J. M., and Van der Hem, G. R. 1986. Dietary protein restriction and the progression of renal failure. *International Journal of Artificial Organs* 9: 77–80.

Ross, W. D. 1930. *The Right and the Good.* Oxford: Clarendon Press.

Rostrand, S. G., Kirk, K. A., Rutsky, E. A., and Pate, B. A. 1982. Racial differences in the incidence of treatment for end-stage renal disease. *New England Journal of Medicine* 306: 1276–9.

Rowe, J. W., Andres, R., Tobin, J. D., Norris, A. H., and Shock, N. W. 1976. The effect of age on creatinine clearance in man: A cross sectional and longitudinal study. *Journal of Gerontology* 31: 155–63.

Royal College of Physicians of London, College Committee on Renal Disease and Executive Committee of the Renal Association. 1983. *Manpower and Workload in Adult Renal Medicine in the United Kingdom, 1975–1983.*

Royal College of Radiologists. 1979. Postoperative chest radiography. *Lancet* 2: 83–6.

Royal Commission on the National Health Service. 1979. *Access to Primary Care.* London: HMSO.

1978. *Patient's Attitudes to the Hospital Service.* Research paper no. 5. London: HMSO.

Sade, R. M. 1971. Medical care as a right: A refutation. *New England Journal of Medicine* 285: 1288–92.

Sagan, L. A. 1988. *The Health of Nations: True Causes of Sickness and Well-Being.* New York: Basic Books.

Samiy, A. H. 1983. Renal disease in the elderly. *Medical Clinics of North America* 67: 463–80.

Sanders, D., and Dukeminier, H. 1968. Medical advances and legal lag: Hemodialysis and kidney transplantation. *UCLA Law Review* 15: 357–413.

Schaefer, K., Asmus, G., Quellhorst, E., Pauls, A., von Herrath, D., and Jahnke, J. 1984. Optimum dialysis treatment for patients over 60 years with primary renal disease. *Proceedings of the EDTA-ERA* 21: 441–6.

Schattschneider, E. E. 1963. *Politics, Pressures, and the Tariff* [1935]. Hamden, Conn.: Archon.

Schelling, T. C. 1984. *Choice and Consequences.* Cambridge, Mass.: Harvard University Press.

Schieber, G. J., and Poullier, J. P. 1987. Recent trends in international health care spending. *Health Affairs* 6: 105–12.

Schmidt, R. W., and Blumenkrantz, N. J. 1981. IPD, CAPD, CRPD – Peritoneal dialysis: Past, present, and future. *International Journal of Artificial Organs* 4: 124–9.

Schwartz, W. B., and Aaron, H. J. 1984. Rationing hospital care: Lessons from Britain. *New England Journal of Medicine* 310: 52–6.

Schweiker v. *Gray Panthers.* 1981. 453 U.S. 1.

Scribner, B. H. 1971. Emerging interrelationships between kidney transplantation and regular dialysis. *Transplantation Proceedings* 3: 1395–1403.

Selected Profiles of Medicare Certified Suppliers. 1981. *ESRD Networks in the United States.* Washington, D.C.: U.S. Government Printing Office.

Sells, R. A., Macpherson, S., and Salaman, J. R. 1985. Assessment of Resources for Renal Transplantation in the United Kingdom. *Lancet* 2: 195–7.

Sen, A. K. 1973. *On Economic Inequality.* New York: Norton.

Shackman, R. 1967. Selection of patients for haemodialysis: Surgeon's point of view. *British Medical Journal* 1: 623–4.

Shaldon, S. 1968a. Independence in maintenance haemodialysis. *Lancet* 1: 520–3.

1968b. Emotional problems in a chronic haemodialysis unit. *Lancet* 2: 1347.

Shapiro, F. L., and Umen, A. 1983. Risk factors in hemodialysis patient survival. *American Society of Artificial Internal Organs Journal* 30: 21–30.

Sherlock, S. 1983. Hepatic transplantation. *Lancet* 2: 778–9.

Shevach, E. M. 1985. The effects of cyclosporine A on the immune system. *Annual Review of Immunology* 3: 397–423.

Short, M. J., and Wilson, W. P. 1969. Roles of denial in chronic hemodialysis. *Archives of General Psychiatry* 20: 433–7.

Shyh, T. P., Bhutt, K. H., Beyer, M. M., and Friedman, E. I. 1983. Excess costs of dialysis renal transplants. *Diabetic Nephropathy* 2: 23–7.

Sieghart, P. 1985. Professions as the conscience of society. *Journal of Medical Ethics* 11: 117–22.

Siemsen, A. W. 1978. Experience in self-care and limited care haemodialysis. In J. L. Anderson, F. M. Parson, and D. E. Jones, eds. *Living with Renal Failure,* 87–97. Lancaster: MTP Press.

Simmons, R. G. 1979. Discussion. *Controversies in Nephrology* 1: 202–3.

Slote, M. A. 1977. The morality of wealth. In W. Aiken and H. LaFollette, eds., *World Hunger and Moral Obligation.* Englewood Cliffs, N.J.: Prentice-Hall.

Smith, A. 1937. *The Wealth of Nations.* [1776] New York: Modern Library.

Smith, M. D., Hong, B. A., Province, M. A., and Robson, A. M. 1985. Does social support determine the treatment setting for hemodialysis patients? *American Journal of Kidney Diseases* 5: 27–31.

Social Surveys (Gallup Poll) Ltd. 1985. *General Practitioners' Survey.* Prepared for the British Kidney Patients' Association, Bordon, Hampshire.

1981. *A Survey among Hospital Doctors of Problems Relating to Kidney Transplants.* London: Social Surveys Ltd.

Solesbury, W. 1976. The environmental agenda. *Public Administration* 54: 379–97.

Spungrin, M. 1985. Excuse my ignorance but what am I doing here? *Health and Social Services Journal* 94: 765.

Stacey, M. 1977. People who are affected by the inverse law of care. *Health and Social Services Journal* 3 (June): 898–902.

Starr, P. 1976. The politics of therapeutic nihilism. *Hastings Center Report* 6 (October): 24–30.

Starzl, T. E., et al. 1987. A multifactorial system for equitable selection of cadaver kidney transplants. *Journal of the American Medical Association* 257: 3073–5.

Starzl, T. E., et al. 1981. Cyclosporine A and steroid therapy in sixty-six cadaver kidney recipients. *Surgery, Gynecology and Obstetrics* 153: 486–94.

Starzl, T. E., et al. 1980. The use of cyclosporine A and prednisone in cadaver kidney transplantation. *Surgery, Gynecology and Obstetrics* 151: 17–26.

Stason, W. B., and Barnes, B. A. 1985. *The Effectiveness and Costs of Continuous Ambulatory Peritoneal Dialysis.* Washington, D.C.: U.S. Government Printing Office.

Steel, D. 1984. Managing health authorities: One member's view. *Public Money* 3 (June): 37–40.

Stewart, J. D. 1958. *British Pressure Groups: Their Role in Relation to the House of Commons.* Oxford: Clarendon Press.

Stewart, R., Smith, P., Blake, J., and Wingate, P. 1980. *The District Administrator in the National Health Service.* London: King Edward's Hospital Fund.

Stocking, B. 1986. Strategies for technology assessment and implementation in some European countries. *International Journal of Technology Assessment in Health Care* 2: 19–26.

Stoten, B. 1982. Planning health care services. In S. Leach and J. Stewart, eds., *Approaches in Public Policy,* 225–37. London: Allen & Unwin.

Striker, G., and Tenckhoff, H. A. 1971. A transcutaneous prosthesis for prolonged access to the peritoneal cavity. *Surgery* 69: 70–4.

Sugimoto, T., and Rosansky, S. J. 1984. The incidence of treatable end stage renal disease in the eastern United States: 1973–1979. *American Journal of Public Health* 74: 14–17.

Suleiman, E., ed. 1985. *Bureaucrats and Policy Making: A Comparative Overview.* London: Holmes & Meier.

Szasz, T. A., and Hollender, M. H. 1956. A contribution to the philosophy of medicine: The basic models of the doctor–patient relationship. *Archives of Internal Medicine* 97: 585.

Taylor, R. M. R., Ting, A., and Briggs, J. D. 1985. Renal transplantation in the United Kingdom and Ireland: The centre effect. *Lancet* 1: 798–802.

Taylor, T. R., Aitcheson, J., Parker, L. S., and Moore, M. F. 1975. Individual differences in selecting patients for regular haemodialysis. *British Medical Journal* 2: 380–1.

Tawney, R. H. 1972 *Commonplacebook* [1913]., ed. J. W. Winter and D. M. Joslin. Cambridge University Press.

Tenckhoff, H., and Schecter, H. 1968. A bacteriologically safe peritoneal access device. *Transactions of the American Society for Artificial Internal Organs* 14: 181–5.

Thompson, F. S. 1981. *Health Policy and the Bureaucracy: Politics and Implementation*. Cambridge, Mass.: MIT Press.

Timmins, N. 1986a. Transplant queues grow as donors dwindle and kidney units face strain. London *Times,* Jan. 13, p. 3, col. 1.

1986b. Doctor shortage puts kidney transplant program in crisis. London *Times,* Feb. 10, p. 3, col. 1.

1986c. Relatives' consent for organs may be sought while patient alive. London *Times,* July 9, p. 5, col. 1.

1985. NHS staff split on proposals to appoint managers. London *Times,* Jan. 12, p. 3, col. 7.

1984a. Plans for new NHS chiefs criticised. London *Times,* Jan. 13, p. 2, col. 5.

1984b. Spending in 4 health regions to be reduced. London *Times,* Dec. 21, p. 2, col. 7.

1983. Transplant cash "a sop", specialist says. London *Times,* Dec. 21, p. 2, col. 7.

Titmuss, R. 1968. *Commitment to Welfare.* London: Allen & Unwin.

Tocqueville, A., de 1961. *Democracy in America* [1840], 2 vols. Trans. H. Reeve. New York: Schocken Books.

Trompeter, R. S., Haycock, G. B., Bewick, M., and Chantler, C. 1983. Renal transplantation in very young children. *Lancet* 1: 373–5.

Veatch, R. M. 1976. What is a "just" health care delivery? In R. M. Veatch and R. Branson, eds., *Ethics and Health Policy,* 127–53. Cambridge, Mass.: Ballinger.

Veitch, A. 1982. Doctors call for revolt against health cuts. London *Guardian,* Nov. 20, p. 3, col. 7.

Verwilgher, R. L. 1981. Audit in renal failure. *British Medical Journal* 283: 556.

Waddington, I. 1985. *The Medical Profession in the Industrial Revolution.* Dublin: Gill & Macmillan.

Walker, P. J., Ginn, H. E., and Johnson, H. K. 1976. Long-term hemodialysis for patients over fifty. *Geriatrics* 31: 55–61.

Walters, V. 1980. *Class Inequality and Health Care: The Origins and Impact of the National Health Service.* London: Croom Helm.

Ward, E. 1986. *Timbo: A Struggle for Survival.* London: Sidgwick & Jackson.

1985. The truth, the whole truth, and nothing but the truth. *Manchester Medicine* 1 (April–May): 6.

Wardle, E. 1983. Over 50 and uremic. *Nephron* 33: 224.

Warren, D. 1979. The doctor's freedom under authority. In G. Scorer and A. J. Wing, eds., *Decision Making in Medicine: The Practice of Its Ethics,* 25–37. London: Arnold.

Wauters, J. P., Brunner, H. R., and Boudry, J. F. 1978. How to reduce the costs of chronic hemodialysis without refusing patients. *Artificial Organs* (suppl.) 2: 373–6.

Weber, M. 1958 *The Protestant Ethic and the Spirit of Capitalism* [1904]., trans. T. Parsons. New York: Scribner's.

1947. *The Theory of Social and Economic Organization.* Trans. A. M. Henderson and T. Parsons. New York: Free Press.

Wennberg, J. E., Barnes, B. A., and Zubkoff, M. 1982. Professional uncertainty and the problem of supplier induced demand. *Social Science and Medicine* 16: 811–24.

Westlie, L., Umen, A., Nestrud, S., and Kjellstrand, C. M. 1984. Mortality, morbidity, and life satisfaction in the very old dialysis patient. *Transactions of the American Society for Artificial Internal Organs* 30: 21–30.

Wetle, T. and Levkoff, S. E. 1984. Attitudes and behavior of service providers toward elder patients in the Veterans Administration system. In T. Wetle and J. Rowe, eds., *Older Veterans: Linking Veterans Administration and Community Resources,* 205–30. Cambridge, Mass.: Harvard University Press.

Wheare, K. 1955. *Government by Committee.* Oxford: Clarendon Press.

Williams, A. 1984. Coronary artery bypass grafting: An economic appraisal. Paper presented at the Consensus Development Conference on Coronary Artery Bypass Surgery.

Williams, B. 1962. The idea of equality. In P. Laslett and W. G. Runciman, eds., *Philosophy, Politics, and Society,* 2d ser. Oxford: Blackwell Publisher.

Wilson, P. G. 1983. When transplantation is *not* the answer. *Clinical and Experimental Dialysis and Apheresis* 7: 325–33.

Wineman, R. J. 1986. Evaluation of automated reprocessed devices for hemodialyzers: a summary. *Dialysis and Transplantation* 15: 32-4.

Wing, A. J. 1985a. Commentary. *International Journal of Technology Assessment in Health Care* 1: 53-5.

— 1985b. Treatment of renal failure in the light of increasingly limited resources. *Contributions to Nephrology* 44: 260-75.

1983. Medicine and the media. *British Medical Journal* 287: 492.

1981. Treatment of end-stage renal failure. In D. Bradley and D. Moras, eds., 1981. *U.K. Transplant Service, Annual Review, 1981,* 71-94. Bristol: UK Transplant Service, South Western Regional Transplantation Centre.

1979. The impact of financial constraint. In G. Scorer and A. J. Wing, eds., 1979. *Decision Making in Medicine: The Practice of Its Ethics,* 151-64. London: Arnold.

Winoker, M. Z., Czaczkes, J. W., Kaplan De-Nour, A. 1973. Intelligence and adjustment to chronic hemodialysis. *Journal of Psychosomatic Research* 17: 29-34.

Winslow, G. R. 1982. *Triage and Justice.* Berkeley: University of California Press.

Woodruff, M. F. A., and Robson, J. S. 1962. Renal transplantation: Effects of publicity. *Lancet* 2: 1221.

World Health Organization. 1958. *The First Ten Years of the World Health Organization.* Geneva.

Yellowlees, H. 1982. *On the State of the Public Health.* London: HMSO.

Young, H., and Sloman, A. 1982. No, Minister: An Inquiry into the Civil Service. London: BBC Publications.

Younger, S. J., et al. 1983. A national survey of hospital ethics committees. *Critical Care Medicine* 11: 902-5.

Zaner, R. M. 1982. Chance and morality: The dialysis phenomenon. In V. Kestenbaum, ed., *The Humanity of the Ill: Phenomenological Perspectives,* 39-68. Knoxville: University of Tennessee Press.

Zborowski, N. 1952. Cultural components in responses to pain. *Journal of Social Issues* 8: 16-30.

Ziarnik, J. P., Freeman, C. W., Sherrard, D. J., and Calsyn, D. A. 1977. Psychological correlates of survival on renal dialysis. *Journal of Nervous and Mental Diseases* 164: 210-13.

Zola, I. K. 1966. Culture and symptoms: An analysis of patients' presenting complaints. *American Sociological Review* 31: 615-30.

Index